## A Bank Street Approach

The basic philosophy of The Bank Street College of Education has been described as the "developmental-interaction" approach. "Developmental" refers to the predictable ages and stages of a child's physical, intellectual, and social growth. "Interaction" refers to a child's external relationships with the environment, adults, and other children. It also includes the child's internal interactions, the blending of intellect and emotion.

This approach to education translates from theory to a way of living with children. It applies to home life as well as to school. Indeed, a child's first and most enduring learning begins at home with parents as their children's earliest and most constant teachers. Bank Street's philosophy offers parents and other caring adults a sensitive and sensible approach to helping children explore, discover, and understand their world. It is a way of sharing ideas and extending interests that match the child's abilities and curiosity. It is a framework that supports and values the child's growth toward independence.

*Kids and Play* is an informal conversation that turns theory into concrete ideas. It translates academic expertise into a practical guide. It explains what, how, and most importantly, *why* play is basic to the child's total development and the Bank Street philosophy.

# Kids and Play

Prepared by the
Bank Street College
of
Education

**Joanne F. Oppenheim**
Author

**Edna K. Shapiro, Ph.D.**
Consultant

**William H. Hooks**
Series Editor

**BALLANTINE BOOKS · NEW YORK**

Cover/jacket design: Andrew Newman
Cover/jacket photos: The Image Bank
Clockwise from upper left: Carol Simowitz; Gabe Palmer;
Mel Digiacomo; Niki Mareschal

Library of Congress Catalog Card Number: 83-45129

ISBN 0-345-31373-9 (hdcvr)
ISBN 0-345-30517-5 (pbk)

Manufactured in the United States of America

First Edition: February 1984

10 9 8 7 6 5 4 3 2 1

# Contents

# Expanded Contents

## CHAPTER 1
## Play

## CHAPTER 2
## Peek-a-Boo and How-Do-You-Do: Playing with Your Infant

## CHAPTER 3
## From Walking to Running:
## The Second Year

# CHAPTER 4
## Terrible/Wonderful Two

## CHAPTER 6
## Giant Steps—The Early School Years

# CHAPTER 7
## Middle Years—Eight to Eleven

## *CHAPTER 9*
## *Playthings*

# Epilogue

# Bibliography

# Index

# Foreword

The message of this book can be simply put—enjoy your children and take pleasure in their pleasure and remember that play is an important part of life for both children and parents.

Adults often take children's play for granted. It seems to come naturally to them. We often forget that play is not a neutral state of being. The actions of play reflect well-being. When children (or adults) are ill or depressed they don't play. Play is active rather than passive, involved rather than detached, and reflects emotional, physical, and intellectual engagement with the world.

Psychologists have looked at children's play, especially the play of young children, from two different points of view. On the one hand, play is seen as a window into the child's emotions. The language of play is the language of feelings. On the other hand, play is seen as a way of learning—learning about social roles and relationships, about objects, and facts about the social and material world. These are not necessarily contradictory views. Both are valid and highlight the importance of play for children's development. They should be seen not as competing, but as two essential aspects of children's play.

Parents and teachers are often exhorted to encourage their children's play because children will learn through playing. "Play is the child's work." And indeed because children do learn through play, hundreds of educational toys are produced and sold on the premise that they will teach new facts, concepts, and relationships, or develop new skills. And many of them do. But it is important to remember that play is not just for learning. Play is also for fun and refreshment. Although much energy can be expended in playful activity, play is not always tiring. On the contrary, it can revive and renew.

In this book Joanne Oppenheim writes about children's play

across a broad age span—from infancy through middle child-hood. During this period the young human goes through dramatic changes in all spheres of development. Naturally the kinds of play that are appropriate also change dramatically—from Peek-a-Boo to playing Monopoly to being umpire at the ball game. The meaning of play for the child and for the parent changes, too. The influence of playmates and peers in the child's expanding world also brings great changes. As Oppenheim notes, many adults have acted as if they should "put away childish things" and play no more. But why shouldn't parents take advantage of the fact that they live with playful creatures?

This book speaks to parents' desires to help children learn more about the world they live in, and to their desire to be with and have fun with their children. One of the cherished pleasures of being a parent is the freedom to be playful, to indulge one's often suppressed sense of silliness and absurdity. For when parents play with their children, they not only enhance their children's pleasure, they enrich their own lives. As adults we are often self-conscious about things we are not very good at. It is not necessary to be a world-class athlete to play catch! Nor do we need to worry about being barely able to carry a tune, to sing with a young child.

Playing offers adults and children a way to be together—not just to be physically present in the same room but to be in active interchange. And play is also what children can do when you don't want to or can't be with them—because you need to be doing something else or because you are tired or need some time alone. When parents provide children with lots of play resources—not merely things, but ideas for play and experiences in using them—children are more able to engage in purposeful and pleasurable play.

Children like to explore the properties of things—measuring cups and plastic beads, sand and stones, clay and paint, magnets and rubber balls. Fooling around with physical objects can be both fun and instructive. Children also express and re-express ideas and feelings in dramatic role play and in drawings and paintings. They can reexperience and reshape pleasant and frightening experiences. Play is a medium for repeating comfortable and familiar formulas, for testing ideas, and also a medium for taking on challenges.

Children can also make real things out of clay, pipe cleaners, sticks, plastic, wooden blocks, "Legos," paper plates, milk cartons—almost anything is material for a child's "constructions."

What children can do is limited only by their developing capacities, by the resources adults provide, and by our expectations. It is here that Oppenheim's book will be a most useful reference and backup for mothers and fathers. She offers, in a very readable form, solid information about children's developing capacities. Children's behavior and language can often be misleading, and parents can seriously underestimate what their children can or can't do. It is helpful to have clear statements of what can be expected from kids.

This book offers a rich array of ideas for activities and games. We live in a world in which a welter of commercial products claim to be essential to our children's happiness and successful development. Oppenheim gives useful guidelines about what kinds of toys to buy for children at different ages and also many suggestions for inexpensive and easily put-together toys that can be made at home. The book is full of simple ways to amuse, involve, and captivate your children. Ideas you once knew and have forgotten, ideas you might never think of, and those that confirm what you already do.

No parent will take advantage of all of the suggestions in this book; parents will have individual preferences, too. But it can serve as a handy sourcebook for ideas to give the baby-sitter or the visiting relative, or an older child taking care of a younger one. Most of all, *Kids & Play* is an antidote to passivity; it offers lively ideas and concrete ways for adults and children to enjoy being together.

Edna K. Shapiro, Ph.D.

## *Acknowledgments*

Grateful acknowledgment is made to Joëlle Delbourgo for her role in conceptualizing the Bank Street College of Education Child Development Series; to Pat Ayres for bringing Bank Street and Ballantine Books together; to Dr. Richard Ruopp, president of Bank Street College, and to the faculty who supported us in this venture; and to Joan Auclair and Mary Fitzpatrick for manuscript preparation.

# Kids
# and
# Play

# Chapter 1

# *Play*

When I was a child, I spoke as a child, I understood as a child, I thought as a child; but when I became a man, I put away childish things.

—Corinthians

## *Take a New Look*

For many of us, "putting away childish things" has included giving up play. We have taken the biblical injunction quite literally. As adults we tend to think of play as:

- something you do after work is done
- a frill to be enjoyed on weekends and vacations
- something that makes you feel a little guilty if you indulge in it too long or too seriously
- something too childish to be a central part of your life.

Try for a moment to discard all of these deeply ingrained feelings about play. Reach deep inside your memory bank and reconnect with the child that remains within each of us. As best we can, let's think about play from the child's point of view.

Children don't separate work from play. To them, play is the all-encompassing business of childhood—their work, their entertainment, their method of sorting out the world. It's very important business. If you can observe the play of children with this in mind you'll begin to see play in new dimensions.

## What Play Does for Children

Playing is more than what children do to fill up their time while growing up. Beyond the urgent survival requirements of food, care, and shelter, children need a wide variety of play activities for healthy physical, mental, and emotional development.

Through play, children exercise and develop their growing bodies. They learn muscle control and coordination. They move from a helpless state to new stages of accomplishment and competence.

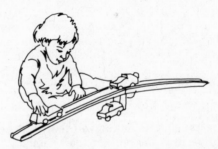

But play stimulates more than muscle development in children. It involves the mind and the emotions. Children don't just jump, bang, run, or bounce. They jump with joy, they bang with anger, they run with fear, they bounce with pleasure. They play out their emotions and thoughts. Through play, they recreate their real life experiences.

Five-year-old Peter, recently relieved of his tonsils, played out this scene with his friend Mike:

Peter:   Make-a-believe . . . this is a hospital. . . .
Mike:   I'll be the doctor.
Peter:   No . . . you could be the nurse.
Mike:   Boys don't be nurses.
Peter:   Yes they do! When I was in the hospital there were boy . . . men nurses . . . listen . . . here comes an ambulance . . . ahoooo! Emergency . . . come on!
Mike:   What's wrong with this sick kid?
Peter:   Tonsils . . . have to come out . . . Give him a shot . . . right away!

Of course, we don't always have time to listen in to the games they play, but when we do, we can hear children playing through emotional events in their lives, clarifying misconceptions, exercising imagination, trying on roles, taking charge, and enlarging their grasp of language and the world.

## *Keeping the Fun in Play*

Let's not minimize the most obvious value of play—PLAYING SHOULD BE FUN! In our great eagerness to teach our children we studiously look for "educational" toys, games with built-in lessons, books with a "message." Often these "tools" are less interesting and stimulating than the child's natural curiosity and playfulness. Play is by its very nature educational. And it should be pleasurable. When the fun goes out of play, most often so does the learning.

If parents only encourage play that is "educational" they may very well be limiting what children can learn about the real world, themselves, and others through play. It has become fashionable lately to replace play with formal lessons. Pushing infants to read before they talk, swim before they walk, recognize Picasso before they paint, and fiddle before they play may lead to fewer long-range rewards than parents expect. Psychologists and pediatricians are reporting a high incidence of tots with nervous disorders attributed to pressure for early achievement. Rushing kids on the fast track may end in derailing both play and a love of learning. Learning and playing do go hand in hand, but when rewards and benefits become the principle objective we run the risk of driving out the pleasure of play—fun for its own sake!

> "I'm making mish-mash!" the three-year-old giggles at the sandbox.
> "Mosh-mush!" Her playmate pats her mudpie.
> "Mish-mash-mosh-mush," they chant and giggle their rhythmic mudpie song.

Hilarious? Only to three-year-olds, still exploring the taste of shaping new words on their lips.

At eight they may be giggling over "Peter Piper picked a peck of pickled peppers." And by eighteen or eighty, if they're lucky, they'll still get pleasure out of a sophisticated pun, a game of Scrabble, or a double crostic.

Playing has value throughout our life span. Naturally the games we play change as we grow older. But the physical, mental, and emotional benefits are there at every stage. With children the stages race by rather quickly—much too fast to allow the luxury of much trial and error. Being aware of the characteristic and general expectations of each developmental stage a child passes through can be an invaluable aid to parents.

## Active Play vs. Passive Pleasure

Unfortunately, both children and adults today are easily seduced by mass entertainment. With a push of a button we tend to rely on watching rather than doing. We expect fun and facts to fall into our laps.

"My three-year-old knows how to count," a proud mother boasts. "She knows the names of all the letters."

Wonderful? Maybe, but that same three-year-old in the company of other children sits, thumb in mouth, close to mama or daddy, passively watching others climb the monkey bars, dig in the sandbox, chanting and laughing at the pure joy of active play. There's nothing wrong with learning how to count, but remember that other things count, too. Besides, not everything is as easy as 1-2-3. Real learning more often than not requires an ability to cope with frustration, not just rote recall of numbers or pushing of buttons.

## How Parents Can Encourage Play

Seeing the value of play, parents can help best by providing materials, space, and opportunities that match the growing child's changing needs. These needs will differ from child to child, from family to family, and from one developmental stage to another.

As parents, you will be your child's partners in play. Indeed, you are your child's first playmate. Before long, your child will be able to play alone for short periods of time. During the preschool years, your youngster will learn gradually how to play with other children.

## Defining Roles

In defining the players in this book we have given "mother" a leading role. But who do we mean when we talk of "mother"? Is mom the only one who can play these games? Although the great majority of mothers are the principal caretakers in their children's lives, they are rarely the only adults. We have used the word mother, in the generic sense, to mean any of the familiar people who play with the child frequently. In using this book you can substitute father, grandmother, grandfather, aunt, uncle, older sister and brother, baby-sitter, and housekeeper as legitimate substitutes for the word mother. Indeed, these "significant others" not only substitute for mother, they can enrich the child's expanding play life.

## Changing Roles of Fathers

Traditionally, fathers have been typecast as outcasts in the nursery. Chances are your dad caught his first glimpse of you through a glass window. In a sense, that barrier between father and newborn was part of a larger distancing pattern that continued throughout infancy and early childhood.

Today's father is more apt to attend prenatal classes, be in the delivery room, and participate to some extent in the day-to-day business of childcare. Although most mothers still handle the chief caretaking responsibilities of young children, fathers are no longer shadow figures in the nursery. Indeed, recent studies show that what fathers do most with their children is play.

Researchers report that fathers and mothers have different but complementary playing styles. Mothers tend to be cuddlers and cooers, while dads are typically more physically active with their little ones, depending less on talk and more on touching. Dads are more likely to stimulate exploration, encourage feats of mastery, and play rough-and-tumble games. Although children are more likely to turn to mom for comfort and security, they tend to prefer their dads as playmates.

Psychologists believe that these playful moments with dad have long-range value to a child's total development. They have found that children who are actively involved with their fathers tend to be less fretful with strangers and more easygoing in new social situations.

In that special relationship between father and child, play is a natural vehicle for shared adventure. Although your time together may be limited, the trick is in making the most of that time. This book can help fathers understand what games and toys match their child's physical and intellectual abilities. It can help dads determine when a game of Roly-Poly makes more sense than bounce and catch. They can use this book as a resource to expand their repertoire of playful possibilities.

## Working Mothers

If you're a working mother juggling home, career, and family, then play may seem like a frivolous frill. But play is not merely an extra to be added when time permits. It should be a basic ingredient in your child's day. It is not an exaggeration to say that play is as basic to your child's total development as good food, cleanliness, and rest.

Since you have less time together, how you use that time becomes even more crucial. This book can help you to zoom in on age-appropriate playthings and activities. You'll find plenty of games in this book that can be played while you're driving to the grocery store, folding the laundry, or fixing dinner. The art of doing two things at once is not really new to most working moms. But don't overlook the value of clearing the decks for

some one-to-one and totally exclusive playtime. We're not talking about sitting back and watching TV together. We mean
tuning out the rest of the world and tuning in to each other.

Take a half-hour for a game of catch or checkers, have a tea
party, take an imaginary trip, share a picture book, pound
some clay. You may be surprised to find that these playtimes
are as refreshing to you as they are to your child. The fact is,
taking time to play with your child is one of the best ways to
balance that old "quality vs. quantity" equation.

You'll also want to be sure that those who care for your child
while you're at work are providing a rich variety of play opportunities. You'll find guidelines in each chapter to help you
know what to look for in child-care settings. Or, if you're leaving your child at home, you may want to share specific chapters
of the book with the important person who cares for and plays
with your child.

## Using This Book

Throughout the pages of this book, you will find few refer-
ences to "boys' play" as opposed to "girls' play." The pronouns
"he" and "she" are used interchangeably throughout and
should not be interpreted to mean this is "a girl's activity" or "a
boy's activity." While it may be that hospitals are still wrapping girl babies in pink and boy babies in blue, there has been
a conscious decision here to help parents, both fathers and
mothers, see beyond the old stereotypes that limit children's
potential to play.

You can read this book from start to finish or dive in at the age and stage your child has reached. If you have several children, you'll discover how and why the same activities and play materials are used quite differently by each of your children. It may help parents and grandparents in selecting play materials that have real value to development.

Each chapter will explore the why, what, and how of providing meaningful play experiences for each developmental stage of childhood.

With any luck—as you and your children grow older—you'll never outgrow the real joys of playing together.

# Chapter 2

# Peek-a-Boo and How-Do-You-Do: Playing with Your Infant

### *"She Doesn't Even Know How to Play!"*

I remember my disappointment as a child when our next-door neighbor's long-awaited newborn turned out to be "just a baby." Of course, what I'd been anticipating was another child—a playmate. But this teeny-tiny baby just slept and ate and slept some more. "She doesn't even know how to play!" I complained.

Well, that was only half-true. The baby—babbling, blowing bubbles, fingering her fingers—does play in a limited way, naturally. But play in its fullest sense is learned through imitation and interaction with people and things. So, I was half-right. But the other half had more to do with not knowing how to play with an infant.

Oddly enough, a good many new parents feel just a little unsure about how, why, and/or when to play:

> Everything was so new and exhausting. There were those diaper pins that might stick him, bottles to sterilize, laundry to fold, bubbles to burp, not to mention the tension of bathing a slippery, wobbly necked wiggler.

My confidence was fading fast. What with feeding, changing, walking, rocking, and feeding again, I began to wonder—what had I gotten into?

Then, early one morning, the doorbell rang. My next-door neighbor, Ellie, was there—offering to lend a helping hand. I had to admit I needed all the help I could get.

"Why don't you just stretch out," she suggested. "You look exhausted."

By midmorning, Ellie had taken charge of everything, including the baby. As I tried to rest, I heard her chattering away, as if the baby could understand: "Now come on, little one, Ellie's gonna change the baby . . . yes . . . she's gonna rock the baby . . . sure." Strangely enough, I realized that the baby had stopped his incessant screaming.

Ellie continued talking: "Yes, you're some sweet baby. Doesn't your mommy know she's got to talk to you . . . and sing to you . . . sure . . . and play with you?"

I hated to admit it to myself or anyone else, but the truth was, I'd been so tense about doing everything exactly right—according to the book—I'd forgotten entirely the possibility of enjoying myself or the baby. I hadn't even considered the idea of playing!

—Mother of a newborn

Unfortunately, many new parents today have few well-experienced models like Ellie in their lives. Family circles tend to spread out in wide arcs all over the country. Even if grandparents live nearby, gram and gramps are both apt to be at work. Then, too, if you grew up with next-to-no contact with young children, playing with an infant may not come quite naturally.

Now the object here is not to give you one more thing to worry about. Remember, Rule #1 is, PLAYING SHOULD BE FUN.

## Playing Is FUNdamental

Just in case you've grown up thinking fun is purely frivolous and play is the opposite of work, let's take a closer look. Fun is not a dirty word, and neither is the four-letter word "play."

Playing does not mean you're wasting time or that nothing else is happening. Playing is the fundamental way infants learn about themselves and others. It is basic to their physical, emotional, and intellectual development.

## Physical Development

"How big is baby?"
"Soooooooo big!"

Anyone who has watched a newborn be startled at the sight of his own mysterious hand knows how little the infant can control his physical being. Indeed, flat on his back or turned on his tummy, the newborn does not even know where he begins or ends. It will be some time before the infant discovers his feet and months before he gains control over the muscles that allow him to sit, stand, and walk. Such milestones of physical development are promptly recorded in baby books and joyfully reported by phone: "The baby sat up!" "She's standing!" "He turned over!" Yet those who live with an infant on a day-to-day basis know that mastering such physical feats comes after weeks and months of effort and physical growth. We don't "teach" the baby to sit, stand, or walk. We can't push the physical growth. But the motivation for mastering motor skills is enhanced by play.

## Emotional Growth

"Mission Control, we have contact!"

Let's go back to that infant who doesn't know where she begins or ends. She cries and sucks and cries when milk doesn't flow from her own mysterious hand. Yet in a matter of weeks she turns her head to the sound of a familiar voice. As she is gently cuddled, cooed to, and fed, the infant drinks in more than nourishment. Intently, with her frequently unfocused eyes, she studies the face that goes along with the warmth of being held, with being fed, and with feeling safe.

Long before the baby can speak with words, a milestone of communication comes with baby's smile of recognition. It is during these early months that a baby begins to develop what psychologists call a sense of being, a separate self. Simply put, growing a sense of self is dependent upon communication with others. Play is one of the major lines for making contact for that communication.

As you come and go, appearing and disappearing from view, baby begins to rely on the fact that you go away and you come back. In fact, that's what the old game of Peek-a-Boo is all about. During the early months, your baby develops long-lasting feelings about the world as being more safe than unsafe. Eye-to-eye as you feed, hold, coo, talk, bathe, sing, and play with your baby, you are forming a fundamental bond of attachment. That bond of trust will affect your child's social relationships for years to come. Unlike a turtle that hatches on the beach and waddles into the sea, a human baby needs human contact to develop into a social being with a positive sense of self-worth. Of all the creatures born into the world, it is the human infant who remains dependent for the longest period of time. And, while many creatures play for a matter of days, weeks, or months, the most intelligent creatures are the ones who play the longest.

## Mental Development

I never played with my own kids—not until they could talk and go to the bathroom—but I can't get over how smart this little guy is. He's really bright! Someone ought to write a book about how intelligent babies are.
—Grandfather of a thirteen-month-old

Let's go back once more to that newborn infant in the crib. Will she be smart? Average? Bright? A genius? According to grandma: "A genius, absolutely!" Will she be a doctor? A teacher? A dancer? Will he be an artist? A detective? An architect? What can you tell or do about a baby's IQ? Isn't a baby born smart or not so smart? Those are the questions the parents ask about the future as the infant's tiny warm hands grasp hold of the present. With no crystal balls to tell us, we do know basically that each child comes into the world with a mixture of gifts. As parents, our objective is to make the most of those gifts.

A baby's mental development is a lot like her physical development. If you feed a healthy baby she will more than likely continue to thrive and grow. On the other hand, no matter how healthy she was at birth, if a baby is not well nourished, she will begin to fail in health. Intellectual growth is much the same.

Given two babies with equal potential, if you offer one a stimulating environment and the other is left to idle hours away staring at a blank ceiling, you will quickly see a striking difference between the babies. So basically it comes down to the old adage: "What you put in is what you get back."

A child who is talked to will generally talk more than a child who is not talked to. Language, like play, is one of the skills children learn in large part through imitation. Learning the names of things in his world gives the child a handle on communicating as a feeling and thinking person. Yet even before the infant can name things, he is learning what is hot or cold, wet or dry, hard or soft, silky or fuzzy. These are the experiences on which meaningful language and thought are built.

In the first year of life mental development can be greatly enhanced by offering infants a multitude of sensory and social opportunities for play. We cannot tell them about the world, but we can provide time and materials that allow them to experience a world they understand. Without such opportunities, the potential for learning may be seriously and permanently damaged.

## *P + I + E (Physical + Intellectual + Emotional) = PIE*

Although we have examined three separate parts of growing, total development cannot be divided like a pie.

Picture your infant dropping toys off the feeding table. Her ability to drop things voluntarily is a sign of physical development. But at the same time the infant is discovering that things make noise, fall down, and still exist even if they are out of sight. She is making the joyous discovery that she is the master of all this action. With this game the infant is also finding out about your patience, your playfulness, and the limits of both. Tie a string on the toys and you have another whole set of PIE experiences. The whole child depends on all three parts of the pie.

## A Matter of Life and Death

Does playing really matter that much? It is not an exaggeration to say that playing or not playing can be a matter of life or death. We do know that an inability to play is a sign of mental illness or, put in more positive terms, playing is good for emotional health. Psychologists made this discovery years ago by studying infants and children left in orphanages and foundling homes.

Despite adequate diets and stringent rules of cleanliness, institutionalized children clearly had a higher mortality rate than normal. Doctors began to ask why. What was going wrong in these homes behind walls where children were tucked away from the world? Why were such children, at best, growing up physically and mentally retarded, emotionally disturbed, and, all too frequently, even dying? Over twenty years ago researchers began to look closely at these children and their environment.

In the course of their disheartening investigations, the researchers discovered one foundling home that was an exception to the rule. At The Nursery, as they called it, infants and children were alert, thriving, and outgoing. Why? What was the difference here?

On the surface, it appeared that The Nursery was a less desirable facility. In "better" homes each infant was provided with a totally separate and private cubicle. In contrast, The Nursery kept many children in one large room, thus providing babies with constant visual and social stimulation. Not only did these babies have each other, they had two other great plus factors going for them. The Nursery was attached to a women's prison. Unfortunately, the children's mothers were inmates, but fortunately, and most significantly, the mothers were allowed to visit, play with, sing to, feed, and bathe their own children every single day. In contrast to this one-to-one relationship, other orphanages offered only one caregiver to eight infants. It was also discovered that babies in The Nursery had an abundant supply of toys while babies in so-called better facilities had none at all!

Obviously, these findings brought about significant changes in the care and handling of institutionalized infants and children. But the true significance of these findings extends far beyond the walls of orphanages and into the lives of all children. Clearly, the well-being of children demands more than attention to their basic physical needs for food and cleanliness. From the child's earliest days onward, we cannot isolate physical, intellectual, and emotional well-being into cubbyhole compartments. They are all intertwined in the baby's total development.

## *Touch + Taste + Sniff + See + Listen = How a Baby Learns*

Most of us grownups are almost totally dependent on words to explain new ideas. If we want to tell someone how to get from one place to another, we may draw a map or say turn right at the second light, and then take the next left. But words and maps are symbols for real roads that we drive on. A baby can't learn from symbols. Babies and young children depend upon real and concrete experiences which they come to understand through their senses.

Watch an infant explore the sound, shape, color, taste, and texture of a rattle and you will witness a child's way of learning. The senses of smell, sight, sound, touch, and taste are tools for testing, comparing, and learning. Words will have to wait a while, but learning will not. A word, after all, is a symbol for something real. Babies and young children need a rich variety of real things to which to attach meaning. You are the first and most essential real plaything to your infant.

## Baby's First Plaything

You, your fascinating face, your sparkling eyes; your lips that sing, talk, and coo; your warm arms, your gentle hands, your tickling fingers; your familiar scent; your soothing and amusing presence make you the first and most perfect plaything in the world.

No toymaker has yet designed a plaything for infants that compares to you. Imagine if one could! Can't you see the commercials:

## U R #1—A First Toy for Baby

- It moves (no switches, buttons, batteries, or wind-up keys required).

- It talks, makes music, plays back baby's first coos and calls.

- It's cuddly (provides security and hours of pleasure).

- It's highly educational.

- It's entertaining, encourages curiosity, fun for the whole family.

- Is composed of resilient, flexible, nontoxic, 100% natural materials.

- It's a unique toy, crafted to meet your individual child's needs.

- Available only through private distribution*.

*To find nearest dealer, check your mirror.

## ECS—Early Communication System

To begin with, babies are far more interested in people than things. Given opportunities, a baby is a social being. While infants cannot talk with words, they soon respond to those who engage their eyes, ears, and bodies with "conversation." Of course, at first you'll be doing all the talking. However, if you imitate baby's gurgles, snorts, and coos, before long you'll have a budding conversationalist in your lap. This early communication system may be built entirely on nonsense sounds. That's all right—nonsense is fun! This is not a speech lesson. Engaging the baby in good fun is the basic objective.

My dad built a little science into his game. Wiggling his fingers to catch baby's eye, he'd say, "Everything that goes up comes down . . . (tickle, tickle, tickle)," as his wiggly fingers reached baby's tummy. The giggling game has action, sound, and touch appeal. Obviously, the words are unimportant. "Coochie, coochie, coo, I love you" has been making sense to infants for generations. Try some funny faces: Puff up your cheeks and pop them. If the baby sticks his tongue out, stick your tongue out. If the baby sneezes, fake a sneeze. If the baby yawns, you yawn. Early communication is something like Follow the Leader. Though to begin with you will have to be the leader, whenever possible, however, let the baby lead.

## Early Toys

Okay, but I thought babies needed toys. Don't they ever play alone? Isn't too much attention going to spoil the baby?

Of course, babies need toys, and you are not going to spend the rest of your life standing on your head to amuse the baby. But there's no reason to fear that playing with your baby will spoil him for life.

Part of what you're teaching the baby is how to play. Until they can manipulate the world of things, babies are totally dependent on the caring people in their lives. Even a simple rattle or soft doll remains inanimate without others to move it about. If you put a rattle in the new baby's hand she may grasp it. Reflexively she will shake it and soon drop it. Until she has control of her reflexes, she cannot voluntarily drop it or pick it up again. So, playing with things at this stage will depend on the willingness of others to provide stimulation.

## Providing a Stimulating Environment

Chances are that when you were a baby your room was painted in a quiet pastel tint. Around your crib there was probably a pink or blue bumper. For the first few months of your life you probably spent many of your waking moments looking at the ceiling.

Today's baby is more likely to be right in the thick of things, enjoying the action. This is not to say that babies never need quiet time, tinkling music, or gentle rocking. But researchers have discovered that a child's total development is enhanced by a stimulating environment. Some of that stimulation comes from people and some from the things people provide.

## Horizontal Environments

Like all of us, babies appreciate a change of scenery. Hang a brightly colored picture on the wall near baby's crib. Better yet, change the picture every few weeks. Studies show that infants quickly become bored with and disinterested in things that never change. This happens to grownups too. Try moving a vase or picture that's been in one place for a year. Suddenly you begin to notice it, almost as if it were new.

### Hanging and Dangling Objects

Soft hanging toys that dangle down the crib side are more interesting if they bounce on elastic ribbons. It takes time for baby to discover the power of cause and effect. But there has to be a cause to have an effect. Accidental jiggling will make a mobile move. Changing the picture or mobile over the crib with some frequency gives the infant a fresh interest to focus on. In time your baby will be mobilizing the mobile—a marvelous discovery of infant power!

### Grasping Toys

Remember, getting baby interested in "things" begins with people

or, as the song goes: "A bell is no bell
till you ring it, a song is no song till
you sing it." Shaking a rattle in
baby's line of vision will attract her
interest. Now shake it so baby has to
turn her head. Newborn babies can't
focus on objects more than seven to
twelve inches away. Hold rattle near
enough for baby to grasp for it, and
only far enough away so that baby
must reach for it. Try to find toys
and rattles small enough for the infant's tiny hands to grasp. Rattles
that are large and top-heavy may
make great fun for later. Right now
you want to find bright-colored objects that make it possible for baby
to grab and explore. Baby's fine
motor tuning, his ability to coordi-
nate eye and hand movements,
takes time to develop. At first, he
grabs hold with his whole hand.
Using his thumb and fingers in op-
position to each other will take time
and practice. Offering him objects
with a variety of shapes, textures,
and sounds adds interest to the practice. Of course, these small objects
must be safe enough for the baby to
taste, since mouthing is one of the
ways he explores everything.

### Cradle Gyms

Once baby begins to grab and
grasp at things, he's ready for a cradle gym strung across the crib (or
playpen). Either storebought or
homemade, a cradle gym is made
with a bar and rings that are attached with elastic across the top of
the crib. Bright plastic bracelets
make eye-appealing rings for baby
to bat at and grab. By about four

months baby will especially enjoy a cradle gym with interesting sound qualities. Most storebought gyms have jingly bells, rattles, or even pull-string music boxes. You can also provide a variety of feel-appeal qualities by changing the things that dangle—a sponge, a pot scrubber, a rattle. Just be sure that the danglers are securely attached and, in the event they do come loose, safe. Stay away from super-noisy jangly cradle gyms which may startle rather than please a very young baby whose movements are still random. Toys are like clothes—you have to find the right fit or they're uncomfortable.

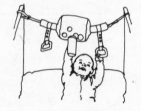

Babies are most attracted by bright colors. In fact, red and yellow are the colors they can best see—so choose their playthings with eye appeal in mind.

## Flat-on-the-Tummy Games

Life need not be flat-out dull. A decoration at the head of baby's crib will attract a young explorer. Crib sheets and bumpers are now patterned with eye interest in mind.

Once your young wriggler shows signs of mobility, put a soft toy or colorful rattle at the outer edge of reaching distance—not out of reach, but just far enough away to make stretching worthwhile. You're not teaching creeping, just encouraging reaching.

As baby catches on, toys can be put a little farther out of reach. The object here is not to tease the baby, so be careful not to set the goal beyond his physical capabilities. Mobility at all ages grows out of realistic motivation to move. For grownups it might be the smell of breakfast coffee that prompts the move from horizontal to vertical. Babies are not that different—they can use a little encouragement, too.

In fact, the horizontal child is not too young for some junior-size gymnastics. Nothing formal, of course. Just some little games to encourage movement and having fun together.

### Heads Up

With baby flat on his tummy, shake a rattle slightly above his eye level but to the left of him. Then move the rattle to the right. This exercise strengthens neck and arm muscles.

### Roll-a-My-Baby

This little action game requires a small round bolster pillow. Place the pillow under baby's chest. Gently lift baby's legs and push her back and forth slowly. Instead of "rock-a-bye-baby," change the lyrics to "roll-a-my-baby."

### Once Over Lightly

One of our babies got the knack of rolling himself over by accident and then howling with outrage because he couldn't turn back over again. It doesn't hurt to help baby discover how this magic comes about. With baby on his tummy, hold an object in his line of vision, then slowly bring it upward and to his side. As baby follows the object with his eyes, slowly bring it behind his head and gently help him turn. When he's flat on his back, allow him to grasp the object. (This game can be played in reverse to encourage baby to turn from his back to his tummy.)

### Squeak Mouse

With baby flat on his tummy, squeeze and move a small squeak toy toward him saying, "Squeak mouse, squeak mouse, squeak mouse . . ." As he reaches for it, finish the chant with "squeak, squeak, squeak into baby's house."

## Propped Up and Playful
## (Position Is Everything in Life)

As your infant begins to spend more of the day awake, why not give him a new slant on the world? By five months, baby will especially enjoy being propped up.

### Slant Boards

These lightweight plastic seats are not unlike the stiff cradle boards American Indians used for centuries. Today's parents often use the slant board as a first feeding chair, especially when the family is eating out or visiting. They're also handy for taking baby from room to room with you, so he can watch what's going on around his world. You are chiefly what he'll watch. If you put your baby on a waist-high surface, you'll be more likely to chat with him as you go about your business. Just be sure the board is securely placed and limit the time baby is strapped into any position.

### Bounce Chairs

This sling-type chair offers another safe holder that puts baby in the center of where the action is. They are lightweight enough to move from room to room, and come in handy when beds and laundry and other daily rounds can't be ignored. Most bounce chairs have the added attractions of a plastic tray and colorful beads which give baby a play surface for a toy or cracker. Best of all, their springy bounce puts baby into self-activated motion. Baby can enjoy both action around him and his own action in the bounce chair. Again, avoid using this for overly long stays that restrict and tire the infant.

### Peek-a-Boo

Propped up, a four- to five-month-old infant will delight in the all-time favorite game of Peek-a-Boo. First, cover your eyes and say, "Where's *(baby's name)*?" Then uncover your eyes and say, "I see————!" Once your baby gets the drift of things, you can play this game as you move in and out of baby's range of vision. Just a word of caution: If your baby finds the game of Peek-a-Boo a trifle scary, play a different game for now. The objective is fun, not fear. A few weeks from now she'll probably love this old favorite. Peek-a-Boo is more than fun. It's a real learning game which reinforces an understanding that you go away and you come back.

To add a new twist, try putting a scarf or diaper over your face, then pull it away. Once baby has the idea, she'll enjoy tugging it away as you say, "I see ————!"

These forerunners of Hide and Seek can be extended later to include objects. Throw a diaper over a doll and ask, "Where's the doll?" It takes time and lots of experience before babies understand that things they cannot see still exist. Until a baby is about six to eight months old, things that are out of sight are out of mind. Games like this help the child make a significant intellectual discovery and are the beginnings of problem-solving, one of the overlooked values of play.

### Pat-a-Cake

At around four to five months, baby also enjoys the gentle rough and tumble of physical games. Taking baby's hands in yours, clap his hands together as you say, "Pat-a-cake, pat-a-cake, baker's man, bake me a cake as fast as you can. Roll it up (rolling baby's arms), and roll it up, and put it in a pan (stretch baby's arms above his head)."

### More Sound/Movement Activities

Babies love the rhythm of your voice and the movement of their bodies. Because they love movement and rhythm, they love dancing in your arms to the sound of music. Dance to a record or croon your own tune. Try composing little songs with baby's name in the lyrics.

Perhaps babies' love of sound explains why Mother Goose rhymes and nonsense rhymes have always been favorites of infants. Combining rhymes with motion will make even a grumpy baby grin.

With baby on your knee or leg, give her a bouncy ride as you chant:

*Ride a cock horse*
*To Banberry Cross*
*To see a fine lady*
*Upon a white horse.*
*Rings on her fingers*
*Bells on her toes*
*She shall have music*
*Wherever she goes.*

With your hands in a fist, say, "Here is a beehive. Where are the bees? Hiding inside. Would you like to see?" Then open your hands and wiggle your fingers, saying "BZZZZZZZZZZZ," as you tickle baby.

Using baby's hand or foot, play on fingers or toes:

*This little piggy went to market.*
*This little piggy stayed home.*
*This little piggy had roast beef.*
*This little piggy had none.*
*And this little piggy went wee, wee, wee*
*All the way home!*

### Who's That?

Catching sight of himself in a mirror brings baby to a new and fascinating discovery. Obviously, he's going to recognize you in the reflection first. He knows what you look like, and now there are two views of you. But wait, he seems to say as he touches the mirror and then touches you. Who's that? he

puzzles as he touches the reflection of his own hands and face. Here, before his eyes, is a new and amazing view of the fingers he loves to finger! Mirrors are a mind-expanding discovery for baby. As he grows familiar with his own image, you can begin to play: "Where's the nose? Where are the toes?" Mirrors give baby a fascinating and otherwise unattainable view of himself. Before he can say the word "nose," he can find your nose and the nose in the mirror. Learning to name the world begins long before the baby can say words.

### Ma-Ma-Ma-Ma

Around five months, the babbling, rhythmic sounds baby makes begin to sound like "talking." Alone in his crib or propped in an infant chair, baby begins to enlarge her babbling sounds. "Ma-ma-ma-ma, da-da-da" are part of the accidental nature of baby's early "words." "Ma-ma-ma" becomes a word when mama or dada responds to the exploratory sounds. In part, we give meaning to words by responding to them. It is our response that motivates a child to repeat the sounds she says and attach names to people and things.

Of course, everyone is eager to teach baby to talk, but too often the playful nature and value of gibberish is overlooked. Babies learn to speak in a multitude of ways. They listen to the patterns, tones, and rhythms of what you say to others and to them. They listen to their own explorations of sounds—volume and rhythm. Putting it all together takes plenty of time and practice.

Talking, singing, and saying little nonsense rhymes as you dress and play with your baby are all part of learning to talk. Knowing the names of things is just a small part of that learning. So chat, chant, and listen when your baby explores the sounds of sounds.

## Sitting Pretty and Raring to Go!

At around six months, your baby will still need a helping hand to go from lying down to sitting up. Eagerly holding on to your strong fingers, baby loves to pull and tug as you say, "Upsa-Daisy!" Playing this game on a bouncy bed can take some of the sting out of toppling over. In fact, learning to topple is almost as much fun as learning to sit when you play "Upsa-Daisy" backward and call it "Downsa-Daisy."

### Beginning of Independent Play

Now your baby cannot only grasp objects, she can let go of them at will. She can use both hands to examine an object, turning it and passing it from one hand to the other, and always tasting it! Along with this newfound coordination comes an ability to focus her attention for longer stretches at a time. Given a few bright and interesting toys to manipulate, she will be content to play independently for a spell.

Banging two objects together, spilling and filling large beads from a plastic see-through container, squealing to the squeak of her soft squeeze toy, the baby discovers she can make things happen to the objects in her world. She can even eat a cracker, all by herself! These short stretches of "independent" play are welcome moments that give parents some free time, too.

### Playpens?

Some parents have strong negative feelings about playpens. They see them as limiting a baby's boundaries too narrowly. Indeed, if a playpen is overused, it can take on the character of a cage—imprisoning both child and curiosity.

On the other hand, used for brief periods, the playpen offers a safe environment that still allows for sociable contact. It's also a great place for learning how to pull up and step sideways. Let's face it: There are household chores that can't be done efficiently with a baby on your hip. Set up in a central location, the playpen need not be an isolation booth.

The real trick lies in limiting the time baby spends inside the playpen. Anticipating his need for a change of scenery, try to remove the baby *before* he becomes restless and fussy. So much of smooth, day-to-day life with young children really depends on this ability to "read" their changing needs.

Note of caution: When buying or borrowing a playpen, be sure the paint is nontoxic and that there are no sharp metal parts that can catch fingers and toes.

My first child used the playpen to store his toys. That was it. He was miserable the moment I put him in there. Now, two years later, I can't keep him out. He's constantly going over the top to play with his baby sister.

I really appreciated the playpen at the beach this summer. Set up under a shady tree, I knew the baby was safe while I watched her brother swim.

## Playthings for Sitting-Up Babies

Remember, your house has plenty of ready-made "toys" that will hold the sitting-up baby's interest. Brightly colored measuring cups, shiny spoons, and empty paper-towel holders are free for exploring, rolling, turning, banging together, and tasting.

A paper bag or box to fill and empty has great play potential. In fact, a simple piece of paper has eye, sound, and feel appeal. Cut off both ends of a cardboard food carton and you've got a tunnel for baby to travel through.

### Bought or, Better Yet, Borrowed Toys

A good many large "infant" toys are outgrown quickly. Whenever possible, try to borrow or trade off some of that high-priced equipment with limited playtime value. Bounce chairs, walkers, mobiles, slantboards, and some of the toys discussed below fall under the heading of short-term useful.

This is the time baby might enjoy one of those "busy box"

boards that toymakers manufacture, with small doors to open, wheels that turn, and bells that ring.

See-through rattles, balls, and boxes with movable parts inside will satisfy the baby's interest in watching things happen. Noisy toys that have clacking parts that can be seen and heard when they are turned upside down are simple yet satisfying. Try to avoid toys that require more dexterity than the baby can possibly have at this stage. Toys for children should provide for built-in success. If the toy is too complex, baby may get the idea that only others can make things happen for him.

Soft, huggable dolls and animals should have slender arms, legs, or tails that are easily grasped. Inspect these for safety first. Buttons, bells, and doodads on dolls can do dreadful damage in the hands and mouths of infants. Make sure that handmade dolls have solid seams that can hold up to active play.

Rubber blocks that squeak and tumble, a music box that starts with the tug of a string, a simple car (minus tiny windows to cut tiny fingers) with sturdy stay-on wheels, a soft clutchable foam or cloth ball, a good solid teething ring, and a noisy dumbbell clown that bounces back when pushed are all good plaything choices.

Remember, no baby needs all of these choices—nor can a baby play with many toys at a time. Avoid clumps of toys heaped up in the playpen. Changing the toy supply keeps alive the element of surprise and interest. Better to reintroduce a toy that's just taking up space than to let it all "hang out."

## Formal Playtime?

A baby who has been played with will now begin to engage others in play. She'll offer her hands for Pat-a-Cake and cover her eyes for Peek-a-Boo. Without getting strictly scheduled, this is probably a good time to establish a "playtime" with your baby. It doesn't mean the "only" time you'll play. What we're talking about is a regular time, set aside for "just" playing together. A time baby can count on for having your relaxed and exclusive attention. It may be a time for fingerplay, horseplay, or any kind of play. Perhaps a time for getting down on the floor and playing Roly-Poly with a bright big ball.

## Bath 'n' Splash Time

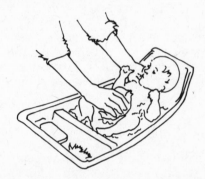

By the time baby can sit up in the tub he's an old hand at water play. Bathtime is one of those formal times that offers a wealth of physical, social, and learning opportunities.

Water seems to satisfy so many sensory needs. Splashing produces surprising sounds and startling changes. Water drips, sprays, and spills if you kick or slap it. Here's another one of those cause-and-effect moments. Splashing certainly gets results, which probably explains why one splash leads to another. Besides, water has so many dimensions! It feels wet, warm, silky, and slippery. A squeezed sponge trickles; a squeezed bottle squirts. There's no need to go out and buy elaborate water toys. With imagination, water "toys" can easily be found around the home.

With the sitting-up baby the addition of a few floating toys, a cup for pouring, or a doll for washing, and you're making a good thing better.

For some infants the transition from small baby tub to big tub seems a bit frightening. There's no need to fill the tub very high. Just a few inches will do. A nonskid mat will add an element of safety, although you will and must remain the most basic safety factor involved. Remember, even though your child can sit independently—*never leave a baby unattended in the tub, not even for a moment!*

## Creepy-Crawly Baby

It wasn't until my baby started crawling that I started wearing glasses. I've always been a little nearsighted, but now I need eyes in front and in back of me. Honestly, she finds every penny, pin, and nail that's ever been lost, and everything goes in her mouth!

At around seven months, most babies begin creeping, although mastering the art of true crawling (up on hands and knees) takes several more months. This is a good time for taking a hard look around your house from the baby's point of view.

### Childproofing

Although it will be a while before the creeping baby is scouting about full steam ahead, the ability to move about represents a developmental leap forward. No longer dependent on someone to "take" him, the creeping infant can take himself!

Childproofing your home is now a must to protect both child and cherished possessions.

Checklist:

- tape over electric outlets.
- move pullable lamp wires out of reach—wires can be taped or tacked out of reach behind furniture.
- avoid overhanging tablecloths.
- check floors for splinters and nails.
- check rugs for tacks and pins.
- put standlamps behind furniture or away.
- install gates at the top and bottom of steps.
- be sure full-length mirrors are secure.
- watch out for tippy tables.

- put medicine, drug supplies, and household cleaning products out of reach.

- barricade or store sharp-edged, glass-topped tables.

## Keeping Up with Curiosity—Early Moves Toward Independence

Once the house has been childproofed, the stage is set for safe mobility and curiosity. In homes where parents are constantly saying, "No, no!—don't touch!" parents run the risk of short-circuiting curiosity, a baby's natural learning tool. This is not the time for teaching baby the difference between mine and yours or right and wrong. It is the time for games and toys that build big and small muscles, his sense that the world is a safe and orderly place, and his sense that he can make things happen.

### Peek-a-Boo Plus

Down on the floor baby will enjoy a new form of Peek-a-Boo. Try hiding by the side of a chair, the back of a door. This is close to the standard game of Hide and Seek, only no one is hiding his eyes and counting to 100 yet.

### Early Pretending

A creeping baby will also enjoy a little pretending on your part. You can pretend to be looking for baby—under a chair, behind a curtain, inside a bag—overlooking (of course) the fact that baby is right under your nose. Teaching children to pretend will spark their pretending, a valuable aspect of play that we'll examine more fully in later chapters.

### Roly-Poly

This is a good time for Roly-Poly. Sitting face-to-face with baby, roll the ball to him and encourage him to roll it back. Don't get uptight if baby doesn't catch on right away. Sometimes it helps to add a third player (brother or sister) to the game for demonstration purposes. Use a big soft ball and patience. This is baby's first cooperative team game!

### Nesting and Stacking Boxes

Baby will also enjoy a set of two or three paper boxes that can be nested into each other. Try putting a toy inside the smallest box and show the baby how to get to the "prize." After you've demonstrated, reclose the boxes and tell the baby to find the prize. This is really another kind of Hide and Seek—with objects rather than people.

### Early Blocks

Now that your baby can manipulate small objects with his fingers he will begin to enjoy a few small soft sponge blocks to stack and tumble. Though block play will be important later, this is the time for soft bright blocks, rather than the hard wooden blocks he'll love later. This may also be a good time to introduce a spindle and ring toy. Although most of these toys are designed with rings of graduated sizes, learning *first* to fit the rings on requires serious concentration and dexterity. Pushing the baby to learn both skills at once will only lead to frustration and/or disinterest. Don't worry about getting baby to make patterns. For starters, getting the rings on and off is an accomplishment worthy of praise.

## Vertical Play

### Up-She-Rises-Early-in-the-Morning

By the time they are eight to twelve months old, most babies have learned how to pull themselves upright. Not knowing how to sit down, they may cry for help. But before long they will perfect the business of going "boom!"

No reason to worry—the backsides of babies are well padded, and basically the only thing that gets hurt is their dignity.

With your reassurance and encouragement they will try till they get it right. An infant's desire to stand and walk inevitably rises above the frustration of falling.

*Reminder:* This is the time to set the crib mattress at its lowest position and side rails should be locked into highest position. Watch out, too, for large toys inside the crib that can be stepped on and jet propel infant over and out.

## I Want to Hold Your Hand!

Once the vertical baby has attained her new upright stature the stage is set for nonstop action. Holding on to your fingers, baby will welcome every opportunity to "take a walk." Walkers on wheels may save some lower back pain and provide support as baby learns to put one foot in front of the other. My own babies really seemed to enjoy the power of racing at reckless speeds in their walkers. So they can't be left just to wander as they will. Remember, too, that the walker is confining and should not be used in excess. Babies still need to learn how to fall down and get up again. Tiring as holding their hands may be, there's really no substitute. You are still number one and supply the human touch that comes from your strong hands and assuring voice.

## Ring-a-Round-a-Rosy

This is a good time to play a slow game.

> *Ring-a-Round-a-Rosy*
> *Pocket full of posies*
> *Ashes, ashes*
> *We all fall down.*

Making light of everyone going "all fall down" puts a little humor into the inevitable. In time, baby will enjoy the added pleasure of anticipating the falling-down part.

## Pop Goes the Weasel

Your baby will also enjoy rolling and clapping hands while you sit and sing:

> *All around the cobbler's bench*
> *The monkey chased the weasel*

*Monkey thought was all in fun*
*Pop (lift baby to feet) goes the weasel!*

Like Ring-a-Round-a-Rosy in reverse—baby will soon be waiting in happy anticipation for the pop-up part.

### Push It Off, or Doll Fall Down

In his playpen or crib, baby will enjoy practicing pulling up and side-stepping. A soft toy animal straddling the rail can be a powerful incentive to build big muscles.

Here's a good game that will probably interest your baby a lot longer than his older brother, sister, or you. Put a doll on the crib or playpen rail and walk it around, then let it perch. Give the doll a poke and let it fall. After a few demonstrations, baby gets the idea and happily knocks it off. Baby has to side-step to reach the doll and also has to hold on with one hand to "knock it off" with the other. Once baby has the idea, you can reverse the game and drop the doll for baby to pick up. Whichever way you play it, this game is great for building muscles—yours and baby's. Better yet, enlist a brother or sister.

### Clear the Path

Of course, "formal" games are something of a diversion for the vertical child. Holding on to whatever is available, the standing child is soon stepping sideways into a new world of possibilities for play. Now chairs, tables, knees, and whatever he can grab hold of offer baby welcome support.

This is the age when three-legged chairs, tipping tables, wobbly standlamps, and oversized planters must be cleared out of range. Sharp-edged tables and delicate objects can also be hazardous.

## Someone's in the Kitchen— I Know-o-o-oh!

In most cases, kitchens tend to be the all-time favorite rooms of mobile babies—and why not? Just consider all the good (and dangerous) things that are to be found. First of all, there's you and all the good things to eat that come from behind doors, out of drawers, boxes, jars, tins, and bottles. Kitchens abound in wonderful smells, sounds, and actions. Instead of fighting it, rearrange it. Making the room off-limits will only provoke a losing battle.

### Making the Kitchen Safe

Your first and foremost concern will, of course, be to make the kitchen safe.

- Install safety locks on cabinets that contain potentially dangerous-to-swallow materials such as:

| | | |
|---|---|---|
| bleaches | cleansing powder | furniture polish |
| detergents | shoe polish | insecticides |
| turpentine | paint | drain openers |

Most hardware stores carry childproof locks you can install and use without being a mechanical genius.

- Put common household items out of sight and reach. Common trouble items include:

| | |
|---|---|
| knives | sewing kits |
| scissors | medication |
| paper clips | smoking items (matches, pipe |
| cosmetics | tobacco, cigarettes) |
| | pocketbooks |

- Tuck and tape tempting cords on appliances out of reach so baby doesn't pull appliances down with a quick tug.
- Use placemats instead of tablecloths that can be tugged.
- Use plastic or paper cups.
- Keep pan handles out of reach.

• By the phone, post the number of a poison control
center nearest you. If you don't know the number,
contact National Poison Center Network, 125 DeSoto
Street, Pittsburgh, PA 15213, 412-681-6669.

## Kitchen Games

Now that you've looked at prevention, let's look at inventions guaranteed to keep your baby content in the kitchen—at
least long enough for you to fix dinner or unload the groceries.

*Invention #1:* A drawer is one of the greatest inventions know to babies. It opens and closes. It can be
emptied and filled. What more could a baby want?
Well, how about a small stock of changeable, colorful
"toys" like plastic cups, spoons, bowls, a stack of cans—
all wonderful items to put in and take out of drawers.

*Invention #2:* One section of a low-to-ground kitchen
cabinet—reserved solely for baby—may be used much
as in #1 (with the added advantage of being less likely
to catch small fingers).

*Invention #3:* A pot with a lid . . . the lid comes off, the
lid goes on . . . add an object to abracadabra inside the
pot . . . peek-a-boo in a pot! What could be better than
a pot lid? Two! Because banging things together comes
naturally, your baby is a cymbal soloist in no time. Add
a spoon and you've got a one-man band. Noisy? Well,
why not add a sing-along to that primitive beat? No
point in fighting it—you might as well enjoy it! (Caution: Do not bake angel food cake during concert. Who
needs it—a fallen angel food cake can't compare with
an angelic child to sing and dance with.)

*Invention #4:* Empty coffee can (be sure edges are
smooth) with slot cut in lid. Provide lots of simple objects to fit through slot (jar lids are perfect) for small
hands that need practice in fine motor skills.

*Invention #5:* Nesting cans—three distinctly sized
cans, large, medium, and small. Can be nested or
stacked, and can be decorated with paint (nontoxic) or
stick-on paper. These help your baby learn about size
concepts.

## Summing Up

In twelve short months your baby has grown from horizontal to vertical—from mostly asleep to more often wide awake—from waiting for things to happen to making things happen—from being a "receiver" to being a "sender"—from learning to smile to knowing how to make others laugh—from needing others to lead a game to leading others to play with him.

# Chapter 3

# From Walking to Running: The Second Year

I couldn't wait for her to learn to walk. Now, honestly, it's as if someone pushed the ON button and the OFF button is out of order!

—Father of a fifteen-month-old

I thought six A.M. feedings were tough. Six A.M. was easy—she went back to sleep! Now, she's like a dynamo. She never stops. I don't know where she gets her energy.

—Mother of a fourteen-month-old

You know, I've never been a morning person. But no matter how groggy I am when I stumble out of bed, there's something about that chattering, smiling, raring-to-go greeting of his that's changed my view of morning. Sure, he's cold and wet, but so delighted with himself and full of enthusiasm. I guess it's catching!

—Mother of a thirteen-month-old

The best way to describe Billy? Busy, busy, busy!

—Father of a fifteen-month-old

## Physical Development

### Wobbly Toddly Tot—First Upright Stage

Watch a one-year-old in action and you'll see a living model of a perpetual motion machine. Between twelve and fifteen months most babies begin toddling (on their two tipsy feet). Able at last to move about in the world with some independence, the upright toddler is physically demanding of himself and his parents.

Though hardly sure-footed, the wobbly tot has a new outlook on life. His objective seems to be to reach the top—of everything. Drunk with power, he climbs to the top of the steps, over chairs, onto tables, into closets. He can wriggle under, over, and in between any obstacles that stand between where he is and where he wants to go. Indeed, in his eagerness to reach his objective, the new toddler is often blind to anything that may block his path. So he may (and will frequently) stumble over a shoe, a toy, or even a large sleeping dog. Having reached his objective, he will soon be off to explore yet another shelf, door-knob, or drawer. These are busy days of discovery.

### Gearing Up for Action

With her new mobility, the tod-dler is ready for new action toys and games. She will also use many of her old toys in new ways. Up on her feet, she loves to lug, push, pull, and carry an assortment of large and small toys. It's as if holding on to something helps her keep her bal-ance.

### Action Toys

- The toddler likes to clutch two small dolls, one in each hand, as she goes from couch to table to chair.

- Push-along toys with stiff rods and clackety-jingly sounds are great favorites that act as balancing sta-bilizers.

- Pull-along toys are a little harder to enjoy since they require better body con-trol. The wobbly toddler can walk forward, but she may not be able to look over her shoulder or walk backward. So save these for a bit later.

- Once she's steady on her feet, small wagons and small carriages are great fun for carting piles of toys. These wheeled toys are also used for that fascinating game of dumping and filling.

- Ball games of Roly-Poly can now be expanded to bounce and throw. Soft foam balls are less damaging to furniture and feelings. Big beach balls are also desirable since they're lightweight and supply the oversized bulk toddlers adore.

- Hang a beach ball in a net bag where baby can bat it with her fists.

- Later in the second year, the toddler enjoys small pedal-less wheel toys to straddle and ride.

- Although it is expensive, many parents build or buy a small indoor slide that's used for several years of climbing and sliding pleasure.

- Toward the end of the year, a rocking horse offers exhilarating action and soothing motion.

## Action Games

In our house, toddlers always assumed that when daddy stretched out on the floor he was available for action games like Giddy-Up or Flying High. A word of warning: Both of these games may be overstimulating and too exciting when played right after dinner or just before bedtime.

Gentle roughhousing and piggy-back riding put the world in different perspectives. Hanging upside down or riding way up high, the toddler shares the sheer joy of derring-do. She views the world from the eye level of an adult and finds that everything looks quite different up there. With your steadying hand ready, the toddler tests and stretches her physical limits. Developing an inner sense of where her body begins and ends, what it can and can't do, takes time and plenty of energy. Yet it is as essential for sound physical development as the food you feed her.

### Giddy-Up

Adult lies on stomach. Baby climbs on back. Adult gently rides on hands and knees, taking the jiggling-giggling rider giddy-upping. Punctuate with whinnying or barking or motor noises (no grunts, please).

### Flying High

Adult lies on back, lifts and lowers toddler up in the air. This is much noisier and more fun than lifting dumbbells.

### Can't Catch Me!

As baby comes toward you, get up on your knees and let baby chase you. Although you call, "Can't catch me!" do allow baby to catch you. That's part of the fun! Toward the end of the year, baby will probably turn the game around and call, "Can't catch me!"

### Active Watching

In contrast to all their physical action, toddlers do (mercifully) enjoy short spells of quiet watching. These are moments when the toddler is actively taking in the world with her eyes. Staring at raindrops running down a pane, cars rushing past, daddy shaving, mommy fixing lunch—all provide spellbinding action for watching how things get done. At times, it can be orchestrated with your running commentary—telling what you're doing, one step at a time. But not everything requires words. Sometimes we grownups need to remember the old saying: Silence is golden.

### Oblivious to Danger

Balancing on their feet demands so much effort, we can hardly expect toddlers to handle the problems of cause and effect. Oblivious to danger, the toddler expects paths to clear as he speeds on his way. So, teetering on his toes, arms spread like airplane wings, he starts the second year with slightly tipsy, staggering steps. In a matter of months his hesitant staggering will have changed to a self-assured swaggering trot. In less than a year the toddler goes from walking step by step to running round and round.

Now, the importance of childproofing (see chapter 2, pages 30, 31, 35) becomes doubly urgent. This is the time for locks on windows and gates on steps. It is the time for locking up medicine chests and cleaning supplies. Pocketbooks with aspirin, jackets with lighters, and other things you have always left around now need to be put out of reach. You may be shocked to know that the poison that kills the greatest number of small children is aspirin!

## Social Development

### Limiting the Limitations for Learning

Quite apart from childproofing for safety, clearing the decks for action can limit the amount of friction that grows from having to say "No, no!" and "Don't touch!" too often. The simple fact is that touching is what toddlers do. Indeed, it is what they *must* do if they are to learn.

Toddlers taught not to touch may get the notion that exploring is "bad." Since exploring is how they learn, such a message can put lasting limitations on the motivation to learn.

### Supplying Touchables

It's really not enough to remove the "untouchable" objects that you don't want broken. On the positive side, parents can provide materials that invite exploration.

> • Instead of putting all books and shelves off-limits, set up a shelf with a few magazines and sturdy books that your toddler can handle. Of course, part of the fun is in emptying the shelf, but don't be surprised to

find him "reading" and chattering to the pictures. Inevitably, pages will be ripped, so supply this shelf with magazines you're finished with.

- In the kitchen cupboard (see chapter 2, page 36), provide a changing supply of "puzzles." Look for boxes or plastic containers that open in various ways (snap top, sliding, screw top, hinged lid, etc.). Putting small toys inside that can be heard adds a little mystery to be solved.

- A nest of cans can be covered with different textures of sandpaper or interesting fabrics (corduroy, satin, burlap, nubby wool, terrycloth, etc.).

### Touching Games

Take the time to lift and let your toddler "make things happen." Best favorites are:

- flicking the light switch on and off
- pushing the doorbell to hear it buzz

Toddlers are also interested in getting a brief but close-up feel of other "unreachables":

- paintings
- wall mirrors
- high-up windows
- hanging light fixtures

Learning to touch "gently" with care takes time. Sitting down with a prized treasure and allowing the toddler to examine it with supervision is one way to begin teaching respect for fragile things.

### Games of Discovery

You can play upon a toddler's love of discovery with little social games that call for a bit of hiding (by you) and seeking (by baby).

### Hand It Over

Shuffle a small ball or cracker from hand to hand, then ask baby, "Which hand?" When baby guesses, hand it over.

### Cover Up

Throw a cloth or pillow over one of baby's stuffed animals, leaving an ear or leg showing. Ask baby, "Where's the bunny?" Variation: Instead of covering the bunny, put it on a shelf where baby can spot and reach it and ask, "Where's the bunny?"

### Squeaky-Eekie

Put a squeeze toy under a cushion, press down and see if baby can find the toy. Extra squeaks are definitely allowed.

### Where's My Baby?

The old game of Peek-a-Boo takes on more action now as baby hides his whole self and then comes running in or popping into view with giggles. Toddlers will enjoy repeating this game again and again if they have a receptive audience asking, "Where's my baby?"

### Lost and Found

This is a pretend game that you begin by making believe that you can't find the baby or someone else who is right there. "Where's ———?" you ask as you search under the table, in your pocket, behind the curtain.

## More Social Development

Thirteen-month-old Matthew totters toward me . . . clutching a small wooden car in his hand. Generously, he thrusts the car in my hand, turns, and totters away from me . . . crossing the room he turns again and races back to me . . . reaching his destination he clutches the car, giggles, and takes off again on the same path . . . again and again he repeats his happy game. . . . "I giveth; I taketh"—he is giddy with his new power to control people, and objects, and his own wobbly feet.

—Baby-sitter

### More Eager Than Able

Upright and mobile, the toddler stands at a developmental crossroads. Those first steps are not merely a physical milestone, but a significant emotional turning point as well. From where he stands, the toddler has a new view, not only of his surroundings, but also of himself.

Standing on his own two feet, he begins to see himself as a separate person. Although he is more eager than able, he strives to do things for himself—to become more self-sufficient. Pulling chairs, lugging boxes, climbing stairs, the toddler tests his physical power. His successes build his inner sense of physical competence and strengthen his view of himself as a "doer."

### Firm but Gentle Limits

Heady with power, he begins to express his budding independence with some negative behavior. He says "no" long before he can say "yes." He does not want to be bossed around or physically restrained. He wants to decide when, how, and where he will and will not go, dress, eat, and play. This declaration of independence need not turn into open war. Just as the child tests his physical limits, he also tests the limits of his power with people. He does not want total victory or total defeat. He wants and needs the security of firm but gentle limits.

For both parent and child, this developmental stage requires a balancing act of "holding on" and "letting go." While he feels powerful with what he can do, he feels frustrated with what he cannot do. Still lacking in language and physical dexterity, the toddler is more dependent than independent. Without allowing the child to become a tyrant, parents can appreciate the positive reasons behind the negative behavior.

All through the early years the child forms his image of

himself as others see him. If his parents see him as more "good" than "naughty," more "able" than "helpless," then the child sees himself as good and able.

Such positive or negative feelings are long-lasting. They are feelings he will bring to the playground and the classroom. These early years shape his view of himself for years to come.

### How to Accentuate the Positive

- Select toys that can be used in several ways rather than one "right" way.

- Give the child time to explore many ways to solve problems.

- Where possible, allow the child to make small choices—a red ball or a yellow ball.

- Praise small gains that have been hard won with persistence.

- Instead of slapping inquiring hands, offer interesting distractions, tempting alternatives.

- Don't worry about "educating" him—keep his love of learning alive.

### Learning Right from Wrong through Play

"But doesn't a child have to learn right from wrong?" (Or, "Whose house is this, anyway?") Sure, he has to learn right from wrong, that it's your house as well as his. And the time will come when the child can be reasonably expected to respect "your things," but this is not the time—not if you value your child's developmental needs.

Rather than living in a state of constant alert, put your treasures away for a while. Bric-a-brac can be kept under wraps—but curiosity can be stunted if it's too sharply curbed.

Instead of getting tied up with a steady string of no-no's, offering attractive alternatives can reduce the sting of off-limit items. Mommy's current pocketbook is not for playing with— but an old pocketbook has miles of play potential and the added attraction of being mommy's—the real thing.

Opportunities to examine "real things" with care and super-vision demystify them as well. Although my daughter had a wind-up music box of her own, she quickly knew the difference between her toy and the glass-topped music box (that was out of reach) on my dressing table. For a while, we watched and listened almost daily to the delicate French folksong it played. Taking the time to enjoy it together was a pleasant interlude that allowed me to teach her how to handle things gently—for enjoyment. Equally important, by letting her listen and watch, her interest was satisfied and soon refocused on other things.

### Constant Supervision Without Constant Interference

Naturally, there are some things that are absolute no-no's— things that are simply never to be played with or dangers that cannot be removed, such as the top of the stove, a blazing fireplace, or electrical outlets. Reserving the no-no's for real danger makes the message more meaningful.

Toddlers don't need lengthy cautionary stories about "a little boy who got so badly burned he had to go to the hospital and he was . . . etc." They do need a simple command and a short explanation: "No, that's hot!" Such direct words and serious tone tell the child what and why, without overloading the communication circuits. Overelaborate explanations and constant cautions ("Watch out . . ." "You'll fall . . .") may overwhelm the child's sense that the world is a safe and exciting place to explore. Better to remove the obvious hazards and eliminate the need for unnecessary hassles.

Of course, short of living in a vacuum there's no way parents can prevent all accidents. No one can devote every waking moment to watching—nor should they. Young children do not need bodyguards hovering over them at all times. Somewhere in between parents have to find a formula for constant supervision without constant interference.

## Intellectual Development

### Learning to Learn

How parents handle the physical and social demands of the upright child will have a long-lasting effect on the child's intellectual development. In fact, research has shown that this second year of life is the most crucial time in the child's intellectual and social development.

Childhood experiences that occur during the second and

third years of life influence later learning in school. These are the years when children "learn to learn."

By understanding the toddler's physical, intellectual, and emotional needs, parents can foster development with play materials that invite independent exploration. This doesn't mean setting the child free to run wild. With all his drive for independence, the toddler still wants and needs to know that those he loves are nearby. He wants them to share his enthusiasm and discoveries. He needs parents to play with him, talk with him, and listen. He understands and communicates far more than his limited power to speak indicates.

### Language and Play

During this exhausting and exciting year, your child's word power is likely to grow from just a few words to more words than you can count. Much of this language development grows out of having and talking about a variety of experiences with people, animals, and play materials. First-hand experiences help children understand the many meanings of a single word. Take "dog" for instance: There's your pet dog, a dog that's a doll, a dog on the street, a picture of a dog in a book, and—of all things—a hot dog. They are all "dog," but the single word stands as a symbol for the many forms of "dogness." Learning to name the world of things demands answers to his persistent question: "What's dat? What's dat?"

But not all of his language is learned through direct imitation. Although he is still limited to single words, he is learning the rhythms and patterns of speaking. That one little word—"no"—can be used to ask, to command, to tease, or simply to answer a question.

Listen to a toddler "talking" on his toy telephone or to his teddy bear and you'll hear the patter of a budding conversationalist.

In a variety of play experiences parents can expand the child's understanding of words without turning language into overloaded lessons. Remember, as with most toddler learning, words are learned in action.

## Language Expanders

### Picture Books

Snuggled in your lap a toddler will enjoy looking at and listening to the very simplest of picture books, books that have clear illustrations of children doing everyday familiar things—getting dressed, taking baths, eating, and playing. Colorful and sturdy, the heavy "board books" can stand up to the poking and pointing of a toddler's "reading."

Toddlers like books with animals and the sounds they make. Books with things that go, like cars, trucks, fire engines, jets. Although "story" books with a once-upon-a-time line may hold his interest a little later, right now "picture" books go along with that drive to name the world, to store up labels. This is no small thing in terms of learning. A picture is, after all, a symbol for something real, just as a word is a symbol. Learning to read symbols is a beginning skill that enlarges the child's use of spoken words and, in a real way, builds a readiness for reading words.

Picture-book games that involve recognizing and naming things are a splendid alternative to the more physical kinds of play for toddlers. The energetic youngster needs this balance between highly active play and quiet-time activities, and it's a welcome relief for parents as well.

Borrowing from the old game "I Spy," you can play a little word game with any of these clearly illustrated books.

To help the baby learn the names of the objects, you can say, "I see a doggie—do you?" Baby or you then point to the doggie and repeat its name. "Yes, here's the doggie." After baby has the hang of it, make the clues a little tougher. "I see something that goes ruff-ruff-ruff." In time your baby will be giving you riddles to solve.

### Singing Games

Enlarging your child's fun with language can also be done through songs. Mother Goose nursery rhymes can be read aloud from books and heard on records. They can be played and chanted for the pure pleasure of their rhythm. Little songs that involve action and naming the parts of the body provide active learning:

> *Clap, clap, clap your hands*
> *Clap your hands together*
> *Clap, clap, clap your hands*
> *Clap your hands together.*

Make up your own variations: stamp your feet, tap your knees, shake your head, roll your arms, etc.

Part of the fun of playing and singing comes from inventing ways to use an old idea in a new way. In time your baby will enjoy inventing her own songs and actions, but for now, you're the model for top-of-the-head ideas.

### The Whole Sentence Game

Obviously, language-expanding ideas will come to you as you play with or respond to your toddler. Without drowning him in words—your responses to his single-word utterances can make a difference in his language development. By responding with sentences that incorporate his single words, you expand his listening and, ultimately, his speaking vocabulary. When your toddler says "doggie!" you can expand his one-word sentence with "Yes, Tony sees a doggie!" or "What a big doggie!" or "That's a brown doggie!" You also show him your interest and respect for his early attempts to be understood. Without drilling for correct pronunciation, you set the model by saying the words correctly. Even if your toddler seems to have a limited number of words, you can be pretty sure, if you're talking to him, that he's storing them up like a squirrel with nuts.

In our family, our second child was a late talker. Looking back, I realize that it was almost impossible for the poor child to get a word in edgewise. His big brother was always talking and seemed to anticipate what the younger child wanted without his having to ask. But the younger one was soaking it all in. As I recall, he hardly spoke in single words. He started in paragraphs the day his brother left for kindergarten.

## Research Scientists

In a way, tiny toddlers and research scientists are very much alike. They both have an abundance of curiosity and persistence. A scientist needs time, quiet, a well-stocked laboratory, and sometimes a grant to pursue his research. He needs freedom to experiment, to make mistakes, and to try again. He needs opportunities to share and clarify his findings with others. A toddler's lab is his home. His research method is play. Most of the materials he needs are there at his fingertips. What he needs most is:

- freedom to explore with safety

- freedom to experiment by banging, turning, shaking, tasting, poking, tearing, throwing, dropping, lifting, and tugging

- freedom to discover that things are hard, soft, heavy, wet, cold, slippery, high, low, big, bigger, small, smaller

- freedom to make mistakes and encouragement to try again

- opportunities to share and clarify his discoveries.

Lacking such freedom limits not only what he learns, but how he learns and even *if* he learns.

A toddler needs time, noise, a well-stocked lab, and adults that grant him enthusiastic encouragement to pursue his research.

## Setting Up the Lab

Quite apart from storebought toys, the home itself offers the toddler fascinating equipment for "scientific" experiments. As an infant he was involved chiefly with people. Now, as a toddler, he spends much of his time playing with objects.

## Appearing and Disappearing Toys

Storebought or homemade form boxes with differently shaped openings add a new twist to the filling and spilling he liked to do earlier. Small blocks dropped into the right opening disappear and then reappear on demand.

You can make your own shape puzzles by cutting one or two block shapes in the plastic lid of a large coffee can or shoebox.

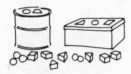

Of course the old favorite, Jack-in-the-Box, does his appearing and disappearing with a turn of the crank or lift of a lid. Some young toddlers find Jack's sudden appearance a little alarming. If yours does, put Jack away for a while.

## Apart and Together

This is also a good time to add two- or three-piece puzzles to the lab. Choose puzzles with whole pieces of fruit, cars, and animals. Whole pieces that can be named are much more meaningful to children this age. Form boards with simple geometric shapes and strong colors will also hold their interest. You can talk about putting the "red" piece in, or the "round" piece. Don't expect your toddler to learn both attributes at once. Concentrate on color or shape.

## Stacking Up and Knocking Down

Frozen juice cans or plastic dairy cups (cottage cheese, ice cream) are fun for stacking up and knocking down.

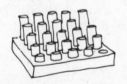

Lightweight but sturdy cardboard blocks are great for lugging and piling.

A small set of (wooden) blocks could be introduced—just a few pieces—to stack in low towers or to line up for roadways.

### Moving Parts

Introduce small cars and trucks that can be lined up or rolled along make-believe block highways.

Hammer boards with bright pegs offer both noise and action, plus that old magic of pegs disappearing and reappearing when you turn the board over.

### Musical Toys

Pianos, xylophones, bells, rubber-headed drums give pleasure to the senses. Pounding produces sounds that satisfy the need to make things happen.

By late in the year, your toddler will enjoy a simple, sturdy phonograph with nothing more than on/off and loud/soft controls. He'll enjoy singing along, dancing along, and marching to the rhythms of his favorite tunes.

### Huggables

Soft, cuddly dolls or stuffed animals which may have been neglected may now become huggable-luggable playthings. This is probably the age when Linus got attached to his blanket. Often toddlers attach great affection to one particular favorite. It may be carted from room to

room, to bed, and on all outings. Facing new adventures just seems to be more comfortable with an old favorite friend in easy reach. So try to choose sturdy, uncomplicated companions that can take plenty of loving and lugging.

Both boys and girls will enjoy a small rubber doll. Choose one without moving eyes or fancy hair so it can be enjoyed in the tub, in a cradle, in a small carriage, or in a wagon. Boys—no less than girls—learn a great deal as they "teach" and "talk" to their doll babies. Practicing to be a daddy is no less important than practicing to be a mommy.

### Other Equipment for Spilling and Filling

Most of the kitchen inventions (chapter 2) will continue to be of interest to the young toddler. He enjoys filling and spilling containers with blocks and beads. Nesting cups or cans, rings that go on rods, jars with screw-on and snap-on lids, boxes that lift or slide open—all of these materials are manipulated now with greater ease.

### Pretend Play

Although playing "make-believe" will become much more important in the coming years, you will see some signs of pretending. Toddlers love to tramp around in Daddy's big shoes. They enjoy putting on Mommy's necklace and bracelet. You can supply them with a damp sponge for cleaning off the tabletop. Provide child-sized dust mops and brooms so

they can "help" clean up. Their ability to play will indeed help you
whizz through what must be done.
At the same time, playing at cleaning gives the toddler a sense of doing
something real and being part of the
family. This is no small thing. Isn't
it funny how toddlers can play at
doing what we call work?

### Problem-Solving

Early experiments in problem-solving often involve taking
things apart. Emptied drawers, tissue boxes, toilet paper rolls,
and bookshelves may be annoying. But comfort yourself: The
toddler is not making mischief so much as he is making discoveries.

He has discovered that something you do will turn on the TV
or open a door. Through trial and error, he tries hitting, jiggling, pulling, turning the knobs and dials and buttons. Short
of frustration or danger, allow the toddler time to figure out
how things work.

In fact, one of the toddler's great experiments is taking off
his clothes. No, he's not a blooming exhibitionist. Undressing
is the other half of dressing, but learning how begins with
taking it off—often, taking it *all* off. You can make or buy a
button and snap book that may satisfy his need to practice
buttoning and unbuttoning, but that's no guarantee he'll keep
his shirt on.

## Keeping the Lab in Order

Although brightly painted toy boxes are highly decorative
and eye appealing, they are rarely the best way to keep toys.
Generally, toy boxes are too deep and difficult for a toddler to
reach into. With so many bits and pieces, toys become jumbled
and useless piled one on top of another.

A low set of wide shelves offers much better access and sets
the stage for orderliness. Of course, toddlers much prefer emp-
tying shelves to putting things back. But parents who take the
time can turn putting toys back into a game.

"Bring me the trucks." "Where does the puzzle go?" "Will the
drum fit here?" This approach works better than firm pro-

nouncements like "Put your toys on the shelf now!" Establishing habits of orderliness is not entirely foreign to toddlers. They are great lovers of ritual. So this is a good time for setting patterns for order.

A collection of baskets for beads, colored cubes, toy animals, and so on are great fun for dumping and are lightweight for toting. So are plastic tool carriers with divided sections. By setting up separate containers for like objects, you are helping your toddler begin to learn important skills of sorting and classifying.

## *The Outdoor Lab*

Action is the name of the game. On the city playground or in the backyard, toddlers are ready for swinging and low slides.

A sandbox with a variety of scoops, pails, and containers offers a new dimension to that favorite experiment of dumping and filling.

In warm weather a tub of water or small wading pool provides more raw material for filling, spilling, and disappearing. With toddlers, remember that water activities need constant supervision.

Water, sand, leaves, pebbles, grass, flowers, and bugs are all there waiting to be discovered. The rich variety of textures, sizes, shapes, and smells provides the young scientist with a wealth of materials to investigate.

Given tools to explore with and listeners to answer their "What dat?" questions, children and the outdoors are an unbeatable combination for all seasons.

## Summing Up

In this second year of life your child has grown from wobbly toddling to sturdy 'n' steady—from walking to running—from jamming things together to trying to make things fit—from rocking in place to dancing a jig—from babbling sweet nothings to saying "no!"—from waving bye-bye to saying "bye-bye"—from spilling things out to filling things up—the second birthday cake approaches—your toddler stands at the threshold of being able to tell you—

"Me do it myself!"

# Chapter 4
# *Terrible/Wonderful Two*

Holding an empty muffin tin, Alexander runs to his mother
calling, "Muffins . . . muffins hot . . . want muffins?" "Delicious!" she says, tasting a pretend muffin from the tin.
"Thank you, Alexander, for this delicious muffin!" Alexander
climbs into the soft cushioned chair where mother is reading
a book. After giving and getting a hug, Alexander begins
jumping up and down . . . "Bounce . . . I bounce . . . I a
bouncer." "Alexander . . ." Mother begins. "Muffins? Want
more muffins?" Alexander hastily changes the subject. Before Mother answers, Alexander is on his way, running to
cook more muffins.

Sure-footed and steady, Alexander runs, climbs, and bounces
through his active day. Between the ages of two and three he
will grow to half his adult height; at twenty-seven months
Alexander has already lost some of his baby fat and is beginning to look much more like a little boy.

Casting aside his muffin tin, Alexander the bouncer runs to
the far end of the room. With no help at all he climbs up five
steps and stands at the top of the slide—he is king of the
universe. "Catch me!" he calls. "Catch Alexander!" Big, bold,
and independent Alexander still wants Mommy there to
watch, applaud, and catch him.

### Big and Little Had a Race

This need to be both boy and baby, this desire to hold on and
let go reaches a new level of intensity as the two-year-old
struggles with his hunger for independence and his continuing
need for dependence. Indeed, two-year-olds are faced with an
assortment of frustrations. They're beginning to know how
things are 'sposed to fit, work, sound, look, and happen. But
their words and actions very often fall short of the mark. They
just don't have the necessary skills.

"Bow," Johnny calls as he marches around the room
humming through a long tubular shaker rattle.

"Bow?" His mother is puzzled as Johnny continues marching to the music of his "bow." "Oh, bow . . . trombone," his mother translates for herself and smiles.

Johnny's daddy had played his old trombone the day before, much to Johnny's delight. Of course, no music came out when Johnny put his lips to the mouthpiece. And moving the slide with Daddy's hand was fun—but not the same. What Johnny wants and says is "Me do it myself!"

## Power of Make-Believe

With his growing ability to pretend, Johnny has invented a *symbol*—his rattle has been transformed into a trombone. This magic of making one thing stand for another is a significant way that children deal with reality. Through make-believe, they bring the big, confusing, and often frustrating world of things down to their own size.

Playing at make-believe, the young child becomes the all-powerful person he cannot be in reality. In pretending, the child takes control of his otherwise powerless position. Not only can he change a rattle into a trombone, he can transform himself into a frisky puppy that yaps and snaps or a hungry lion who growls and prowls. He can flick himself on and off, from real to make-believe, from boy to tiger. His world is full of magic. Playing pretend he can turn real events into make-believe. While real birthdays come just once a year, he can make a birthday cake of mud and candles of twigs in the sandbox any day.

## Replaying the Familiar

A few months before our second child was born, James picked out a baby of his own, an Italian doll named Tonino who became his constant companion. Although the doll had no gender, there was never any doubt that Tonino was a boy baby. Tonino took naps, rode in the wagon, ate dinner, and took baths. He went everywhere with us. He was a member of the family. In fact, when James's brother was born, it just seemed altogether natural to name him Tony.

—Mother of a three-year-old and infant

Pouring milk from teapot to cups for his teddy bear, the child "controls" liquid matters as teddy's cup runneth over. Teddy is the one who "is so messy," who "needs a nap," who has "wet his pants again!" These two players, teddy and the tot, understand each other completely. Teddy understands who's the boss and every word the boss has to say. Teddy is a willing, flexible, and uncritical partner who can growl like a bear, sleep like a baby, and listen like a pal. So the two-year-old "replays" the familiar events of his day-to-day life.

Since few little children really get to see the outside work their parents do, they play at the familiar household tasks of mopping, vacuuming, cooking, and caring for their pretend children. They act out the grownup nurturing roles they know best. Although boys most typically play these games with toy animals (because dolls are often not provided), we know that boys and girls benefit from playing pretend. There's no reason to fear that a boy who plays with dolls will turn out to be a "sissy." Caretaking is part of being a parent—a role both fathers and mothers play in real life.

Unless Daddy works at home, children can rarely imitate more than his departure and arrival. In a world where both men and women increasingly work outside the home, boys and girls can benefit from opportunities to play at roles in child care and housekeeping. But pretending is not so much practicing for the future as it is a way of understanding the present and immediate past.

After a visit to the pediatrician, Alexander is very likely to be playing doctor, not patient. Giving shots or medicine to all his patients and listening to their hearts, looking in their ears, noses, and mouths—Alexander is able to unload some of his natural fears. By reversing roles he plays at being the powerful one. In make-believe he makes all the rules—a welcome relief from the real world where others seem to make all the rules. He is the master of right and wrong, good and bad.

## Providing Props for Pretend

Understanding the value of playing pretend games, parents can provide a variety of props that support make-believe.

- Rubber dolls that can be bathed, fed, and "go pee-pee" (go to the potty) are basic. Clothing should be minimal, and simple to get on and off. The fact is, two-year-olds are more likely to undress than dress their play children.

- A storebought or home-made crib or cradle should be supplied with small blankets for covering and uncovering baby. A small carriage will cart baby, blocks, and assorted treasures that are loaded and unloaded (an old play pattern from infancy).

- A plastic dishpan or toy sink is basic for bathing baby and dishes, pots and pans. (See "water play," page 29.)

- If room permits, a toy stove and toy refrigerator can be bought or made from large cardboard boxes and painted with burners and dials and doors that open and close. Small replicas of ovens that heat up are more appropriate for older preschoolers.

- Toy pots and pans, plastic teapots and dishes, plastic fruits and vegetables, plastic baby bottles, cutlery— all lend themselves to pouring, feeding, washing, and cooking up fun.

- A toy iron (no heat necessary) and ironing board are also fun—yes, if you're two, ironing can be fun.

- A child-size table with at least two chairs will be used for everything from tea parties to fingerpaints. Since scrubbing the toys with plenty of suds is one of a youngster's great joys, choose a table that can stand up to a frequent "cleaning."

- A small chest of drawers or a shallow "treasure chest" of wicker can be useful for storing dress-up clothes. Elaborate "costumes" are not important to twos—they do enjoy stomping about in a pair of mommy's or daddy's shoes, a hat, a tie, a pocketbook, bracelets, necklaces, briefcase, and scarf.

- A toy telephone will now be used for "private" conversations.

## Values of Pretend Play

Although a crowded apartment may not permit establishing a total "playhouse" for your child, providing some place and realistic props for pretending will lead to valuable learning. Playing make-believe, children enlarge a variety of very real skills. Manipulating the props provides opportunities for eye/ hand coordination in dressing and undressing their dolls, filling and spilling tea cups, opening and closing lids, jars, doors, and drawers. Along with developing motor skills, pretending enlarges the fluid use of language, through dialogues and monologues. In playing many parts, the child explores a broader range of feelings—in acting out roles they might never play in reality. This ability to use the imagination needs to be fostered and encouraged. It is the basic raw material for the creative thinking and problem-solving that they will need to do throughout life.

## Physical Development

Action for the sheer joy of action is still the name of the game. Two-year-old Johnny climbs the steps, not because he wants to get something upstairs, but because the stairs are there and climbing is fun. He can now climb up although he must use both feet for every step. By midyear he may be able to go down the steps in the same way.

On flat ground, running is his favorite style. By midyear he is such a good runner he hardly falls or trips over toys or misplaced obstacles along his path. It is as if his feet have radar that carry him round about or over the debris he scatters as he goes.

Although action for its own sake is still the prime mover, two-year-old Johnny is not totally aimless. He may be attracted to someone or something and run for a "look-see." Chances are his interest will be short-lived. His attention is still limited.

Opportunities for twos to stretch, flex, and build their big muscles should be part of the daily scheme of things. No, they don't need a gymnastics class or formal exercises. But they do need room to run, jump, and climb. Although a crowded urban apartment has space limitations, parents can provide indoor action with various kinds of simple equipment.

### Indoor Action Toys

No one child needs everything on this list, but here are some ideas to choose from.

> *Walk-the-Plank:* A simple (but smooth) two-by-eight plank of wood makes a great balance board for walking.

Young twos may need a steadying hand to start. Once they have the knack of it, suggest they try to walk the plank sideways or backwards. As they become still more proficient, you can raise the board up off the ground with two fat phone books. This adds challenge to conquering space. As for storage, the plank can be stored under a bed or in a closet. Later in the year, a narrower two-by-four board presents a whole new challenge.

*Rocking Horse:* Twos love the soothing back-and-forth action of a rocking horse, which also lends itself to pretend trips to town.

*Swings:* Indoor swings can be hung in doorways if getting to the park is impossible. Twos can't quite "pump" their own swing, but they love being pushed, "more" and "more."

*Tunnels:* Storebought cloth-covered tunnels give twos an opportunity to explore moving their whole selves through a space problem. Large cardboard boxes, though less durable, offer the same kind of adventure.

*Wagons:* Loading and unloading small wagons provides plenty of action. These are good for playing make-believe deliveries . . . also terrific for playing Pick-Up (though Put Away is not so much fun).

*Big Hollow Cardboard Blocks:* These lightweight but sturdy cardboard blocks are great for stacking and knocking down. They can be carted by the wagonload and eventually will be used with wooden blocks (see chapter 5, page 100).

*Ride-On Trucks:* Pedal-less riders that children can straddle and drive are great for exercising legs and imagination.

*Big Bounce-On Balls:* These oversized balls with a handle for holding are great fun for bouncing about on.

## Outdoor Action

Whether you live in the country or in the city, your two and you will really benefit from some outdoor action. Either playground or backyard, both offer that wonderful expanse of space for running, jumping, and climbing.

*Sandboxes* are the best of all possible places—where a pail can be filled and emptied and filled again. Other props can be added to the sandbox: a strainer or sieve, cups, spoons, small realistic trucks or cars.

*Basket-Type Swings* give

more security and are en-joyed so long as you are will-ing to push.

*See-Saws* are great fun for up-and-down action, if an older child is available for the ballast.

*Low Slides and Low Climb-ing Gyms* need supervision, but provide that big muscle stretching action they thrive on.

*Tire Swings:* If you've got a sturdy tree, one of the best climber/swinger combos is an old tire hung with a solid stout rope. This is great for sitting on, standing on, and spinning in. Drill holes in the bottom of the tire so that rain water doesn't collect. In addition to swinging and spinning on, the old tire is fun to throw a ball through. For longevity, it's probably best to buy heavyweight nylon rope for your tire swing.

*Trikes:* By midyear, most twos are ready to learn how to pedal a small trike. It does take time to learn how ped-als work, but a little push from behind will get the ped-als turning and get the ac-tion going. Too big a trike is worse than no trike. Since little trikes are outgrown so soon, see if you can buy or borrow a used one. Blocks added to the pedals may help beginning riders get a firmer foothold on driving.

*Low Wooden Climbing Gyms* proved to be one of the best investments we made. It could be climbed (with close supervision) up and over. By adding wide cleated planks to the climber, the children could walk, run, slide, and jump up and down the slanted planks. For years, the climber was used for sheer physical fun and pretend play as well. It outlasted the metal swing and gym set and had greater versatility.

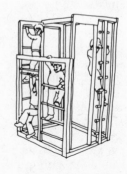

Depending on your location, outdoor equipment might also include child-size shovels, rakes, and gardening tools. Obviously, in warm weather, water play (see pages 75–76) can be extended to the out-of-doors.

## Values of Active Play

Obviously, twos are not old enough to take themselves to the park or to play outside independently. When our first child started toddling, my father-in-law gave us an extravagant gift—a fenced-in play yard. Three children and two dogs later, I can tell you that except for the birds and chipmunks (which were free to come and go), no living creatures were ever contained by that fence without an adult companion.

Perhaps it's just as well. Getting outside for some fresh air is probably as beneficial for you as for your child. Taking time to watch a bug crawling, a worm wiggling, a jet soaring is part of the shared adventure. Away from the phone and the confines of home, your two-year-old gives you another chance to see the world with fresh eyes, to rediscover the excitement and wonder of it all.

Unfortunately, in too many cases today, "getting out" means going to the mailbox or going to the mall. While some of these excursions are interesting and valuable, they tend to be even more confining than home. They do not invite the kind of exhilarating play and motion that young children need.

Active play provides an acceptable way for a young child to use his natural storehouse of energy. Lacking a legitimate place for spending that energy may lead to explosive backfire. Indeed, what grownups often call "misbehavior" is really "misplaced" and natural behavior. Like playful kittens and frisky puppies, young living creatures need time and space to stretch and test their growing bodies.

Naturally, supervision is an absolute must. You can't childproof the world or put pillows on every path. There are hazards you'll need to be aware of in the backyard or park. Glass in the sandbox, going too close to the swings, standing at the bottom of the slide, running into the street after a rolling ball—all of these are real and potential disasters waiting to happen.

Yet none of these dangers are reasons not to get outdoors and play. It does mean, however, that you'll need to take an active role in supervising their play. One of the great tricks in parenting is anticipating predictable trouble before it happens and finding ways to skirt it. For instance, it may be better to go to the city playground while the big swingers are in school. It may mean sitting near the sandbox and talking instead of

reading a book or magazine. It may mean getting outside when you'd rather watch television or talk on the phone. Let's face it, living with a two-year-old can be a tiring, full-time job. On the other hand, it's a temporary job (with long-range rewards). At least being out-of-doors gives both grownup and child a change of environment that can have a positive effect. It can lift you out of that cut-off, stifled feeling of being cooped up all day. You don't have to live on the frontier to develop cabin fever.

Digging, climbing, running, and jumping, the child tests the limits of his physical self. Finding out what his body can and cannot do, practicing and mastering the physical challenges he creates for himself builds a basic inner sense of well-being.

These feelings of being in control of one's body and one's actions, of feeling able, are carried into other tasks that are challenging to mind and body, and may bolster later success in the classroom.

## *Fine Motor Tuning*

In contrast to the expansive whole-body action, your two-year-old is also actively refining her fine motor tuning. Now she can use her eyes and hands together better than just a few months ago. Happily, she uses some of her old toys with greater ease and is also ready for some new challenges to her new-found dexterity.

*Big Wooden Beads* to string on a stout shoelace present a good challenge for eye and hand. Be sure the lace has a long stiff casing on one end and a solid knot at the other.

*Shape Sorters:* Once the three-shape sorter (see chapter 3, page 52) becomes old hat, a more complex sorter can be made or bought. Some offer eight or more sizes and shapes and may require a few demonstrations.

*Caution:* If the frustration level is too high the toy will be abandoned. So, if the puzzle's too puzzling, put it away for a while. Unfortunately, parents often overlook the satisfaction children find in playing with toys they have mastered. Sometimes we need to remind ourselves that every-

thing doesn't need to be hard to have value. Children love successful repetition. Feelings of success are valuable in motivating a child's further struggles for new successes.

*Nesting Cups, Barrels, Blocks, and Eggs:* These are still easier to take apart than to put together completely. Yet who says they have to be put together completely?

*Simple Puzzles* with large pieces may still require a little parental help. While adults usually do a jigsaw puzzle just once, children do and undo their puzzles again and again. In fact, twos love to memorize their puzzles and show how fast they can do them. So there's no need to worry about spoiling the fun of a puzzle by helping along. You don't have to pick up the piece and fit it in—but you can make some helpful suggestions about trying the "red piece next" or "Where does the big wheel go?"

*Sewing Cards* can be made with a hole punch and cardboard . . . draw a bold picture of a simple object and punch scattered holes along the outline. Sewing is done with a long colorful shoestring. (Remember to knot one end.)

*Plastic Construction Toys* that screw, snap, or link together give small hands and fingers the kind of repetitive activity they need. Nuts-and-bolts toys that screw and unscrew, oversized blocks that snap and unsnap, bristle blocks that stick and unstick—all invite the child to use his eyes to guide his hands, to get his toys together and apart. Storing toys with multiple pieces can be simplified with straw baskets or plastic tool boxes with tote handles.

*Miniature Settings:* Farms, garages, houses, and other playscapes lend themselves to little pretend dramas. Though storebought buildings are costly, a handy parent can make a barn or garage with a sturdy cardboard box and paint. These can be furnished with inexpensive cars, trucks, animals, and people. One of the toys our children enjoyed most was a Noah's Ark that was more like a houseboat with a lift-off lid. Inside the ark lived a sturdy collection of creatures. Two by two the animals were matched and marched in and out of the ark.

## Art Materials

Art supplies will now be welcome tools for exploration. Remember, at this stage the child's interest is in the doing—not the artistic end product. Since permanence is not important, a chalkboard and colorful chalk are quite satisfying to young scribblers. Erasing is almost as much fun as drawing. In fact, painting with water on a chalkboard is sometimes more fun than chalk. In our house we finished the sliding doors of a low closet with charcoal-colored paint and created a big enough chalkboard for several children to work on at once. In later years it was used for playing school, Tic-Tac-Toe, math homework, and, finally, family messages. For the youngest, the broad expanse gave their early drawings free range and kept them off the other walls.

> *Crayons and Paper:* Large sheets of blank paper will be welcome tools for scribbling bright squiggles, lines, and circles. Their early scribbling is really a form of experimenting with the many kinds of lines they can make. In time, they discover they can join lines to make shapes and enclosures. This is not the time for teaching the child to write letters or to draw a flower. Don't worry about how your two-year-old holds the crayon or which hand he uses. One crayon at a time is sufficient and fat crayons are sturdier for small fists than skinny ones. Most twos will shift crayons from one hand to the other and have not settled on right- or left-handedness. Nor is there any reason to believe that righties are better off than lefties. Letting the child decide which hand he commands best requires a hands-off attitude by parents.
>
> This is not the time for coloring books that demand keeping the scribbles inside printed lines. Limiting your twos artistic exploration to paper (as opposed to walls) will require supervision and a generous supply of paper.
>
> *Paint and Brushes* can be enjoyed by some two-year-olds, although two and a half may be time enough for most. Start with one color of tempera paint, a fat-handled brush, and a good stack of paper. Remember, the two-year-old paints for the pure sensory pleasure, not to create an end product for framing. Parents should avoid asking the child, "What's that supposed to be?" Chances are it's not "supposed to be" anything. Rather than making positive or negative value judgments, parents can show their appreciation by commenting on some dominant features: "What a bright red circle!" or

"You really make a lot of blue dots!" In other words, describe what you see.

*Caution:* Keeping the paint and its drips on paper (as opposed to floors, tables, and clothes) is no simple task. All the value of painting will be lost if the child has to worry about making a mess. Naturally, you can't allow your child to run around with a loaded paint brush. You can provide an oilcloth or plastic dropcloth to protect a contained area and a cover-up smock (a cut-down shirt) to protect clothing. A word to the wise: Some twos simply aren't ready to abide by any territorial restrictions. Better to postpone paint and brushes for six months than to stir up tempera paints and temper tantrums.

*Fingerpainting:* Although it's messy (maybe because it's messy), two-year-olds seem to put their whole selves into the act of fingerpainting. Although some twos are very reluctant to get their hands dirty, most really relish getting up to their elbows in the stuff. Unencumbered by a brush, fingerpaints invite knuckles, nails, fingertips, and whole hand action. In fingerpainting, the child usually uses both hands at once to swirl, dabble, and draw. Moment by moment the picture changes with paint responding to the child's motions.

While the demands for staying clean (and dry) are very much a part of the two-year-old's daily life, fingerpainting offers a legitimate way to muck about and mess around. Naturally, for everyone's sanity, fingerpainting requires a contained area where the artist can swirl and slide his hands without fear of messing up. A

large sheet of oilcloth or plastic should be draped on a
child-sized table. Since the accent here is on doing—
rather than creating a finished product—you need not
use paper. A large tray, formica tabletop, or sheet of
oilcloth makes a fine surface for paint and hands in
motion. Standing seems to be the best approach. If you
choose to use paper, you'll need to find some with a
shiny surface (shelving paper is perfect). Using a
sponge, wet the paper to smooth it down. Next, put a
blob of paint in the middle of the paper and your artist
is ready for action.

### Fingerpaint Recipe

3 TBS cornstarch
3 TBS cold water

Combine to form a paste.
Then stir in 1 CUP OF BOILING WATER.
Stir till smooth.
Add vegetable coloring or tempera
    paint to desired color.
Cool and serve up for fun.

*Homemade Playdough* is fun to make and then to
pinch, pull, pound, squeeze, and cut up. Again, the finished product is unimportant—action and making
things change is what it's all about. With the addition
of plastic forks, knives, and plates, children may make
pretend pies, cakes, and what-not. Of course, you can
buy nondrying plasticine or playdough—just be sure
they're marked *nontoxic*—or use this simple recipe
that will keep if stored in a plastic bag.

### Playdough Recipe

1 cup flour
⅓ cup salt
A few drops vegetable oil
Enough water to form dough (⅓ to ½ cup)

Optional: dough can be colored with
    vegetable color or splash of tempera
    paint.

Aside from paint, clay, crayons, and chalk, don't overlook the pleasure of a pencil and small note pads for young children. Felt-tipped markers with their bold, easily flowing colors are one of the best treats imaginable to a two-year-old. Just be sure they're marked *washable* and *nontoxic*.

None of these artistic ventures will fill up the whole morning. Twos are not likely to work more than ten to twenty minutes at any single activity. But even if it's only ten minutes, it has enormous value to the child. Of course, the follow-up action of washing out brushes and sponging off tables and cleaning off hands (and possibly noses) should not be overlooked as part of the fun.

## Water Play

In a pool or tub, a hose or pail, in a cup or a puddle, a sink or the sea, frozen solid or liquid flowing—water remains an all-time favorite of young children. Of course, water play is both soothing and full of surprises. It can be sprayed, sprinkled, spilled, squirted, and sipped.

Naturally outdoor water play requires less mopping and sopping up. However, a bathmat or thick layer of newspaper can soak up spills from indoor play. A plastic dishpan placed on a towel-draped low table will catch drips before they hit the floor. Plastic runners with treads tend to be less slippery than a sheet of wet plastic. They come in handy for painting sessions, too.

Add a dash of soap and an egg beater and it can be whipped into a froth of bubbles to wash dishes, dolls, clothes, tabletops, and hands. It can be spilled and filled from teapots to teacups. It can be squished out of sponges and squirted out of squeeze bottles.

In a puddle or a sandbox there are scientific experiments waiting to be explored—bugs that swim, leaves that float, pebbles that sink. Watching water vanish in sand, studying snow turn to water, an icicle melting—seeing these things first-hand lays the groundwork for understanding basic scientific concepts. Remember, always supervise water play.

## Two Sides of Two: Terrible and Wonderful

Sometimes at night I look at him sleeping so peace-fully—looking like a perfect angel—and I wonder, what in heaven's name is going on inside that head of his . . . what makes him so stubborn, so obstinate, so downright aggravating!?

—Mother of a two-and-a-half-year-old

My son just used to say "no"—but my grandson is something else! He looks me straight in the eye and says, "No way, grandma, no way!"

—Grandmother

## Just What Does "No" Mean?

There's no use denying it—two-year-olds (and most typical two-and-a-half-year-olds) can be trying at times. Indeed, in their play, *trying* is exactly what they're doing . . .

- trying to test their power and yours
- testing the limits of what's acceptable and unaccept-able
- trying to find out what's possible and impossible.

If twos had a theme song, it would be:

> *I want what I want when I want it—that's all that
> makes life worth the while! I eat when I'm hungry and
> drink when I'm dry—yes, I want what I want when I
> want it!*

Of course, not even a two-year-old with the most patient, loving parents in the world can have everything he wants when he wants it. Furthermore, given too many choices, a two-year-old often can't even decide what he wants. So there are days (or parts of them) when life with a two-year-old seems like a no-win situation.

Yet, this relatively short-lived time need not become a game with winners and losers. At the heart of the matter is a child who (in spite of all evidence to the contrary) wants to please himself and the people he loves best—his parents. But, just as he gains physical skills with practice and more practice, learning what is acceptable and unacceptable takes repetition and more repetition.

### The Role of the Adult

Knowing right from wrong is not the same as being able to choose right over wrong. That kind of control does not come so early nor so easily. Yet, there are signs that the child is learning:

> He knew the wedding cake was not for touching. It was almost comic, the way he made a straight line for the forbidden cake. With his little finger trailing through the icing . . . he kept watching over his shoulder. . . .
> —Uncle of a two-and-a-half-year-old

Indeed, two-year-old David looking over his shoulder knows someone had better be coming to save him from what he cannot save himself from.

For some time to come young David will remain dependent on adults to set firm but reasonable outside controls until he can take control of his own impulses. Of course, this leads to some confrontations between parents and child. But in many instances, a parent armed with a sense of humor and good timing can offer stimulating and satisfying play activities to redirect unacceptable behavior.

> You can't allow two-year-old Jackie to comb baby's hair—yet she can comb her doll's hair.

Andy can't cut his own meat with a knife—but he can cut up pieces of playdough.

Mary can't go to school like her big brother—but she can play school and have lunch from a lunch box.

Jonathan can't pinch or poke the new baby—but he can pinch, poke, and pound a piece of clay or a rubber doll.

By its active nature play opens new channels for venting the child's energy and emotions.

### More Than Toys

Providing not just toys but an interest in the child's curiosity and enthusiasm will help you to match her energetic style with appropriate activities. Like all of us, children need a variety of rhythms to their day. We need time for physical motion, quiet relaxation, being with people, and being alone. Teachers of young children understand these changing needs and schedule the day's activities accordingly. At home, the two-year-old's needs are no different. Taking time to get them started, making a pretend telephone call to your little doctor or TV serviceman, setting up tea for the doll family, help to extend the pleasure in playing pretend. Taking time to sit down with a book or puzzle makes for a refreshing pause, heightened by your undivided attention.

Obviously no one can or should spend the entire day entertaining a child. Toys and activities should be chosen that offer a good balance for playing alone and together, playing quietly and noisily, playing with big muscles and small, balancing challenges with plenty of success. But toys alone are not enough. Young children learn through interaction with the important people in their lives. They learn through their everyday, real life experiences.

Trying and time-consuming as your two may be, these are also days of tremendous growth and learning. With their gift of gab, two-year-olds are warm and wonderful companions. They are lavish in their affection, and thrive on positive attention.

## Social Development

### Early Playmates

While the infant and toddler are almost entirely dependent on willing playmates within the family circle, two-year-olds become increasingly interested in playing near (and, in their own way, with) other children.

For years, child-study experts have used the phrase "parallel play" to describe the way twos play *next* to each other rather than together. Yet, increasingly, day-care specialists are reporting that two-year-olds who spend their days together form relationships that go beyond playing next to each other.

As in all things, twos are inexperienced in the "social graces." When it comes to possessions, the two-year-old's philosophy is simplistic—"What's mine is mine and what's yours is mine, too!"

So they grab, jab, clutch, and cry, "Mine! Dat's mine!" Naturally, parents worry and wonder, "Why is my child so selfish, so self-centered, so spoiled?" But selfishness in a two-year-old is not a sign of a weak character—just an inexperienced one. It is part of the struggle to define one's self.

### Parents' Role

In trying to understand the big confusing world of things and people, two-year-olds have a mind set something like the three bears, who have a mama's chair, a papa's chair, and a baby bear's chair. In making sense of the world, twos tend to be very rigid in their orderly view of things. His possessions are almost a part of himself, and not to be "broken all to pieces" like the baby bear's chair or bed. So, in a way, a two-year-old is protecting part of his "self" in what appears to be selfish behavior. Learning the business of give and take, sharing and taking turns, requires time, plenty of practice and, most especially, supportive adults who can help the child become a social being.

Often, the ideal playmate is a four- or five-year-old who has already learned some of the techniques of playing with others. The older child is delighted to "show how that works" and offers the two-year-old a model for playing cooperatively.

Bringing twos together for short playtimes does require some planning ahead.

- Putting away prized or favorite toys makes good preventive sense.

- Setting out the toys that "they" will play with helps the child prepare for the onslaught.

- Where possible, supplying materials that are easily divided (this takes the sting out of sharing). For example: playdough, fingerpaint, sandbox, water play.

- Sharing a snack together also provides a pleasing interlude after active play.

### You Mean They Need Two of Everything?

Having two of everything might sound like the ideal arrangement. Certainly, having two kinds of wheel toys, sand toys, or whatever will smooth the way. But even with a cribful of dolls or a boxful of trucks, one doll or truck is apt to be "the" toy of everyone's choice. This, too, is part of the learning that comes through play. Accepting an alternative toy or waiting for a turn can be hard for a time. These early playtimes are another form of exploration—of trying the limits of others and seeing "what happens."

You can help by assuring your child that "when Tony is finished, you'll have a turn." Chances are, his interest in the desired object will be forgotten or quickly spent when Tony is finished. But do follow through by offering him his turn and making good on your word. Keep the visits short. An hour is probably maximum time for your twos. Better to end a playtime on a positive note than allowing it to run itself ragged. Or, as they say in show biz—leave them wanting more.

Although learning to play with others may seem like more "work" for you, the benefits to your child are both immediate and long-lasting. By providing occasional playtimes with others, you help enlarge the child's circle of friends and build upon the pleasure of becoming a more social being.

## Forming a Playgroup

Given the two-year-old's growing interest in others, many parents today have joined together and formed playgroups. For parents and children in small apartments or rural settings with no easy access to playgrounds, meeting a few times a week helps break up the isolation. These "co-op" playgroups are usually supervised by parents on a rotating basis. Such arrangements offer benefits for both parents and children without large expense. They do require planning and a willingness to cooperate. You may find *The Playgroup Handbook* by Laura Peabody (St. Martin's, 1974) useful reading.

## Day Care

Obviously, playgroup arrangements are inadequate for families in which both parents work on a full-time basis. Such schedules demand a regular day-care program that both parents and child can rely upon week in and week out. Depending on where you live, you'll want to take the time to visit the various programs that are available. Most day-care centers will welcome your interest and allow you to visit the center while it is buzzing with children.

What should you look for?

Basically, day care should offer a "homelike" atmosphere with enough space and material to invite and extend opportunities to play alone and together. Most essential of all is the availability of caretaking adults who treat children as individuals, not as a group. Day care for two-year-olds should not be "schooling"; rather, the center should be a place where learning goes on every day. The bottom line in choosing the "best" place for your child is: How does it feel? Would you want to spend the day here?

## At Home and Away—The Importance of Play

Children who spend part of their day away from home are likely to encounter a broader variety of toys and play experiences than the child at home. But having toys in school doesn't mean they don't need toys at home. Some toys are so basic they're needed in both places. Dolls, wheel toys, pencils/crayons and paper, balls, simple puzzles, and picture books are certainly minimal needs.

The sense of ownership—*mine* as opposed to everyone else's—may be all the more urgent for the child who lives among many children on a daily basis. Remember, the young child sees his toys as an extension of himself.

On the other hand, the child who is at home full-time will need adults to provide a variety of play experiences. It may mean importing playmates or seeking them out in the park. It may mean going visiting or inviting visitors even though you've got tons to do. It may mean sitting down and playing with your child, even though he can play alone or watch TV.

If you're a working parent with a surrogate caretaker at home, you'll want to be sure that person understands the importance of play to your child's development. Why not share this chapter with your caretaker? Or, give that person specific play suggestions, just as you probably leave word about lunch or dinner. Discuss your feelings about limited TV viewing directly. You don't need to leave "lesson plans," but don't leave things to chance either.

## Language and Play

Just as a dancer moves to the sound of music, your two-year-old at play provides his own soundtrack. He talks to, with, and about whomever or whatever he is playing with. It is as if he must tell himself what he is doing. His language is part of his organizing process. So he describes his own action like a sports announcer describing a game. Only he is also the player, the listener, and the announcer all rolled up in one.

### Playing with Words

Combining play and language, the two-year-old's vocabulary grows beyond naming things. He plays with words and the rhythms they make. Listening to his language gives parents an opportunity to tune in and help clarify the child's understanding and misunderstanding. Little words such as *in, up, on, under,* words that describe places in space, are used and misused as children run their trucks, feed their bears, and stack their blocks. Playing and talking is the active way children get hold of these basic concepts we grownups take for granted. Interestingly enough, these little words are the very words young schoolchildren have trouble with in beginning reading. As a first grade teacher, I often found that some problems in reading really have their roots in language development that begins long before the child is six or seven.

Without drilling or formally teaching speech, parents can extend the fundamental language learning that goes right along with playing.

- You can replay what the child does by describing it: "You're putting the doll in the carriage."

- You can replay what the child says and expand it. For example, child says, "Truck bwoke." You say, "Your truck is broken! What happened?" He says, "Torn, wheel torn." You say, "I see, the wheel came off."

- Try some humor. Say very seriously, "Let's put your mitten on—give me your foot." This upside-down or topsy-turvy form of humor is the first kind of joking that children enjoy.

Language can also be used by parents to smooth the way between playing and going on to other activities. Often, in our rush to get on with the day, we forget that children have trouble shifting gears rapidly. Instead of saying, "Put your toys away now," try to prepare them for what comes next: "We're going grocery shopping soon."
Or,
"In a few minutes we're leaving for grandma's."
Or,
"Pretty soon we have to put the doll to bed."

## Music and Language and Play

Twos continue to love singing and saying nursery rhymes and songs with patterns that repeat.

- Row, Row, Row Your Boat
- Jingle Bells, Jingle Bells
- Are you Sleeping? *(Frère Jacques)*

This is a good time to learn some new fingerplay games and action songs.

Check with your local children's librarian for some song and game books for this age group. Some of my favorites are:

- *Finger Frolics,* compiled by Liz Cromwell and Dixie Hibner (Partner Press)

- *American Folk Songs for Children,* by Ruth Crawford Seeger (Doubleday & Co.)

- *Treasury of Songs for Children,* by Tom Glazer (Songs Music, Inc.)

- *Jim Along, Josie,* by Nancy and John Langstaff (Harcourt, Brace, Jovanovich)

### Dancing Feet

Dancing and marching to music is one of the great joys of life when you're two. Extend your twos' listening and possible dancing repertoire to include a variety of music. Twos will really respond with different body movement if they're offered new sounds. They'll move to everything from waltzes to cha-chas, marches to minuets—especially if you dance along or at least act as audience.

## Read It Again

By now you will have been sharing books with your child for some time (see chapter 3, page 49). In addition to books, your two-year-old will also love hearing you tell stories about "when you were a baby" and the familiar pattern stories of *The Three Bears, The Three Little Pigs, The Gingerbread Man,* and *The Little Red Hen.*

While many parents save picture books as part of the night-time bedtime ritual, don't overlook the possibility of a quiet-on-your-lap storybook after lunch or in between busy times.

Twos are also ready for books with simple stories about everyday things they see or do. Your two-year-old will probably memorize every word of his favorite story and catch any at-

tempt to skip a page or two. Don't worry if he insists on hearing the same old book again and again. It may be boring to you, but not to your two-year-old. Knowing what comes next is part of the pleasure of being a big, smart two-year-old.

## Summing Up

In his third year of life your child has grown from speaking words to simple sentences . . . from saying not just "no" but (miraculously) "yes" . . . from diapers to training pants . . . from imitating what you do to pretending to be a mommy, a daddy, a lion, and a mouse . . . from playing not only with you or alone, but with others . . . from being your baby to being your big boy or big girl.

# Chapter 5
# *Preschoolers*

From the moment they bounce out of bed till the last big hug, little "dwink," got to go, and just another kiss goodnight, preschoolers spend their days at play. Even when they're eating, dressing, or washing, there's an element of play at work.

> Clutching a spoon in one hand, Danny seriously takes a long sip of milk through a straw . . . then, switching from straw to spoon, he tries another method of getting milk from cup to mouth. "Are you drinking or playing?" his mother asks.

The truth is, Danny is doing both. Satisfying his thirst is only part of Danny's experiment. Like Kipling's Little Elephant, he is "full of 'satiable curiosity." This interest in trying many possibilities rather than one "right" way is an expanding form of playfulness that leads to new discoveries. In testing out his own skills and how things work, your preschooler continues to enlarge his understanding of himself and the world through play.

## The Need to Know

His curiosity is heavily punctuated with "Why?" and "How Come?" While the whys may become wearisome, the need to know should be satisfied with simple answers. It helps, too, if occasionally you turn the questions around to "Why do you think——do——?" Listening to a child's explanations may help you understand better what the question is about, or at least the kind of answer that will clarify. Children are especially delighted when they can discover their own answers.

Sometimes, a why question is better answered with "Let's see how we can find out."

Although preschoolers are big talkers, adults often mistake the child's ease with words for genuine understanding. Thanks to TV, today's toddlers may learn to count by rote, but understanding what "threeness" or "fourness" means requires more than flashy lights and singing one-two-three. Lacking objects or reasons to count, saying numbers is little more than a rhythmic chant of nonsense words. Truth and half-truth, fact and half-fact, logic vs. magic—all are a mixed bag that needs sorting out in a rich variety of experiences.

> As a child, every time I heard Kate Smith sing "God Bless America," I'd rush to the window and sing along, so she could hear me. After all, Kate was just down the street at the "station." How was I supposed to know a bus station from a radio station?

### Showing vs. Telling

A lengthy explanation of sound traveling on the air waves from stations to radio receivers was not the answer, either. A child of the 80s, even one who can count, still may think that the people he sees on the TV screen are actually right inside the set.

In listening, talking, and playing with young children, try to remember that understanding does not come through words alone. Preschoolers are still dependent on real experiences they can feel, touch, taste, smell, and see. This sensory style of learning remains the dominant way children build solid understanding rather than surface glibness with words. Oddly enough, one of the most important ways children clarify their understanding of the real world is by playing at make-believe.

### From Here to Reality

Indeed, one of the great developmental tasks of the preschool years is sorting out the real from make-believe. Drawing from both his inner and outer worlds, he creates fantasies from realities and deals with realities through fantasy. If this two-way switch sounds confusing to you, it is even more so to the child. He is not yet sure that good or bad dreams do not come true. His own angry thoughts are so real that he is sure others know what he is thinking. He isn't even sure that thinking or wishing will not make things come true. Even in adulthood most of us still cling to some bits and pieces of magical thinking—we may knock wood, or walk around a ladder, and laugh at our superstitious foolishness. But the preschooler is not superstitious—for him the line between fantasy and reality is not so clear.

> Mother: Mike, I found one of your shoes—where is the other?
>
> Mike: (thinking) I don't know . . . maybe it's hiding.

## More Let's Pretend

Preschoolers play much more elaborate games of pretend than they did earlier. (See chapter 4, pages 60–63.) While the two-year-old played out simple little domestic scenes, the preschooler of three and four plays roles ranging from reality to fantasy.

> "Fire!" the new chief calls, "Ahroom!" He sounds his siren, pops his hat on his head, and hastens to put out the blaze. "We're on our way!"

### Creating Fantasies from Realities

Although he may never have seen a real fire, he has seen and heard firetrucks on the road. With his parents or nursery group, he may have visited the firehouse, sat on the truck, touched the hose, and rung the bell. Putting together what he's seen, he can make a giant leap of imagination that places him in the powerful role of the fire chief.

### Safe Scare

> Rick: Wanna play Vampire?
>
> Chip: Vampire?
>
> Rick: Yup. R-R-R-R- (making menacing faces and sounds).
>
> Chip: No, I don't wanna play that (he walks away).
>
> Paul: I'll play. I'll be the vampire!
>
> Rick: No, YOU can't be a vampire.
>
> —Three three-year-olds

Although some games are scary, there is a need to conquer fear. What better place than in an imagined realm of safe-scare? Obviously, in dramatic games the child can also choose not to play as well. Unlike games with rules that must be followed, the child is in control of what he will or will not do.

Dramatic play is a child's way to rehearse and practice for fearful occasions—both past and future, both real and unreal. This new ability to imagine makes it possible for preschoolers to become terrible tigers and hulking giants, growling angry feelings that would be unacceptable in reality. "I'll eat you up!" he growls at his powerful daddy who an hour earlier told him to be gentle with the baby. So, playing pretend is a safe way to cope with fears and get rid of tensions.

### You're My Friend, Right?

First Child:     After school, you're coming to my house, right?
Second Child:    If my mommy says.
Third Child:     I'm coming, too, right?
                                —Three three-year-olds

Unlike two-year-olds, who are largely content to play next to each other, preschoolers gradually discover the shared adventure and pleasures of playing with each other. Even the squabbling over possessions or who will be the daddy helps the young player in learning how to negotiate with others. Although there are not real winners or losers, in games of pretending children soon learn that the game ends when mutuality ends. "I don't want to be the tiger anymore" can bring a halt to a pretend game whenever the child feels uncomfortable with the role. As the old song says: "It takes two to tango." These early experiences help children learn to predict how others will respond to their words and actions.

So pretend play is a significant way for a child to develop a sense of the needs, feelings, and expectations of others. Although the ability to see things from another's point of view may take several years, playing with other children moves the child closer to becoming a social being. He has come a long way from the two-year-old who played and talked mostly to adults, to the preschooler who plays and talks mostly to other children, and who is beginning to form strong friendships.

Studies show that children who play pretend games together have greater ease in expressing themselves and understanding others. Their play helps them become better at problem-solving and coping with frustration. Preschoolers who are given opportunities to play pretend games with others also seem to be more self-disciplined and better motivated to achieve.

## Imaginary Playmates, or "Choolie Did It!"

Even children who have real playmates may play host to one or more imaginary playmates as well. Just when I thought our family was complete, a little stranger arrived. . . .

"No, no, Choolie!" I heard my four-year-old warning someone in the next room, "Never touch matches!" I thought we were alone, but I soon discovered that "Choolie" was to become a regular member of the household.

It was Choolie who spilled sugar, tracked mud, left water running, and broke the candy dish. When we went shopping, Choolie needed reminding to "buckle that seat belt." It was Choolie who "needed" new crayons and Choolie who opened the crackers. In fact, on one memorable occasion, "it was Choolie's idea" to take a pack of gum at the check-out counter.

### Is It Normal?

Now, there wasn't a doubt in anybody's mind that Choolie was not the sort of friend mother would invite home on purpose. But it should be some comfort to know that magical imaginary playmates do serve a very real purpose in the lives of young children.

Parents often have uneasy feelings about the arrival of imaginary playmates. Just in case you've had those nagging little doubts—or your neighbor has been asking bluntly, "Is this normal?"—you can relax! Research shows that one out of three children between two and a half and four has one or more Choolies in his or her life.

Some children entertain imaginary "human" companions while others host a menagerie of animals or totally mythological creatures. Although some visitors like Choolie come for an extended stay, others come and go and take on new names in a matter of days.

Imaginary playmates are more common among girls than boys, and seem to indicate not only a well-developed imagination but also a high IQ (grandma should love that!). It should be comforting to know that the invention of Choolie does not spring from loneliness or indicate some deep-seated disturbance. Research shows that children from large families and even twins have imaginary playmates during the preschool years. For some children, Choolie remains on the scene until they are five or six.

### Forming a Conscience

Knowing that Choolie's presence is normal may still leave you wondering: Who is this Choolie and what should we do with him?

At first glance, it may seem that Choolie and other imaginary companions are just convenient scapegoats. Of course, they do fill that very human need we all have to "put the blame on Mame" or, as we often say, "The devil made me do it!" After we've broken our diet or lost our temper we often ask ourselves, "Why did I do that?" As adults we can accept and generally control the good and bad impulses within us. But little children of three and four find it less threatening to deal with bad impulses by dumping them on Choolie. By externalizing them, Choolie and his naughty ways can be thoroughly unlovable, while Choolie's creator remains lovable to himself.

Having Choolie out there instead of inside makes it easier for the young child to be critic, teacher, and controller. In creating Choolie, the child takes a long leap toward a significant developmental goal—the forming of a conscience.

This slow and ongoing process of conscience-forming cannot be done with a wave of a wand. A child of three or four is concerned with right and wrong only insofar as they bring praise or punishment from caring adults. It will take several more years before a true conscience is formed—that is, when controls come from within the child rather than without. In a sense, Choolie is a tool the child uses to teach himself the rules of right and wrong.

### The Power of Fantasy

With a magical playmate the young child has opportunities to be both teacher and learner at once. Through fantasy the child becomes all-powerful, practicing out loud the parental dos and don'ts, as in "No, no, Choolie, never touch matches!"

In fantasy, the child can do what he cannot do in real life. Real friends, parents, and siblings will not take the guff that silent Choolie takes. So, Choolie offers a harmless release from the tensions of being powerless. With Choolie, the child is in the driver's seat, playing parent to a part of himself.

### What Should Parents Do?

Occasionally a "bad" Choolie gets under the bed or inside the closet at night. Some imaginary playmates can be more frightening than friendly. Parents will need to reassure the child that his room is safe and that nothing will harm him. Taking time to check out the closet is more helpful than saying Choolie is a fraud. For the young child the fear is very real. Time and repeated experiences with reality will eventually help the child to replace magic with logic. However, this long-range goal cannot be achieved with lengthy speeches about real and make-believe. We cannot make Choolie vanish with our abracadabra words of wisdom.

Parents can help the most by casually accepting Choolie without entering too far into the child's fantasy and enlarging it into a game of their own. Allowing Choolie to sit at the table does not require setting a formal place and providing a bowl of soup.

Without banishing Choolie, parents will need to stress the reality of who actually spilled the milk or tracked in the mud. Slowly but surely, the child will become better able to accept responsibility for what Choolie does—for his own actions. As Choolie becomes less and less useful, the child will banish his imaginary playmate, letting go of a piece of magic that's no longer needed.

# Understanding Reality through Fantasy

Not all dramatic play springs from the child's emotionally charged inner world. Preschoolers also play at what they see and experience in the real world.

Delivering mail, washing windows, drilling cavities, building roads, directing traffic, piloting jets—the preschooler plays seriously in order to understand the work people do. His excursions into the bigger world outside his home are all raw material for his play.

## Parents' Part in Priming Pretend Play

Trips to the zoo, the supermarket, the library, the post office, the garage, the fire station, all supply the ingredients for dramatic play. Nearby visits to interesting action-packed places are more rewarding to the preschooler than extended trips to cultural or historical sites. Preschoolers are far more excited by the here-and-now action of a road being repaired than a trip down memory lane. Save the long-ago facts for the school years.

Allow enough time on these short visits for the child to linger and watch, and wonder and ask questions. Make comments about the sounds, smells, shapes, and feel of things. Try to find books in the library or pictures in magazines that extend the memory of your small excursions.

## More Props

In addition to the props suggested (chapter 4, pages 60–62), preschoolers love more realistic props. When they play fire chief, they like a fireman's hat and/or slicker and boots. Nurses need hats and stethoscopes. Policemen need whistles and badges. Storekeepers need a register and stock to sell.

A chest or drawer can hold quite a costume collection of dresses, jackets, hats, scarves, necklaces, rings, bracelets, pocketbooks, briefcases, and shoes. Sometimes the clothes suggest a game or a game demands a quickly made "costume."

Dressing up is much more fun when there are choices and changes enough to share with a playmate. Naturally, a full-length mirror (unbreakable) enhances the pleasure of preening and giggling.

By providing a wardrobe of costumes, parents give their stamp of approval to a valuable form of play. Adding to or changing the props from time to time also sparks new play ideas. After seeing *Camelot* it became urgent for my young King Arthur to have a crown and cape. The cape was an old velvet skirt hooked with an old bracelet and was used for years by many children.

Oversized cardboard boxes from washing machines or refrigerators can be converted into a versatile playhouse. Cutting a door and window provides a terrific place for everything from puppet theater to spaceship. Sometimes a sign is needed, or a curtain and some paint.

If you haven't room for a cardboard box, a table covered with a blanket or tablecloth can also create a little playhouse to go in and out of or a puppet stage to squat behind.

Toymakers are now making painted "house" cloths that fit a card table and can be put away. These "prefab" houses are a bit more fixed and finished and may therefore limit the scope of pretending. A box or tablecloth lets the child do the imagining.

Playing house and dolls becomes even more elaborate now. Dolls with hair to brush, easy-on/easy-off clothes, and eyes that open and close will get fed, bathed, dressed, spanked, scolded, and taught how to behave. Housekeeping equipment (see pages 61–62) is especially important to the sociable preschooler and visiting friends. Stuffed animals, too, are playful companions for playtime and bedtime.

### Puppets

Simple homemade or storebought puppets invite dramatic play for the child alone or with a playmate. Controlling both the body and words of a hand puppet gives the preschooler a total command of what "another" says and does. With a puppet on each hand, the puppeteer has the pleasure of composing both sides of a conversation, much as a novelist or playwright creates dialogue. Speaking through a puppet allows the shy youngster to say things—silly or saucy—that the child can't or won't say or sing.

For beginners, the easiest puppets to operate are sock or mitten shaped.

These can be made with an old mitten or sock and decorated with eyes, ears, or hair with yarn and bits of felt. Remnants of fake fur or plush can be sewn by hand or machine.

Puppets with arms require more dexterity to operate and may be more desirable for older preschoolers and their school-age brothers and sisters.

Of course, paper-bag puppets are easy to make, though less sturdy. Brown lunch-size bags make quick and inexpensive puppets with features added by magic markers or crayons. Rod puppets, made by anchoring a juice can or paper plate on a stick, will also serve.

Although one can purchase drawstring "talking" puppets, their novelty is short-lived and may even short-circuit the playful and unpredictable things puppets are capable of saying.

Children who have experience in playing with puppets will in time create little stories of their own or play out familiar stories they love. These early excursions in oral composing are a form of readiness for writing skills in the school years.

When children play with puppets together, puppets provide another mode for cooperative play. The players need to send and receive, listen and be heard. Puppets can punch and poke, tease and shout, tell each other off without offending the puppeteer's dignity.

"Puppet to puppet" allows for asking and saying things one might not talk about "face to face." This quality of being once removed—of talking indirectly through the mouth of a pretend character—is a useful technique for parent and child dialogue. Conversations that might otherwise be embarrassing or provocative are somehow defused through puppetry.

One of my children used a puppy puppet to ask some big questions that needed answers.

"You be the doctor," he would say, handing me a white-robed doctor puppet.

| | |
|---|---|
| Puppy (child): | Woof, woof—hello doctor! |
| Doctor (adult): | How are you feeling today? |
| Puppy: | Fine, except I gots a baby growing inside me. |
| Doctor: | You do? |
| Puppy: | Not me, my mommy has. |
| Doctor: | So, you're going to be a big brother. |
| Puppy: | Only thing is, how does the baby get out? |
| Doctor: | No problem—the baby comes out of a special opening. |
| Puppy: | Why can't it come out right now? |
| Doctor: | The baby is too small. |
| Puppy: | When will it come out? |
| Doctor: | It needs more time to grow. |
| Puppy: | Oh . . . let's have some cookies, doctor. |

## Sex and the Preschool Set, or Tony and the Tulips

During the preschool years most children are sexually curious about themselves and others. Some of this interest is expressed in sexual questions and in sexual play. Most threes and fours are likely to ask: "Where did I come from? Or, if a new baby is on the way: "How will it get out?"

When we were expecting a new baby, I made the mistake of telling our three-and-a-half-year-old son Tony that the new baby would be born when the tulips bloomed. Although my physical appearance was noticeably changing, young Tony kept his eye on the garden and anyone who might step on it. In spite of all explanations to the contrary, he held fast to the notion that his new baby would spring—not from a cabbage patch—but the tulip bed.

While it's fine to give preschoolers answers about their sexual questions, don't expect them to understand or even remember from one or more tellings. The important thing is to tell them what they want to know simply and honestly. Often you'll hear that information played back in their dramatic games of pretend.

Chances are your preschooler will also express his interest in sexual curiosity with the age-old games of Doctor, or "I'll show you and you show me." Parents are often alarmed to find their preschoolers giggling and naked, exploring each other with great interest.

Most experts agree that such games are altogether normal and natural. Rather than overacting with alarm, parents need to deal calmly and firmly with the situation. "That's enough of that game . . ." and "Put your clothes on" will convey what you want and expect here and now. This is not the time for lengthy lectures or stern punishment. Nor should parents assume it's the other child's fault. Neither blame nor shame are the key issues here. At no time should children be made to feel there's something dirty or shameful about their bodies.

On the other hand, there's a huge difference between casting shame and conveying an attitude of anything goes. Kids need and want parents to set limits. They need parents to teach them what is socially acceptable and unacceptable.

### What Is the Question?

Basically, when children play sex games they are sending out signals about their natural curiosity. They want to know how their bodies compare to others . . . from bellybuttons to buttocks, from tummies to toes. They want to know how boys are different from girls. What they're looking for together is more in the way of sexual information than sexual stimulation. These questions are particularly compelling to the child who has no siblings or no siblings of the opposite sex.

### What Is the Answer?

Parents who understand the basic questions their kids are asking can provide a variety of alternative ways to satisfy the child's curiosity. Arranging to visit where an infant is bathed or changed supplies some of the answers kids are looking for. Frank and honest answers will take away the mystery and worry children sometimes have about their bodies as compared to others. In a casual way, nursery school bathrooms have been providing these everyday lessons in unisex bathrooms for years.

Basically kids want simple and direct answers to their questions. They don't need elaborate details, diagrams, or demonstrations. When five-year-old Jennifer asked her parents, "Where do I come from?" they immediately sat down and explained all the facts about eggs, seeds, and fertilization. Poor Jennifer listened with glazed eyes as the discourse droned on. When they were finally finished, Jenny said, "But that's not what I mean. Karen comes from Philadelphia. Where do I come from?"

### Your Values

In recent years, some parents have thought that their own openness in dressing/undressing in front of their children would answer all the child's questions. Yet, in reality, a little girl's body is nothing like a grown woman's body. And a small boy's body is hardly like a man's. Indeed, for some children, unable yet to formulate questions, the differences may be more worrisome than helpful.

Then, too, there are many adults who are simply uncomfortable with a lack of physical privacy. Sexuality is a sensitive and personal affair. How you handle it with your child has to fit into your own value system. In passing along parental values just remember that early feelings about sexuality are part of the long-lasting baggage children carry into adulthood. So go easy on heavy guilt trips here. Remember, they're not acting promiscuous—just curious.

## Blocks

If you could buy only one special toy for a preschool child, there's probably none better than a big set of wooden building blocks. Unlike wind-up toys that lose their novelty or plastic toys that break or lose their parts, blocks offer years of play that enrich the child's social, intellectual, and physical growth. Even children who attend nursery school enjoy playing with blocks at home.

> The day after Alan called his mom to tell her she was going to be a grandmother, he called back and told her to please pack and send his blocks.
>
> —New mother

Of course, this new father is going to have quite a wait before his daughter is ready for blocks. During the toddler years blocks are used largely for carting about and dumping. But, real block building comes into its own during the preschool years.

Observe a group of three-year-olds in a day care center:

| | |
|---|---|
| Molly: | OK, I'll build with you and nobody else will. |
| Kate: | We have to close it up, right? |
| Molly: | Be careful—take all the blocks. We are using *all* the blocks! |
| Teacher: | You're using lots of blocks. |
| Kate: | We're going to make a playground, right? |
| Molly: | I think we have too much blocks. |
| Kate: | Going to fall down! (Purposely knocks them down.) |
| Molly: | We build it again . . . we're cooperating making this building. |
| Kate: | These should be closer, right? |
| Dean: | (Arrives on scene, says nothing.) |
| Molly: | You can't build with us, Dean! |

Molly and Kate have gone well beyond the beginning stages of block play. Their "playground" is a complex series of four-sided enclosures. Molly is not only building walls, she intends to keep others out. Her game is closed to others. Kate is her exclusive friend and they will use "all" the blocks. While Molly is far more involved with social issues of "cooperation," Kate defines what they are building, how to build it, and how to rebuild it "closer."

Not far away, Sam and Mike have been lining up blocks. Their "barn" goes all the way from one wall to the end of the block corner. "It's big!" Sam boasts. "You forgot the animals!" Mike rushes to remedy Sam's oversight. He lines up one animal next to another. "Trucks!" Sam shouts. Now Mike and

Sam begin lining up truck after truck. "Just big ones!" Sam commands. "No little trucks!"

Neither Molly and Kate nor Sam and Mike spend much time actually playing with their buildings. The act of building is more important to these three-year-olds than the end product.

### Advanced Block Play

In contrast, the more complex block buildings of the four- and five-year-olds are often remarkable structures—spectacular studies in symmetry, intricate patterns, and creative works of art. Not only does the child enjoy the act of building, he has great pride in the end product. "Look at what I made!" he insists. "See, this is where the cars go in and up the ramp." He happily explains every minute detail, the ins and outs of his marvelous inventions—which, if at all possible, he wants to keep standing for as long as possible. From his own actions, he brings life, drama, and motion to the small people, planes, cars, trucks, and animals that inhabit his miniature world. He supplies the rumble, roar, and reason. Such elaborate little worlds can be built alone or in the company of two, three, or even four other players to manipulate the miniworld.

Unlike structured toys which "come as they are" and must be played with one way, blocks invite the child to invent an ever-changing toy world of his own. Molly's "playground" and Mike's "barn" are symbols that stand for something else. This ability to invent, imagine, and represent reality is a giant step in learning how to think in new ways. It takes the child one step closer to dealing with more abstract symbols, like words and numbers. Parents who are eager to hurry their children into reading and writing often overlook the prereading skills that support learning to think symbolically.

### Block Play and Language

Going back to Molly and Mike, it's obvious that playing together makes social dialogue necessary. But the language of block building has an equally rich value in the understanding of little words that define big concepts. *Up, in, on, under, in back of, in front of, longer, bigger, shorter, thin, top, bottom, wide, higher, wider, even, less,* and *more.* In handling blocks the child feels, sees, and slowly learns the word symbols we use to compare and define, to locate and describe.

Children who have grasped these concepts through their everyday play experience are likely to have fewer problems learning to understand such words. And when they begin to read, they bring meaning to their reading rather than sheer mechanics of "sounding out" letters.

### Math Concepts

Math concepts such as more, less, same, and different; curved, straight, square, rectangular, triangle, etc. are built into the blocks children play with. In experimenting with building they discover that you can use four square blocks to balance off one long unit. They discover that two triangles put together form the same shape as one square.

> Get the other half.
> Get one more.
> That won't fit.

Without formal lessons preschoolers build the foundations of math concepts in their block structures.

### How Many and What Kind?

A preschooler can never have too many blocks. Unpainted

hardwood blocks can be cut and sanded from scrap lumber if you have the tools, skill, and space. They should be cut in units that are the same width and thickness and cut in lengths two or four times as long as the basic unit block.

Storebought blocks also come with a few ramps, curves, and cylinders that add extra dimensions and possibilities. The illustration below shows the possible shapes and varieties and number of blocks recommended for a nursery school. Scaling the numbers down to home use will depend on your budget and space limitations. Costly as blocks may seem, their long-term and flexible use will outlast many flashier toys.

If buying or cutting wood blocks seems prohibitive to your budget, you might consider a set of unit blocks made from milk and cream containers. These will need some cutting and taping to square off their tops. Between half-gallons, quarts, pints, and half-pints it's possible to assemble a plentiful block set in several weeks. Although they lack the variety and weight of wooden blocks, they are a good and inexpensive alternative.

How blocks are stored can affect their usability. If you dump them in a box or toy chest they may become just part of the clutter. Better to provide a low shelf where blocks can be sorted and stored in size order. Even the business of putting blocks away has built-in learning possibilities.

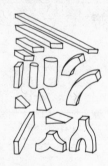

**Accessories for Block Play**

Simple wooden trains and snap-together tracks are used alone or in concert with block building. Lengths of track may be elevated on blocks or snake under block bridges and tunnels.

Accessories are especially important for enriching block play.

| | |
|---|---|
| small trucks | people |
| cars | animals |
| planes | carpet samples |

These are the toys that will inhabit the miniworlds your child constructs. Stored in open shoe boxes or baskets on the block shelf they provide another sorting activity when clean-up time rolls around. Label the boxes with a picture and the word.

Older preschoolers may enjoy having signs taped to thir buildings: "Post Office," "In," "Out," "World Trade Center," whatever. Taking the time to admire their work and suggesting a sign post here and there adds support to their play. It is also another small connection between words and print and prereading skills.

While blocks require an investment of money and making space available, they are among the best-loved toys your children can have. In playing with blocks your children will make an investment of themselves—of their physical, intellectual, and social selves. Toys that stimulate doing and thinking have the added value of enlarging children's ability to stay with a task and stretch their staying power. Learning to solve problems of balancing bridges, ramps, and towers also helps children to accept some frustration in exchange for the pleasure of getting things to work.

Building up or pushing down their mighty creations—there is no fear of breaking things that should not be broken. Indeed, there is an element of power in this being able to break down what they have built. It is theirs and that, too, is a pleasing notion.

## Other Construction Toys

Building with Lego blocks and Tinker Toys provides children with another form of building miniworlds. These smaller bits and pieces call for greater dexterity of small fingers and hands. They require less space and are easier to cope with in small apartments. Since most construction toys come with pictured end-products, your child may get stuck on the business of what "they" show on the box. While reproducing a copy of something predesigned is a worthwhile skill, it should not be the sole objective of the toy. Encourage your youngster to explore and invent designs and structures of his own.

## Art Materials

In addition to the art materials suggested (in chapter 4, pages 71–75), the preschooler is ready to explore the possibilities of blunt scissors for snipping paper, and glue, tape, and paste for sticking things together.

While your two-year-old scribbled, painted, pinched and pounded clay for the sheer joy of doing, preschoolers become increasingly interested in the outcome of their actions.

> "Look at this!" Amy announces proudly as she holds her painting in front of her and walks around the room. "I made this! See what I made!"

With growing control of hand and eye coordination, pre-schoolers' paintings and scribbling become less accidental. Often they will name what they've painted after the fact, but the three-year-old doesn't set out to paint a cat or a tree. Usually, it is the shape of what he's painted that suggests itself and then gets named by the child. In large part, there is still a great deal of exploration of color, lines, and shapes. The pre-schooler's love of repetition is one of the ways he explores the materials and how things happen.

### Setting Up the Paints

Here's what you will need:

- tempera (poster) paint. You can find it in most art supply stores. Buy the three primary colors (red, blue, and yellow). Add white and black later.

- long flat-handled brushes—½ inch and 1 inch. Those called "brights" are the best choice.

- a plastic container for water.

- a sponge for cleaning brushes.

- jar lids or plastic furniture coasters for mixing paints.

- a tray to hold supplies.

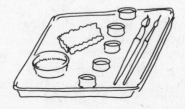

- newspaper to cover tabletop. A flat surface is easier to paint on than an easel where paint drips.

- paper—there are all sorts of papers perfect for painting. Ideally it should be 18 x 24 inches and may be purchased by the pad or in a ream. Ask for newsprint (without the print, of course) in the art supply store. Real newspapers can be used, too. The classified ad pages have such small print that they disappear into the background. Large sheets of old wrapping paper are useful too. Anything in quantity is a better choice than opting for a short supply of quality paper. Kids need plenty of freedom to experiment and discard.

A few pointers:

- Pour a small quantity of each color in a lid or coaster. Close jars tightly, so paint does not dry up. Older kids will be able to do this themselves. (Syrup jars with lids or squeeze bottles will make this easier.)

- Show your child how to clean the brush in water and test for cleanliness on the sponge. With threes you may find it simpler to introduce one brush for each color and avoid the water and sponge business until the child is older.

- Don't forget a smock or big cover-up shirt to protect clothing.

- Show your child how to clean up after painting. Learning to work in an orderly way begins at the beginning.

You can show your appreciation of the child's work best by describing what you see. "You've used three kinds of green." Or "You painted a big red circle and two little ones."

Some children may have a good deal to say about their paintings and drawings. They may even have whole stories to tell. Your child may be delighted if you offer to write down the story of all that is happening. On the other hand, some kids find questions an intrusion and have no stories for sharing just now. Don't be too pushy about getting a story out of every painting they make or they may limit their painting or drawing. Actually, children's drawings tend to be far more representational or "realistic" at this stage than their paintings. So pencil and crayon drawings may be a rich source for beginning storytelling.

Don't overlook the pleasure kids get from seeing their work displayed and admired. A plastic frame that allows for changing paintings can be hung in the child's room or in more public places. Without making too much of end-products, children like to know that you value their efforts.

### Printmaking

Tempera paint may be used in a variety of ways for print making.

- Sponges cut in various shapes make interesting stamp designs—especially good for making gift wrapping and cards.

- Fruits and vegetables can be "inked" by dipping them in paper saturated by watery paint and then stamping them on paper. A slice of potato, the tops of carrots, zucchini, an eaten half-grapefruit, a slice of apple—all make interesting prints.

- A waxy crayon or chunk of paraffin can be used to draw a design or picture—then washed over with thinned paint. Since paint will not cover wax, the result is an interesting "resist" print which children find rather magical.

- Wet, colored construction paper makes an interesting surface for drawing on with colored chalk. Dip paper in tray of water, then put on flat surface. (Protect surface as color comes off.)

### Clay

Preschoolers bring a new approach to their clay play, too. While a two-year-old is interested in simply exploring what clay is like, your preschooler is likely to poke his fingers into the clay and show you his "cup," his "bowl," or a "swimming pool." They love to make cakes, snakes, and all kinds of shapes. Permanence is not nearly as important as the pleasure they get from the three-dimensional and changing material in their hands.

Actually, there are a variety of modeling materials to choose from:

- Playdough may be bought or made (see page 74).

- Moist clay can be bought in art supply stores by the pound and must be kept moist.

- Plasticine, which is mixed with oil and never hardens, comes in a variety of colors.

Each of the materials is exciting to work with and responds very differently to the touch. You may need to work the plasticine with your hands to warm it up and make it soft enough for the child to manipulate. Playdough is fine for patting and pounding, but doesn't respond to the hand or hold its shape the way clay does. A box of clay from the art supply store will last a long while if reasonable care is taken to keep it moist and firmly wrapped. If the clay you buy seems too hard to mold, add some water to the bag and tie it up. In another day or two it will be ready for action.

Although three-year-olds tend to do and undo their modeling efforts, fours tend to name what they have made and add on to their creations. They begin to be more inventive and enjoy saving some of their work for display.

### Construction

Once children have had plenty of hands-on experience with clay, they may wish to explore the three-dimensional world of constructions. Using clay or large styrofoam scraps as a base, the child can construct compositions with a variety of pliable, stickable elements:

| | |
|---|---|
| toothpicks | telephone wires |
| tongue depressors | straws |
| pipe cleaners | shells |

### Collage

This is a great time to start collecting bits and scraps for making two-dimensional collages. A basic collection could include:

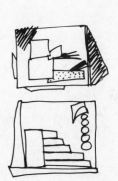

- bumpy cardboard from cookie boxes

- tissue paper in many colors

- bits of fabric in different textures (rough, smooth, shiny, patterned)

- cotton, net, gauze

- foil.

All of these lend themselves to cutting, aranging, and pasting in pleasing designs. White liquid glue can be watered down and applied with brushes. It tends to hold better than white school-type paste that dries and hardens in lumps.

Since much of the collage material is heavy and paste is wet, it's best to provide a cardboard base for the background. Often the results are highly imaginative and purely decorative. Yet collage gives the child still another opportunity to explore the contrasts of texture and feel of many materials.

As with their block creations, preschoolers are often eager to tell a willing listener a long story about their creative masterpieces. Not every collage has a story, so don't press the issue. Rather than asking "What's that?" you can show your appreciation by admiring a dominant feature—lumpy and smooth textures, the arrangement of their design. Often, preschoolers will pick it up from there and tell you a name or whole adventure that goes with their pictures. Older preschoolers may enjoy having you write down their story so you can read it back to them. Making this early connection between spoken words and written squiggles is a big step toward learning to read. In truth, the act of being a storyteller comes long before becoming a story reader or story writer.

## Developing Fine Motor Control

Colored markers, crayons, and all sorts of paper invite the child to use smaller muscles and finer control than paint brush and paint require. Although coloring books are widely available, the business of learning to stay inside the lines of other peoples' drawings really limits the bigger possibilities of coloring in one's own pictures. If a child has plenty of opportunity to create his own pictures, then an occasional coloring book will probably do no harm. But the exclusive use of coloring books can discourage children from drawing pictures of their own at all. If learning to control hand and eye is an objective, better to provide blank paper of various shapes and sizes with an assortment of writing tools. Pencils, wide and narrow markers, crayons, and chalks all produce very different results. A scroll of shelf paper, a little note pad, or a blank artist's pad each invite very different approaches. In contrast to the simplistic pictures of things children find in coloring books, the drawings children create are another road to making symbols that represent other things.

Older preschoolers often express an interest in learning how to write their names. Without making a big lesson, show them how to print their name—using a capital for the first letter and lower case letters for the other letters. Parents often print the whole name in capital letters, thinking they are easier to write. But teaching them to do something that then has to be unlearned seems unfair. In school the name will need to be written in capitals and lower case. Better to learn it that way to begin with.

Actually the interest in printed words may mislead parents into the belief that their preschooler is ready to learn to read. Some preschoolers do show a high interest in knowing "what dat says." By all means tell them, encourage them, but don't drill them. Learning to read at three or four is often done at the expense of far more engaging tasks that are more appropriate. Making "labels" or signs for their block buildings, puppet shows, and art work provides a meaningful connection between spoken words and print.

## Value of Art Experience

In working with art materials, you are giving your child rich learning opportunities for physical, intellectual, and emotional growth. Paint, clay, and paste do not come formed and ready to be played with by pushing a button. They are unstructured materials which the child must shape and form in a personal way. The only rules are built into the nature of the material and how it responds. Using eyes, hands, and mind the child is in charge of making something of nothing, of solving problems, in making decisions, and using his own imagination. It is not merely a way for the child to express himself and release tension. Nor is it merely an exercise in discovering that red and yellow make orange. Art experiences offer the child the active excitement of discovering by making things happen. It is another step toward making personal symbols for real objects or feelings. Children who have rich experiences with creating their own symbols are more likely to understand the symbol systems of others who draw, paint, write, and compose. Art experiences—in addition to being fun—open doors to aesthetic and intellectual growth.

## From Print to Play

Visiting in the three-year-old nursery class, I overheard a literary tea party:

Kara: Want some tea?
Billy: (sits down) Sure.
Kara: (stuffs blue dough into teapot and begins pouring) Want cake, too?
Billy: What kind of cake?
Kara: Just cake . . . or chicken soup and rice is nice.
Billy: Oh, I thought (he giggles) it was Mickey cake!

Why literary? Well, both Kara and Billy were playing with soup and cake that came right out of two of the most popular children's books in print—*Chicken Soup and Rice* and *In the Night Kitchen,* both by Maurice Sendak. In making the connection from print to play Kara and Billy demonstrate one of the ways children use their storybooks to reshape and enlarge their play and language.

Reading books to your preschooler provides more than shared moments of pleasure. Children of three and four are ready now for the little dramas found in storybooks that have a beginning, a middle, and an end. They especially love storybooks with repeated refrains, like "Millions and Billions and Trillions of Cats" or the little engine that says, "I think I can, I think I can, I think I can." In storybooks, they find people and creatures not unlike themselves—who get frightened, feel angry, sad, happy, and loving. In books they find detailed pictures of machines and creatures that they can study down to the smallest whisker. They can "read" the pictures and tell you a story or listen to the words you read. Either way, they are learning how a book unfolds from left to right, from page to page. They can understand words they will not be able to read for years. Yet it is during the preschool years that children begin to become "literate." These are the years when children get the idea that books and reading and words provide pleasure that enlarges their play. Here's a very short list of preschool favorites just to get you started:

> *The Noisy Book Series,* by Margaret Wise Brown
> *Runaway Bunny,* by Margaret Wise Brown
> *The Color Kittens,* by Margaret Wise Brown
> *What's That?* by Tana Hoban
> *The Story about Ping,* by Marjorie Flack
> *Ask Mr. Bear,* by Marjorie Flack
> *Nutshell Library,* by Maurice Sendak
> *Caps for Sale,* by Esphyr Slobodkin
> *A Baby Sister for Frances?* by Russell Hoban
> *Bread and Jam for Frances,* by Russell Hoban
> *The Carrot Seed,* by Ruth Krauss
> *Make Way for Ducklings,* by Robert McCloskey
> *Best Word Book Ever,* by Richard Scarry
> *The Tale of Peter Rabbit,* etc., by Beatrix Potter
> *Millions of Cats,* by Wanda Gag
> *Bank Street Two-Gether Books.*

## Outdoors

Hot, cold, rain, or fair—it really doesn't matter, daily time out-of-doors is a must for your preschooler. This is valuable time for refining coordination and expanding those big muscles in their arms and legs. It's not merely a matter of developing strong muscles, but physical activity is basic to building a positive sense of feeling able (see chapter 4, pages 63–69). At two your child may have spent much of his outdoor time watching other children. Now he is ready to climb, slide, dig, tumble, and swing in the company of others.

Outside, preschoolers can screech, laugh, hoot, and howl

without being "shushed" because of the neighbors. Outside, they can run, jump, skip, and spin without constant cautions to "watch the furniture!" or "You'll break something!" Outside, they can splash in water, squish in mud, stamp in puddles, play in sand, or jump in leaves. These seemingly carefree times are not a frivolous way of filling up the day. It is through physical play that the child

- gets welcome release of high levels of physical energy

- stretches his own physical powers and sense of self

- begins to play cooperative games

- explores the physical world from many perspectives: high up, under foot, far away, and up close.

### *Outdoor Equipment—Playing Safe*

If you're installing swing, slide, or climbing equipment, do be sure it's safe to play on. You may be appalled to know that about 166,000 people a year are injured on playgrounds. Many of these accidents could have been prevented with some foresight and planning for safety. Here are some suggestions from the U.S. Consumer Product Safety Commission:

- Select equipment scaled to the child's physical and developmental growth.

- Install equipment on surfaces that can cushion inevitable falls—grass, sand, rubber matting.

- Install equipment at least six feet from fences, walls, walks, sandboxes.

- Use concrete or anchoring devices underground to give equipment stability.

- Cover exposed screws and sharp edges with tape.

- Don't hang exercise rings that have a diameter of 5–10 inches; they might choke a child.

- Alert the child to danger of moving pieces that may pinch fingers—gliders, see-saws.

- Buy lightweight soft swings rather than heavy swings that may hurt.

- With pliers pinch ends of "S" hooks that might catch fingers and clothing.

- Check the equipment regularly for rust, loose bolts, and rusty parts. Replace when necessary.

Naturally, you'll need to supervise the use of even the most secure equipment. Young children must be taught not to stand in front of moving swings and gliders, not to climb on wet equipment, and how to look out for others and themselves.

### Young Naturalists

Encourage your preschooler to begin to notice the small differences in similar things. How many differently shaped leaves can you find together? Examine the bark on a maple tree. Feel it. Talk about the color. How does it compare to the oak tree or birch? Which is smoother, bumpier, darker, etc.?

On a visit to Cape Cod we absolutely got "rocks" in our heads, admiring the wonderful colors, shapes, and feel of the rocks and shells washed up on shore. Collecting became a passion. Once home, the rocks lost the sparkle and sheen of being bathed by water and sun. Yet they were sorted by color and displayed with pride.

In city park or backyard garden, preschoolers are fascinated by the changing nature of growing and living things—if the adults in their lives encourage them to look, touch, and listen. Take the time to watch an earthworm moving, an army of ants on the march, a butterfly hovering. Try some of these:

*Adopt-a-tree* that is nearby and easily noticed as it changes through the seasons.

*Watch-a-worm:* Fill a large jar with moist earth and add a worm or two. Punch air holes in the jar lid and close it.

*Sort Shells and Stones:* Encourage children to sort stones by color (dark/light), texture (smooth/bumpy), shape (flat/round), size (big/tiny).

*Grow-a-Potato:* Preschoolers are interested in growing things (with quick results). If you have no yard for a garden, the windowsill will do. Start with some magic from your kitchen: A sweet potato will sprout a marvelous showy vine. All you do is rest part of it in water, in a narrow glass. Roots will grow down and vines will climb up. Just be sure your potato has not been coated with wax or preservatives.

*Grow-a-Carrot Forest:* Buy a bunch with leaves (rather

than bag), snap off the leaves, and cut off about an inch or two of carrot.

Stand the stubby little carrot in a shallow dish of water. In no time at all, you'll have a little forest of carrot trees.

*Plant Seeds:* Leftover grass seed will germinate rapidly if it is sprinkled on a moist sponge. Place sponge in a dish and keep it moist. Better yet, sprout your own beans in a jar and enjoy eating them later.

Keep window gardens simple enough for a child to water and care for. Giving the child responsibility for these relatively cost-free plants makes more sense than purchasing extravagant plants that may be neglected. Besides, it's easier to notice changes when you start with next-to-nothing than if you buy a big and mostly grown plant.

*Feed-a-Flock:* Although I grew up in the country, one of the great memories of my childhood was feeding the ducks and swans in a city park. Whenever we visited the city, my aunt had a bag of dry bread waiting and ready for our visit to the duck pond. On a windowledge or from a tree or in the park, children are fascinated by the small dramas that can be seen while feeding birds. Noticing the variety of birds, their names, colors, songs, and eating preferences enlarges the child's understanding that b-i-r-d means many things.

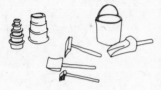

### Still-Wonderful Water & Sand

While washing and suds are still entirely pleasurable, water outside is less messy and can be experienced in a wonderful variety of ways:

| | |
|---|---|
| sprinkling cans | measuring cups |
| squeeze bottles | plastic tubing |
| funnels | pitchers & pails |
| strainers | colanders |
| shovels & spoons | sandmills |
| boats | trucks |

In the sandbox, water can make floods and landslides, lakes and rivers, and marvelous mud forts, castles, and islands.

In the wading pool or plastic dishpan, water can be sprinkled, poured, siphoned, and sprayed. A splash of liquid soap in a frozen-juice can of water will make mountains of bubbles with bubble pipes or ordinary drinking straws.

Don't overlook the scientific discoveries to be made about:

*Sinking/Floating:* Interesting to discover what will or won't float . . . leaves, nuts, paper, toy boats, stones, feathers, flowers, etc. can be tested out in a puddle or pond.

*Melting/Freezing:* Icicles brought inside or a dish of

water brought outside make for first-hand understanding of hot and cold, liquid and solid.

—A pailful of snow turns into less than a pailful of water—why?

—What's air? If you can't see it, how do you know it's there?

You don't have to worry about "teaching" all of the whys and hows of wherefores. "Learning" as opposed to "teaching" grows out of the child's questions and observations. Preschoolers aren't ready for lectures on photosynthesis—they are ready and eager to observe and formulate questions of their own. Answer what you can in simple terms. Don't be embarrassed to say "I don't know, but we can find out in a book (or by watching)." Your big job is to provide experience that keeps the child's expanding curiosity alive. If you can help the child make meaningful connections between what he knows already, you will aid him in enlarging his understanding of the world and its living things, which he, too, is a part of. Giving children that sense of the natural may lead to science and/or art, to wonder and logic.

## Sporting Equipment

Big three-wheel trikes, kiddie cars, tractors, and scooters are standard fare for action.

Preschoolers enjoy a whole range of earth-moving trucks (dump, crane, fire, sandroller, tow), which are great in the sandbox or on the beach.

Sleds and slick saucers add pleasure to snowy downhill runs. In a
family of skiers, the preschooler may
long to do what's "in" with brothers,
sisters, or parents. If you can offer
instruction with the accent on play
and safety, go to it. Older preschoolers are often ready for double-
runner ice skates or simple roller
skates.

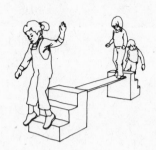

All the equipment listed in chapter 4 is still appropriate at this age.
Climbers, swings, tunnels, rope
tires, balancing boards, slides, and
see-saws are used with greater independence and self-assurance. Instead of "Push me," your preschooler
will be calling "Watch me!" But he
may be calling to a friend as often as
he is calling to you.

## Parents' Role

Parents are still needed within easy eyesight or hearing. Not
so much because the child wants constant attention, but because he still needs supervision for his own safety. Preschoolers have an expansive way of climbing up and not
knowing how to climb down. While direct rescue operations or
constant prohibitions and warnings are not called for, you may
be needed to supply assurances that he can do it. You may even
have to tell him how. "Put your foot here and your hand there."
Children who know they can rely on parental support are freer
to test their own power and develop their independence.

Providing playmates and time and space to play actively and
noisily may require some juggling of your time. Even the child
who goes to a playschool benefits from opportunities to play
with a friend at home or in the backyard. Going visiting or
having a visitor are two very different sides of the coin, but
both are valuable.

Taking turns with other parents can give each of you some
free time or an opportunity to visit together. Often, parents of
preschoolers find great comfort in sharing ideas about handling inevitable problems that they thought no one else ever

had. So, getting your preschooler together with a playmate may be of great benefit to both you and your child.

## *Counting Games, or What's in a Name?*

Preschoolers can often recite their numbers (with varying degrees of accuracy). But knowing how to say a long string of number names is not the same as knowing what they mean. It's what's in a name that counts. So preschoolers need repeated opportunities to count real objects in meaningful situations rather than merely reciting numbers.

Fortunately, their everyday play offers many counting opportunities. You can help your child by counting such things as:

- stairs you climb together
- buttons on daddy's or mommy's shirt
- chairs in the room
- forks on the table
- cookies on a plate.

You can find opportunities to have the child use his counting skills with requests and questions that call for action as well as words:

- Please bring enough napkins for everyone at the table.
- We'll each have ten raisins.
- How many blue towels did we fold?
- How many toy cars do you have?

You can help your child begin to recognize the number symbols he sees. The world is so full of numerals:

- on clocks and calendars
- in shoes and coats
- on scales and cans
- on buses and street signs

- on dials and switches
- on buildings and boxes
- on pushbuttons and pages
- on pricetags and stickers.

It takes lots of time and a variety of experiences before children firmly grasp the number concepts under the symbols we use. Just consider the number 5 from the preschoolers point of view:

- His big brother is 5.
- He has 5 fingers on each hand and 5 toes on each foot.
- He has a nickel which his brother says is the same as 5 pennies—but how can 5 things be the same as 1?
- His favorite show comes on at 5 o'clock.
- He sees it on channel 5.
- He has 2 red trucks and 3 blue trucks—that's 5 trucks.
- He lives at 5 Hammond Street.
- There are 5 steps up to his house.
- Playing a game with dice he rolled 4 dots and 1—he gets to go 5 moves on the board.

Learning the complex and multiple meaning of "fiveness" is often confusing—but it is a source of fascination to young children. Indeed, once preschoolers get started, their love of playing with numbers is apparent. Parents can capitalize on this interest by using numbers in different ways. If the child wishes to learn how to write numerals, by all means show the child how.

$$1234567890$$

But keep in mind the large goal—it's what's in a number that counts.

You can make simple board games that are played with the

roll of one die or a pair of dice (or by drawing from a stack of number cards).

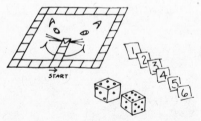

Decorate the board with any theme—a trip to the zoo, the circus. The game illustrated above is called the cat's whiskers. The winner is the one who gets around the board to the cat's whiskers first—with plenty of counting in between. (Your last move must end up in the whiskers, no more, no less!)

Games with old playing cards are good for a challenging game of concentration. Select several sets of matching cards—two 5s, two 10s, two 4s, two 8s, etc. Now lay them out face down:

First player may turn two cards over. If they match, he takes them. If they don't, he turns them back over in place and the next player tries his luck. The winner is the player who has taken the greatest number of "tricks." (Once kids get the knack of this, they're much better than most grownups, or at least this grownup.)

Don't overlook the value of fingerplay songs and picture books that have built-in number concepts. Long before children are ready for 4 + 1 or 5 − 1, they develop an understanding of adding and subtracting. Consider this old fingerplay:

*5 little squirrels*
*Standing by the door.*
*1 ran away*
*Then there were 4.*

*4 little squirrels*
*Playing in a tree.*
*1 ran away*
*Then there were 3.*

*3 little squirrels*
*Sitting in a shoe.*
*1 ran away*
*Then there were 2.*

*2 little squirrels*
*Nibbling on a bun.*
*1 ran away*
*Then there was 1.*

*1 little squirrel*
*Has no fun.*
*He ran away*
*Then there was none!*

## Games for Quiet Times

In contrast to the motion-packed action on the playground, preschoolers enjoy and need stretches of time for quiet play. Too often, both parent and child automatically turn on the switch, depending upon TV for taking a break. Sitting for hours on end, the child comes to expect to be entertained without having to do anything but watch. This passive way of spending time can become habit forming.

Given other options, your preschooler can benefit from more engaging activities. Unlike the flighty two-year-olds, preschoolers can get really wrapped up for long stretches of time in quiet but actively stimulating play material.

## Puzzles

Wooden puzzles with pieces (ten pieces or more) provide a quiet challenge to eye, hand, and mind. Since these puzzles are expensive, you may want to create some homemade cardboard puzzles.

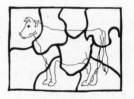

Mount a clear picture from a magazine on heavy cardboard and cut into large jigsaw pieces. (A piece of see-through contact paper stuck over the picture before cutting will give the puzzle a longer life.)

## Pegboards and Play Tiles

Pegboards and play tiles help the child develop fine dexterity with small muscles in hands and fingers. Don't get hung up on the pictures of things on the package. Preschoolers need free time to explore the mechanics of pegs before they "copy" the designs on the box. Like their paintings, they may name what they're making or simply enjoy filling every hole on the pegboard. Comments like "You used a lot of red" or "What a nice design of stripes!" tell the child you value his own creations.

If the child is seriously frustrated by attempts to reproduce the manufacturer's designs, you may wish to help him find some strategies for reproducing designs. For instance, looking at a pattern helps your child zoom in on one row at a time. Ask what color tile goes in the top left-hand corner. What goes next? If the next few are the same color, count how many. After the first line is in place, help your child move on to the next line. Slowly but surely, you're guiding the child toward an orderly way of building a whole picture from many parts. Don't belabor the point. This is tough going for young children—but it beats no strategy at all.

### Bead-Stringing Toys and Sewing Cards

Bead-stringing toys offer a challenge to dexterity and fine muscle tuning. Instead of beads, you can use pasta in a variety of shapes (ziti, wheels, macaroni) to introduce your child to the excitement of creating patterns.

Example:

What comes next?

Buttons and empty spools of thread are also useful for stringing.

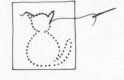

Sewing cards can be bought or homemade. These, too, develop coordination of eye and hand skills.

### Stickers and Plastic Stick-Ons

Games with precut forms give further practice in developing small muscles in fingers and putting together a whole picture from small parts.

### Lotto-Type Games

These are basically matching games with playing boards and a deck of cards. Each player has a playing board. Players take turns drawing cards. If the card matches a picture on the board, player uses it. The winner is the first to fill his board. Lotto games can be made or bought. Try making your own:

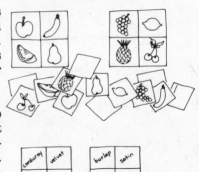

You can also make your own lotto games with duplicate pictures cut from magazines and pasted on cardboard squares and old playing cards. Or you might use patches of wallpaper (or gift wrap scraps) with similar but different patterns, or try fabrics all of the same color but different textures.

Using the lotto idea, my friend Gloria made up a terrific game for shopping. She pasted pictures of brand-name products she purchased regularly on index cards. At the grocery store she used a shopping list, but gave her four- and five-year-olds the shopping cards. While she waited at the end of the aisle the kids matched their cards with products and brought mom the goods. Obviously, she stuck to nonbreakable items and did not send them wandering alone in the supermarket. She also avoided some of the "Can I haves?" and replaced them with a challenge of "Can you find?"

These simple games are won on chance but many skills are learned in the process. Simply learning the names of the objects expands the child's easy use of language. Since game boards are often designed around themes—fruits, vegetables, animals, utensils, clothing—they teach the child how to sort and classify things that go together. In fact, your child may enjoy playing a solitaire-type game with all the boards and cards.

Such games encourage your preschooler to sharpen his attention to details. This kind of visual and sensory discrimination will help him later in learning to read and write.

Playing with others offers yet another opportunity to learn the social skills of taking turns and both winning and losing. Since the luck of the cards puts everyone on equal footing, chances are he'll get to be both a winner and loser without too much frustration or need for cheating. Preschoolers are not ready for long lectures on good sportsmanship or cheating. Time and experience will teach these lessons better than long moral lectures. How you win and lose will teach more than words.

### Dominoes

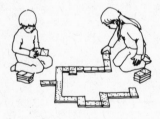

Giant-size wooden or cardboard dominoes are fun for sharpening up counting and matching skills. Picture-type dominoes can also be made or bought:
Dominoes can be played as a game of chance with others or as a solitaire-type game.

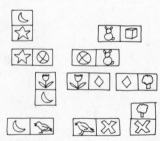

### Board Games

Simple games like Candyland and Winnie the Pooh which require no strategy have been long-time favorites for beginning players. Remember, learning to play by the rules is no small task, so go easy on games that have too many rules.

## New Kinds of Peek-a-Boo

*Abracadabra:* Have your child put four (or five) small toys on the table. Tell her to close her eyes, and say, "Abracadabra." While her eyes are closed, remove one toy. When she opens her eyes, ask her to tell what toy has vanished. Switch roles. Let her be the magician.

*Alacazam:* Put the five toys in a row. Tell her to look at the toys carefully, because you're going to move one of them. Tell her to close those eyes and not to open them, till you say "Alacazam."

Say, "Alacazam, which one did I move?" Try rearranging two objects when one is too easy. Use silverware, trucks, cookies, fruit, what have you.

*Shazam:* Put objects on a table. Explain that you are going to put just one of the objects in a bag. Ask the child to close eyes, and remove one from sight. Put one in the bag. "Shazam— tell me what's in the bag." Child must feel, not look.

## Riddle-Dee-Dee, What Do I See?

Riddles make good games to challenge the child to listen and look. These are games that require no special equipment. Try this the next time you're waiting in the doctor's office.

"I see something brown . . . it stands on legs . . . it has arms but no hands . . . you sit on it." Once your child gets the knack of riddles you can graduate to things that aren't even there: "I'm thinking of something you can eat . . . it's hot . . . it comes in a bowl . . . you can eat it with a spoon."

Encourage your child to make up riddles to stump you (and please be a little stumped).

Magazines in the waiting room can be used for riddles, too. Leaf through magazines and find a large, full-color ad. Give a clear riddle about something in a full-color ad. The child must find the item that the riddle describes.

## Following Directions

Learning to follow directions can be fun when you play at it. The old favorite, Simon Says, provides both a visual and spoken clue, but the trick is to follow only the spoken clue. The caller says and does what players are to do:

> Simon says touch your nose.

> Simon says touch your knees.

But when caller says "Touch your lips," the players must not follow because all commands must begin "Simon Says." Simon Says helps children to learn to name parts of their bodies— knees, elbows, wrists, waist, chin, forehead, etc.

Not all directions need to be spoken. Follow the Leader can be played with small movements indoors or expansive movements outdoors. Remember to give your child a chance to lead as well as follow.

## Playing Group Games

Ring games with preschoolers don't last long. But if you've got a birthday party or a group of visiting nieces and nephews, try a whirl with The Farmer in the Dell, the Hoky-Poky, and Ring Around the Rosy.

Another sure crowd pleaser is a sit-down song with active hands. "Where Is Thumbkin?" or "This Old Man, He Plays One" are easy songs to follow even if children don't know all the words. They will enjoy coming up with suggestions once they get the drift of "If you're happy and you know it, clap your hands."

If you play the piano or a phonograph or can beat a drum, try Start and Stop. Explain to the children that as long as music is playing, they must dance/march/clap, but when music stops, they must stop moving and freeze. This surprisingly simple game has the built-in charm of action and the need to listen.

Of course there are activity records with action songs that tell the child just what to do. These are fun for a limited time and in a limited way. Preschoolers have lots of good ideas of their own for fitting music and movement into their own harmony. Try not to get between them and their music with too many directions.

## Musical Moments

Homemade instruments are great for keeping time with the music. Try:

- shakers made with boxes and beads

- drums made with coffee cans and spoons

- tambourines or wristbands with jingle bells

- cymbals made with two pot lids or one lid and a spoon to strike

- zither made with rubber bands stretched over a box.

Instead of relying on records made for children, look for music with varying tempos and dramatic content. Marches, ballet, and symphonic music invite the child to move in many different ways. Add a silk scarf to twirl with for special effects. Don't just sit there—don't fight it, join it!

Singalongs in the car or while you're making dinner or whenever the mood moves you can give the day a special lift. Threes and especially fours love to sing. Folk songs with repetitive lines are their favorites. "Row, Row, Row Your Boat," "Old MacDonald," "Jingle Bells," "*Frère Jacques*," and "Three Blind Mice" are just a few that come to mind. Don't worry if you think you have a terrible voice. Your kids won't think so. Singing on key is not nearly so important as opening the key to singing. Singing can help moods and miles fly.

## Schools for Preschoolers

Although threes and fours are called PREschoolers, the fact is many children in this age group go to school on a regular basis.

For both parents and children the separation from home to school can be a bit bumpy. Nursery school teachers are often able to ease the process in small steps, allowing preschoolers to come for short "visits" and inviting mother to stay for a while, as well.

Giving your child that little extra time to feel safe is a short-term investment with long-term benefits. Occasionally, preschoolers are simply not ready to make that break from home, even for a few hours. Better to postpone the separation for six months or a year than to force the issue. Visiting friends at your house and theirs, going to story hour at the library or playtime in the park may be a more gradual and appropriate way for your child. There are no absolute rules about the right age for all children to begin school. It has to feel right for your child, and if it doesn't, then accept it without making an issue over it. Don't be pressured into thinking that your child's college entrance depends on formal preschool training.

### What Preschoolers Learn

Of course, there are parents who doubt the value of nursery school.

> "It's nothing but a baby-sitting service," they say, or "They don't do anything there but play!" or "By the time he gets to kindergarten, he's going to be bored stiff with the whole thing!"

Obviously, for working couples or single-parent families the question of nursery school can be more a matter of necessity than choice. But to view the nursery school as nothing more than a convenient babysitting service is a mistake. Schools designed for preschoolers offer learning opportunities that even the best-equipped home cannot provide.

Just what do they learn there, anyway?

- Nursery school has a natural supply of what children want most—other children. Playing cooperatively with others necessitates learning social skills of give and take, or learning how to negotiate and communicate.

• At home the child is one of just a few or even the only one. In school, he is one of many. He must share the teacher's attention with others. Being a part of a group requires greater independence and self-reliance.

• Until now, the child's parents have been the prime caring adults in his life. In nursery school the child learns that there are other caring adults who can be trusted. Knowing this helps the child feel safer in the bigger world.

• In school there is likely to be a wider variety of equipment for active play. In a setting designed for action and messy play, the preschooler is freer to act his exuberant age.

• In living with others the child begins to discover that his fears, enthusiasm, and angry feelings are not unique to him alone—these beginning feelings of commonality with others are significant steps toward becoming less egocentric. Although preschoolers still see the world chiefly from their own point of view, experience with others helps them to begin to think less rigidly.

• Since a skillful nursery teacher fosters both individual growth and a sense of belonging to a group, the child participates in cleaning up, preparing snacks, going on small trips, sharing songs, and participating as a member of the group. Finding pleasure in the routines and responsibilities of the group adds to the child's sense of well-being as a doer. Not only does the child participate, he delights in the predictable rhythm of the day—which makes him feel safe.

• In playing with others, your child has a greater need to make himself understood with words that communicate.

• Since the nursery school group is generally smaller than the classroom in elementary school, nursery school makes for an easier transition from being a one and only to being one of many.

- A skillful nursery school teacher gives time and attention to providing materials that nurture the child's curiosity about the world and the things in it. She does not stand in front of the class and teach, she sets up a variety of learning situations and is ready to step in when needed.

- In the natural flow of events, the nursery school child has many experiences with counting, comparing, sorting, and classifying, as well as building basic concepts that are fundamental to academic skills.

### Won't They Be Bored?

Contrary to fears that preschoolers will be bored with nursery school, kindergarten, and "nothing but playing," both threes and fours use the learning materials in their nursery in different but constructive ways. Fours use the same materials in far more elaborate and cooperative ways than their three-year-old counterparts. Just a look at the art work and block building of threes as compared to fours will satisfy any doubters. A good nursery school program is neither boring nor "just" playing. It is not a watered-down program to hurry children in learning their letters. It is a place which is stimulating and supportive of the child who is learning about herself and others. It is a safe place where children can play with clay, paint, puzzles, blocks, swings, sand, and each other. And this is how threes and fours best develop their physical, emotional, and intellectual skills.

### Alternatives to Preschools

Lacking nursery school or good daycare experience, many children must telescope all of these social and intellectual skills into the kindergarten year. Unfortunately, kindergarten classes tend to be larger and more formal. So, too often children who are inexperienced socially are overwhelmed by being one of many. They lack the feeling of being at home away from home.

Without the option of a good nursery school, parents may find a reasonable alternative in forming a playgroup with other parents of preschoolers (see chapter 4, page 81). If this is not possible, parents may need to fill the void with play materials suggested in this chapter and a regular round of visiting playmates.

## Basic Toys

Whether your child attends a nursery school or not, there are some toys and materials that should be available in both home and school:

| | | | |
|---|---|---|---|
| blocks | dolls | miniature cars, trucks | crayons |
| balls | dress-up | trikes | paints |
| books | records | simple puzzles | paper/ pencils |

Naturally, in school there will be a greater variety of toys which must be shared. But your preschooler's personal toys are still very important to his sense of self. It's not just a question of "mine." Preschoolers still see their possessions as extensions of themselves. Their favorite doll, truck, or book holds a special place of endearment and safety. It is a familiar friend in a world full of so many unfamiliar things and people. The doll in the play corner at school is quite different than the doll who listens lovingly to the complaints and fears of its four-year-old playmate. Alone with blocks and cars, the child at home creates dramas and constructions unhampered by others. There, he can use all of the blocks just as he pleases. At home, he has time to explore without the distraction of others who may want him to play monster when he's building a skyscraper.

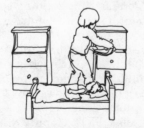 

While the importance of playmates and others is real, it is no less important that the child continue to develop his ability and pleasure in playing alone. Not everything we do can or needs to be done with others. So, children need a variety of materials that invite their active exploration and individual attention. Lacking such play material, they may turn to the TV as a way of spending their time alone. This is the time to establish your own "standards and practices codes for selective viewing" (see chapter 9, pages, 270–75). Recent studies show that preschoolers watch more TV than any other age group. The average preschooler is spending over twenty-six hours a week in the passive role of viewer. Indeed, this is when the passive TV habit really takes hold unless parents provide active alternatives that are more attractive and valuable.

## Summing Up

During these exciting preschool years, your child becomes a more social being, learning to play cooperatively with other children. While your child still loves to talk to you, he or she will talk more to other children if they are available. Your

preschooler has gone from asking "What's dat?" to asking "Why?" "How come?" and even "Where do babies come from?"—and has some pretty fancy explanations of his own. During these years he has gone from depending solely on you to knowing there are other adults he can count on. In playing make-believe, your preschooler has gone from little domestic dramas to directing traffic and putting out fires. He not only laughs when he is tickled, he makes little jokes out of absurd things, putting his boots on his hands and mittens on his feet. His jokes are funny only because he knows what goes where and with what. He's come a long, long way in understanding his own small world and his place in the family. In the coming years he will take giant steps toward finding his place among his playmates in the bigger world of school.

# Chapter 6
# *Giant Steps—The Early School Years*

> *It:* Joey, take two giant steps.
> *Joey:*(takes the first step) Two?
> *It:* Go back, Joey! You forgot to say "May I"!

In a way, the old game of Giant Steps captures the essence of the early school years. Entry to kindergarten marks the giant-size step out of the home and into the big world of school and group life. In the classroom and on the playground the child takes everything from umbrella steps to giant strides in developing a variety of physical, intellectual, and social skills.

While developmentalists generally call the years from six to twelve the middle years of childhood, the early school years from five to seven are more closely related to each other than to the years that follow. Entrance to school marks, for children, the beginning of a time of transition—

- from home to school

- from family life and small group life to more expanded group life

- from informal learning to more formal learning

- from making their own symbols—with blocks, paint, and clay—to using standard symbols like numbers and letters.

Even if your child has been attending a nursery school, going to real school with the big kids is a new giant step forward. For many children, kindergarten is the first daily separation from the familiar home and family life they have known. Increasingly, kindergartners are attending school for a full day. They climb on board the school bus with their older brothers and sisters. They carry their lunch on a tray, rest on a mat, and spend five to six hours in the company of other children. They meet with a whole new set of rules and regulations.

Unlike their nursery group with ten to twelve children to one teacher (and maybe an aide), the kindergarten may have twenty or more children and one teacher (and probably no aide). Your child goes from being one of a few to being one of many, and sharing the teacher's time and attention and needing to become increasingly self-sufficient.

Learning to wait his turn at the easel or water fountain, the give and take of sharing and using equipment together, changing from one activity to the next—these are just some of the new demands your five-year-old faces. Although schools vary, many kindergartners spend part of each day in formal lessons. Increasingly, workbooks, worksheets, and pencil/paper tasks have filtered from first grade down to kindergarten.

## Play Still Counts

While the value of play to preschoolers is widely accepted, parents and teachers of school-age children tend to draw an artificial line between work and play. It is as if suddenly, at the age of five or six, work and play have become opposites—meaning one is hard, the other easy; or one is a chore, the other fun; or work is worthwhile, whereas play is a waste. But if by *work* we mean *learning,* then we had better not banish play. The connections between play and learning continue to be very real during these early school years.

In our eagerness to teach them to read and write, many fives and sixes must be reminded to "sit still," "pay attention," "raise your hand," "don't talk," and "stay in line." Programs that demand fives to sit passively for prolonged lessons require adult-imposed control. Although many children will conform, most of the learning energy may be spent on sitting still, while the teacher's lesson is missed or quickly forgotten. Indeed, too many demands for quiet and uniform orderliness tend to run contrary to the very nature of healthy, noisy, active five-year-olds.

Skilled teachers try to balance the schoolday with varied activities that foster the child's physical, social and intellectual growth. Just as they do not all wear the same size shoes, not all fives or even sixes are ready for the same tasks. While the 3Rs are important, they are by no means the only skills a child needs to learn during these important years of transition.

One of the most overlooked skills learned in play comes in the child's stretching his STICKABILITY. Just watch a child searching for the right puzzle piece or sewing a puppet or shaping a pinch pot of clay. No one needs to remind them to sit still or pay attention. Learning to ride a bike, jump a rope, or finish a drawing, children invest their minds, bodies, and souls in the tasks they choose. They cope with frustration, setbacks, and occasional failures when the bike tips, the threads twist, the paint drips. Yet they are likely to persist with a minimum of assistance and outside direction. While adults may be needed to assist—with tying a knot or steadying a hand—it is the child who insists on persisting, even if it's hard. This willingness to stick with it can't be suddenly mastered at a desk and chair. Yet it is as basic to learning as A-B-C.

## Combining Work and Play

Five-year-olds are not ready for diagrams or wordy explanations about electric currents—but they are ready for a flashlight that can be taken apart and put back together. Six-year-olds are not ready for detailed studies of maps of the

world—but they are ready to draw maps of their room, of their school, and of the street where they live. Seven-year-olds are not ready for text books that explain photosynthesis—but they are ready to see what happens to two seedling plants if one sits on a windowsill and the other sits in a dark corner.

During these early school years, children continue to learn in active, hands-on ways. They have a great hunger for information, but they cannot learn simply by word of mouth or even pictures.

## *Fact + Fancy = More Understanding*

Recognizing children's active learning style, schools often arrange short trips out into the real world. If your child's school is not providing such trips, you may need to fill in the gaps with small journeys that fuel both learning and play. Here are some readily available choices:

| | | | |
|---|---|---|---|
| butcher shop | factory | museum | apple orchard |
| post office | firehouse | zoo | farm |
| bottling plant | newspaper | airport | circus |
| lumberyard | ferry | barber shop | bus station |
| restaurant kitchen | hospital | bakery | greenhouse |

All of these places are alive with people and machines at work. You can call attention to the tools people use. If possible, encourage your child to ask questions of the people at work.

In today's world, it's difficult to see how things are made. Visits to see "things happening" help children make the connections between people and products. A trip to the apple orchard that includes picking, weighing, paying for the fruit, carrying it home, paring, coring, and cooking the apples, is a live demonstration that applesauce doesn't originate in jars. In a world full of processed and packaged foods, children need many first-hand experiences to understand the connection between people and products.

After a trip into the real world, children enjoy playing elaborate games of make-believe that are a rich mixture of fact and fancy. Playing restaurant, they take the roles of waiter, chef, customer, and cashier. They invent menus, checks, food, tables, chairs, trays, money, and a cash register.

Flying to Florida, they need make-believe pilots, flight attendants, passengers, tickets, food, and safety belts. There may be a crash landing, a brave rescue, or a terrible disaster.

Clearly, this make-believe play is heavily laced with reality. While these games have no rules, there are conventions that must be followed:

> "In school you must raise your hand!" the pretend teacher says.
>
> "You get a ticket—you went through a red light!" the state trooper says.
>
> "This shot will make you better!" the pretend doctor says.

In their active play, children try on adult roles of power which serve emotional needs. But the real world is very much a part of play. They are sorting out big chunks of information about who does what, where, how, and with which tools. Playing student and teacher, doctor and patient, pilot and passenger, is the child's way of making sense and order out of what they see, hear, and feel.

## *Proper Props*

Delivery men carry boxes, mailmen have letters, doctors have stethoscopes. While the real thing may not be possible, reasonable substitutes are necessary—the more realistic the better.

This is the age when costumes are desirable: astronauts, clowns, ballerinas, sailors, nurses, cowboys, railroad engineers, and conductors.

Here are some of the proper props for pretend play:

| | | |
|---|---|---|
| cash register | doctor/nurse kits | tickets |
| toy money | chalkboard/chalk | briefcase |
| whistles | small pads of paper | badges |
| assorted hats (pilot, police, etc.) | empty cans and food boxes | checkbooks |

Many of these props can be made with materials scrounged from around the house. Large cartons can be converted into stores, tickets booths, puppet theaters, houses, space stations, you name it.

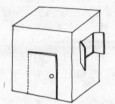

Windows—just fold back

With sharp knife
cut dotted lines for door

## More Miniworlds

Just as children's games of pretend demand more elaborate and realistic props, their miniworlds of make-believe demand more detailed miniature objects.

### Dollhouses

This is the age when dollhouses with furniture and family figures are used to play out little dramas. Where space and privacy are restricted, the dollhouse allows for dramatic play on a small scale.

Alone or with a friend, the child can replay (or rewrite) reality. In the dollhouse, wishes can come true. All power rests in the small hands of the child—a breath of freedom from the demands of everyday life. Here the child holds mother in her left hand and the child in her right—but she is in charge of them both. She is playmate, actor, director, and scenic designer.

Some frightening and angry thoughts can be played more safely by these little dolls than playing them in dressed-up costumes. In a way, they are once removed from the child. Playing a variety of roles demands saying what other people say and having a taste of how that feels. It is another route toward understanding other people's points of view.

### Buying or Building

Dollhouses need not be elaborate to be enjoyed. They can be bought or built of wood or cardboard boxes. One of my friends built a replica of the family's house, down to the finest detail. It really became an adult craft project rather than a child's toy. A cardboard box that's playable is preferable to a castle that must be cared for with fear.

Props for dollhouses:

- basic furniture for bathroom, kitchen, living room, bedrooms

- scaled figures—bought or made (but sturdy)—should include family like the child's own. Also useful: figures of doctor, police, animals, cars, trucks, planes

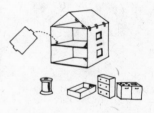

- scraps of wallpaper, rugs, and paint for decorating

- children may make pictures, dishes, food, bedcovers, and other accessories from clay, cloth, and wood scraps.

My own dollhouse had a doorbell and lights with a little help from my dad, who rigged up the wires and batteries and flashlight bulbs and buzzer.

While dollhouses are generally of greater interest to girls, boy visitors or brothers often enjoy entering these little worlds to play pretend roles. They should not be teased or told "that's for girls." After all, men and women, boys and girls live together in houses. If you tune in, you're likely to hear that many roles they choose to play are adult roles they have seen their fathers and mothers play.

### Other Miniworlds

Children enjoy recreating what they have seen by constructing miniworlds of scrap materials. They may enjoy illustrating their trip in a homemade book, with or without a text that they dictate.

They may also like constructing small "scenes" that capture a place in the space of a shoebox. Using cardboard, clay, paper, paint, glue, and small toys, they may build a little model of a barn, a zoo, or the firehouse. For some children the total play value may be in the making and displaying of their miniworld. For others, the construction may be used like a dollhouse for playing out small dramas.

Both boys and girls enjoy constructing or playing with miniature models that duplicate places in the real world:

- garages with lifts and ramps and elevators
- farms with silos and stalls and livestock
- airports with hangars and towers and airplanes.

These worlds also need props that enlarge the possibilities for little dramas. They need:

- little people
- cars and gas pumps
- roadways and ramps
- ships and sailboats
- small signs and signals
- animals
- trucks (fine detail and large variety).

Many of these toys are used together with unit blocks (see chapter 5, pages 98–103).

Unlike preschoolers who are just beginning to play cooperatively, fives and sixes plan, construct, and model these miniworlds with greater attention to detail and working parts. Elevators, steps, gangplanks, walkways, bridges, and tunnels have a purpose. They do not link blocks together and say, "Look—it's a bridge!" They begin their play with "I'm making a bridge—the George Washington Bridge."

## Puppets

Though interest in puppets may have begun during the preschool years (see chapter 5, pages 94–96), puppets continue to provide another dimension for acting out little dramas.

Often the content of children's puppet play reflects their personal feelings. So, through the mouths of puppets, children find emotional release. Hidden behind the puppet stage they are free to let go. The small plays they create also reflect their heightened interest in each other. Shy and otherwise inarticulate children often find it easier to talk to another child through the characters at the end of their fingertips. Puppets offer a path to connecting with others and playing together.

While five-year-olds generally prefer making up their own stories, sixes and sevens enjoy replaying stories they have heard from storybooks, TV, and movies. In effect, this kind of acting uses skills similar to those needed for reading comprehension. To recall the characters, the order of events, and to make the words they have heard come alive in action are significant kinds of comprehension skills. Playing a story requires planning ahead, cooperation, recall, and restating in one's own words.

When two of my kids were in first and second grade, they loved the story of Tiki-Tiki-Tembo so much that they created stick puppets of all the characters. Not only did they play out the story for the family, but they delighted in doing it for their neighborhood friends. Their friends took an active part in the performance, chanting with the puppets each time the line "Tiki-Tiki-Tembo-No-Sa-Rembo" came up. Children who could not remember what number comes after twenty-nine could remember that chant.

—Mother of a first and second grader

Hand puppets may be made or bought. The simple sock puppet (see chapter 5, page 95) continues to be useful. Simple rod

puppets can be cut and colored on stiff cardboard or poster board which may be taped to slender sticks. Seven-year-olds may like to make jointed figures that require more manipulation and action.

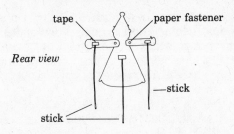

tape — paper fastener

*Rear view*

— stick

stick —

Simple puppet stages may be improvised by throwing a sheet over a table.

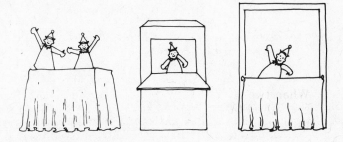

## *Dolls, Dolls, Dolls*

Interest in dolls really blossoms between five and six. Children of this age use dolls as friends to confide in, as companions at bedtime, and as pretend children to care for. There's nothing strange about boys of this age playing with dolls, nor should they be teased about it. Jeffrey may find his doll or teddy bear just as comforting at bedtime as Debbie does. His toy monkey will share great adventures of pretend and listen to sad tales of woe. If a new baby has arrived in the family, he may enjoy playing with a model baby doll of his own (see chapter 4, pages 60–61). Boys particularly like small action dolls (firemen, po-

licemen, spacemen) that they can use in their pretend games.

While the preschooler's doll spends much of its time being undressed and put to bed, the fives' (and up) dolls lead much livelier lives. They are certainly better dressed. You could even call them clothes horses. Homemade or storebought, a doll just "has to have" everything from pajamas to bibs. Clothes still need easy fasteners that small fingers can manipulate independently. Dolls with flexible arms and legs are easier to dress, sit up, and put through their paces in carriage, stroller, crib, or cradle.

This is not the time for teenage dolls with their complicated clothes or foreign dolls that just stand there looking pretty. Fives to sevens want dolls that are ready to have their hair brushed and their bottoms dusted. Their dolls use dishes and bottles, blankets and rattles. Their clothes need ironing and washing, hanging and drying. Although there are dolls that do everything from talking back to spitting up, remember that novelty features get played out quickly. That doesn't mean they have no value; just be sure there's still playability left when the buttons don't work.

Paper dolls with cut-out clothes are also appealing at this age. Do look for large and easy-to-cut-out clothes for the fives and sixes. Sevens will be able to snip the more complicated tabs and hems with ruffles. Look for blunt-ended scissors designed for safety. But be sure they really can cut. Some manufacturers are now making plastic scissors that work equally well for lefties and righties. If your child is left-handed you need to find scissors designed for her.

## Outdoor Activity

Often the importance of physical activity is overlooked by parents (and teachers). After six hours of sitting still and paying attention, most kids have a stored-up pool of energy that needs releasing. At the end of any schoolday, you can witness this explosive burst as children make their way out of the school building. It's like a cork popping out of a bottle.

### Then and Now

Years ago some of that stored-up energy was released on the long walk home. In fact, if you attended a small-town or city-neighborhood school, you may have been let out at noon. It was time for a romp and run home, a quick lunch, a fast hug, goodbye, and back to school. A few hours later, the last bell was the signal for play. It was time for snowballs and puddle jumping, for "I'll race you to the corner" or "Watch out for the cracks or you'll break your mother's back." There was time to watch the streets being repaired and holler, "Hold your breath!" when the tar was poured. There was time for window shopping and often a quick stop for deciding between a stick of gum and a pretzel.

From schoolhouse to home, you and your friends were on your own. For that short time, you were free to shout, tease, run, skip, or drag your feet through puddles. It was on the way home that friends planned what and where they'd ride bikes, jump rope, go skating, or play potsy.

Today's child goes from schoolroom to schoolbus and home. He may or may not ride the bus with his best buddy. Chances are, in cities or suburban sprawl, the only way they can get together is by prearrangement and parents willing to pick up and deliver. There is little or no time for small independent adventures in the big world. Many suburbs have no sidewalks and our city streets have become too threatening for un-escorted young children.

So they travel from teacher to driver to parent or baby-sitter—all with varying thresholds of tolerance for kids' bot-tled-up energy and noise. Instead of letting off steam, many children are scheduled into another round of activities directed by adults. Some need appointment books to keep track of ballet, scouts, skating lessons, gymnastics, piano, crafts, and guitar. There is next to no time for making up games and thinking up their own fun. Lacking a scheduled event, there's always "something on TV."

Yet today's children have the same needs that children have always had to be with other children. They need to use their muscles and their minds, to shout out loud and whisper secrets, to scrape their shins and scuff their shoes. Given the realities of working couples, transportation, and tightly scheduled lives, children today still need time for fun with other children.

## After-School Programs

Some school districts and communities now have after-school programs, making use of playgrounds and gyms that were otherwise locked up with the last school bell. If your school or community center has no such program, perhaps you can bring this to the attention of the parent group or a civic organization. Unfortunately, some after-school programs have become another kind of school with "lessons" and "no talking." So, the six-hour schoolday is extended to seven or eight hours of adult-imposed activities. While adults must play a role in selecting activities and supervision, this should not be an extension of the schoolday.

Ideally, after-school hours should be a mixed bag of flexible choices. School-age children are eager to try their skills at handstands and weaving. By seven, some want to learn how to ski and swim, to sculpt, skate, and bat a ball. But they also want time to be less than serious, even to be silly. They want and need time to dream up games with rules of their own. They need to know there is an adult nearby but not in the center of their play.

### At Least Now and Then

Lacking an after-school program, parents will need to make the child's friends welcome. For working parents, such visits may need to be on weekends or just now and then. Often, several working parents, with different work schedules, can make arrangements for exchanging visits that satisfy everyone's needs. You may think you're taking on extra work, but you may be pleasantly surprised to discover—happiness is having your friend over!

### What Games Do They Play?

After school hours, on the playground, and in the backyard, children of this age play age-old games of chasing and catching, hiding and seeking, danger and rescue. The danger may be a girl who will kiss the boy, or vice versa. The hiding may be a simple game with a leader who's *It*. Though the rules may change in midstream, there are agreed-upon ways to tag and boundaries for being safe or out.

Such games call for cooperative play, for rules, and for taking turns at being the chaser or the chased. All players are automatically part of the group. So, being accepted into the group is not dependent on being best or better than someone else.

Games such as Cops and Robbers, Cowboys and Rustlers, Giants, or Monsters are essentially fanciful versions of these hide-and-seek, chase-and-catch games. They are also another form of dramatic play, related to the preschool games of pretend.

These games do not come in a box with given rules and directions. They are passed from child to child, but constantly reinvented on the spot by the children who bring their active imaginations into play. Playing together, they combine their intellectual, social, and physical skills to keep the game going.

## Play Equipment

### Trikes and Bikes

Your five-year-old will still enjoy a stout and sturdy trike. If it has a bell and basket, so much the better. In fact, a good many six-year-olds continue to ride their trusty trikes. This is especially true of physically small sixes. However, most sixes and sevens eagerly long for a two-wheeler.

This first bike must be small enough for the child's feet to fit the pedals comfortably. He should be able to straddle the bike with both feet on the ground. Better to buy or borrow a used bike that fits than to buy a big new bike to grow into.

Learning to balance on two wheels takes time, persistence, and often some parental assistance. Training wheels can be helpful in giving a sense of security while the child gets the hang of pedaling and braking. Ultimately, when training wheels are removed, a parental hand on the back of the seat gives that extra touch of balance and assurance the child needs.

Since riding a two-wheeler is what the big kids do, the motivation to learn often offsets the frustration of scraped knees and wobbly wheels. It's important for parents to understand that being able to ride is something of a status symbol—proof of coming of age. It is one of the ways kids measure themselves and each other. So, being able to ride a bike is one of the tickets into group life which will be increasingly important during the middle years of childhood.

### Safety

Not only do kids need a steadying hand, they need a firm hand on where and how far they can ride. You may be uneasy about where your child rides her bike. You may want her to be accompanied by an adult until she has mastered the skill. You may want to limit her to a specific area that you think is safe. Whatever your reservations, you must be clear about your conditions. Setting realistic limits will naturally depend on where you live. But make the rules clear and certain. Here are some basic rules that kids need to observe:

- Always ride on the right side of the road.

- Always ride single file.

- Watch out for bumpy surfaces, potholes, and wet, slick pavement.

- Look both ways before crossing.

- Never show off or try tricks on a bike on public roads.

- Stop for lights.

- Put reflectors on bike, even if night riding is a no-no (you never know).

### Roller Skates and Ice Skates

Although fives get tired easily, learning to skate is another balancing act they long to try. However, wanting to do something is not the same as being able to do it. Parents will need to provide supervision and other safety precautions. A pair of knee pads can go a long way in saving wear and tear and tears. As with bikes, kids need definite limits on where and how far they are to skate. Beginners may need a steadying hand—or a pro to show them how to glide and fall without doing serious damage to bones or teeth. Since skating is another one of those activities that kids do together, learning how to do it well is a move toward belonging and participating in group life.

### Other Wheels

| wagons | dump trucks | cranes |
|---|---|---|
| scooters | plows | tractors |
| earth movers | wheelbarrows | fire engines |
| | sturdy, large trucks for sandbox | |

Of course, no child needs all of these. It wouldn't even be desirable for a child to have one of everything. These are simply choices that have lasting play value and appeal.

### Balls and Bats and Baseball Caps

Interest in baseball often begins in the early school years. By six, most boys and many girls spend a good deal of time and energy learning to hit, pitch, and catch a ball. For starters, they need a lightweight bat and soft ball. They are also going to need plenty of practice and a little coaching. Since playing baseball is one of those group entry tickets, a little parental time in the backyard or playground is as important as supplying the equipment. Here are some tips for practice time:

*Batting:* A soft ball suspended by a length of elastic can be hung from a tree branch. A tetherball arrangement can also be made with a sturdy post in the ground. Neither arrangement is a substitute for some sessions with parent pitching and child batting.

*Catching:* Practice with catching balls need not be limited to a softball. Kids who are having trouble may get the knack with a larger ball. Remember, kids need feelings of success as well as skill. If the practice session ends up with "How could you miss that?" you're likely to strike out in the coaching department. Kids at this age don't need much help in seeing their shortcomings. They need positive assurance that they're getting better—a little bit at a time.

*Pitching:* Marking a target on a solid wall can provide independent practice time. As with batting, solo pitching needs to be supplemented with the presence of a live, moving, eager batter on the receiving end of the pitch.

Few children of the early school years are ready for true competitive games. Team sports with winners and losers will be more appropriate in the coming years. But developing the skills and using the gear is another first step toward group life. Even the baseball cap is a signal of wanting to belong—a positive sign of belonging to the group.

## Other Equipment for Eye-Hand Coordination

Magnetic darts, ring-toss games, and horseshoes help the child develop eye-hand skills. Balls to bounch, catch, or pitch in a wastebasket or through a tire are basic equipment.

## Big-Muscle Action

On the playground or in the backyard children continue to stretch their growing arms and legs, climbing up monkey bars, slides, and chinning bars. Swings, see-saws, and trapeze rings to swing from offer the kind of acrobatic action children love.

Learning to somersault, walk forward and backward on the balance beam, and jump with a rope are physical challenges they work at in earnest.

## Other Sports

Depending on where you live, this is the age when many children become keen on learning how to ski or swim. Many seem to learn better with special instructions from the ski or swimming pro. Often, group lessons are offered at community centers or by youth groups. Some schools include such group lessons in the after-school or weekend activities. Struggling to conquer the hill or dive for a penny in the company of other children can motivate some and build tension for others. You'll really have to keep your ears perked on their progress. Without overprotecting them, remember their feelings about themselves are as important as their athletic prowess. If class isn't something they look forward to and enjoy now, they may be ready to do so in six months or a year from now.

## Golden Oldies—Games for the Young

Although fives to sevens are not ready for competitive games, they do enjoy an occasional group game. If you're having a party, a family pow-wow, or the young neighborhood gang seems to be in your backyard, you may find it useful to know some of the games that kids have loved for generations.

These golden oldies have a preimposed structure with simple rules. Once children know how to play them, they need little more in the way of adult interference. Of course, if you can't resist, just remember you have to take turns at being *It!*

### Farmer in the Dell

- Children form a circle around the child who is the farmer.

- All sing, "The farmer in the dell, the farmer in the dell, hi ho a derry oh, the farmer in the dell."

- Then with each succeeding verse, the appropriate character chooses someone to come into the middle of the circle:
      The farmer takes a wife
      The wife takes a child
      The child takes a dog
      The dog takes a cat
      The cat takes a rat
      The rat takes a cheese

- At this point, all those who have been chosen, except the cheese, run back into the ring and sing: "The cheese stands alone."

- The cheese becomes the new farmer.

### Duck, Duck, Goose

- Children are seated on the ground in a circle.

- *It* walks around outside rim of circle, tapping each child on the head (lightly) saying, "Duck, duck, duck" until he taps someone and says, "Goose!"

- Now the Goose chases *It* around the circle, trying to catch *It* before *It* can sit in Goose's old space.

- If *It* gets caught by the Goose, he goes in the pot in the middle of the circle until someone else is caught.

- This game takes a long time and everyone really wants a turn to be *It!*

## Green Light Go

- All the children line up on a starting line, except *It*.

- *It* walks a distance away, turns his back and says, "Red light; green light; one, two, three!"

- The others run toward *It*.

- But if *It* sees anyone moving after he says "three," *It* can send them back to the starting line.

- The object is to be the first to tap *It* and become the next *It*.

## Giant Steps

- The Giant stands at one end of playing area and others stand at starting line.

- The Giant calls the name of each child in turn and says, "Take one (or more) giant, baby, or umbrella steps (twirls)."

- The child must ask, "May I?"

- If a child moves without asking permission, the Giant sends him back.

- The object is to become the new Giant by getting close enough to tap the old Giant.

- *Variation* Once the Giant is tapped, he may race all the players back to the starting line. If he catches one, that player becomes the new Giant. (Most kids long to be the new Giant and get caught willingly.)

## Statues

- *It* closes his eyes and starts counting to ten.

- All children but *It* start to move.

- When *It* finishes counting to ten, he yells, "Freeze!"

- Children must hold their position without moving.

- The first person to move is out.

- *It* keeps moving among the statues, waiting to send out anyone who moves.

- Last person to "melt" becomes new *It*.

### Shadow Tag

- You need a sunny day.
- *It* tries to step on the shadow of other players.
- Player is out when *It* steps on his shadow.
- Last shadow to be caught becomes *It*.
- This is a running and chasing game without physical grabbing—but it still can get wild, with head-on collisions, so supervision is needed.

Check your library for other outdoor group games.

If you're having a party and get caught indoors, here are several games worth having in your magic hat.

### Chief

- Everyone sits in a circle.
- *It* goes out of sight.
- Someone is chosen to be Chief and begins clapping hands.
- Everyone must do what the Chief does.
- Chief keeps changing actions.
- *It* returns and watches, and gets three guesses to find out who is the Chief.

### Who Moved?

- Everyone sits in a circle.
- *It* goes out of the room.
- A leader chooses four kids (or more) to change places.
- *It* returns and must discover who has moved. (Great for powers of observation.)

### You're Hot!

- *It* goes out.
- A child hides a beanbag or other object somewhere in the room.

- *It* returns and others guide him to object by shouting, "You're cold!" or "Freezing!" when he's nowhere near the object, and "Getting warmer, hotter, hot, hot, burning!" until the child finds the object.

- *It* picks next *It*.

### Hot Potato

- Use a record or drum as a signal for starting and stopping this game.

- Everyone sits in a circle and passes the Hot Potato until the music stops.

- The person holding the Potato is out.

- The game continues until everyone but the winner has been caught with the Potato.

- Use a bean bag, a ball, or—why not?—a potato.

## Gameboards

Formal games with rules are still pretty hard to deal with. Kids with older brothers and sisters may want to play like the big kids. But the fact is, the young child really can't stand to lose.

Not only are their strategy skills unequal to the older child's, but so is their moral fortitude. Faced with defeat, some children would rather cheat. So playing with an older child, the game is apt to end with tears and anger. And playing with agemates may end with shouts of "You cheated! No fair!" Knowing the rules, he expects others to follow them exactly, but sees no fault in himself if he makes a new rule in midstream.

Nevertheless, some kids at six and seven manage to sidestep the moral issue by a kind of gentlemen's agreement—they both cheat by rewriting the rules as they go. This lasts only until one of them goes too far or wins too often.

### Parents' Role

Learning to play takes experience with both winning and losing. The truth is, few of us voluntarily do things we're likely to fail at all the time. In games between parent and child, it's best not to come down too heavily on issues of ethics. If you're the type who always has to win, you'd better warn the child and be prepared for the game to end soon. Letting the child win more than he loses may mean bending the rules or being purposely a bit behind. It may also mean giving a little hint when the child has not noticed an obvious move. Now, purists might say that's cheating. But helping the child to see how to play is not exactly the same as letting him win. Learning skills of strategy and how to plan ahead are big ideas that some sevens can begin to grasp. By seven, many are also better able to live with the rules—sometimes. Just remember that learning to lose takes a lot longer than learning to win. And learning to play by the rules for the pleasure of playing takes longer still.

### Choosing Games

While fives may still thrive on games of chance (see chapter 5, pages 122–28), sixes and sevens are ready for games like:

| | | |
|---|---|---|
| Chinese Checkers | Chutes and Ladders | Dominoes |
| Regular Checkers | Parcheesi | Bingo |

Rules for simple games like War, Old Maid, Snap, and Rummy-type games can be found in many books on card games in the library. Of course, the shelves of toy stores have a wide variety of board games featuring superheroes and TV characters. Their packaging is often more interesting than the game inside. Yet they offer a framework for future game playing. Their novelty is usually short-lived. If you're buying, look for games with simple rules and not too many pieces that can get lost or broken.

## Great Expectations

My daughter knows all the letters of the alphabet. She can count and even add. I think it's ridiculous for her to go to kindergarten. She wants to learn to read.
—Mother of a four-and-a-half-year-old

There's no doubt about it, many kindergartners come to school knowing more than five-year-olds of a few decades ago. Many avid TV watchers do know the names of the letters and they can count, too. In fact, on the surface, some of these kids look like they might be blooming geniuses. But knowing your numbers and letters extra early is no guarantee of being the best student in the world. Basically, it means that someone has taken a great deal of time to teach the child letters and numbers. It may also be that, a year later, the same tasks could have been learned with much more ease and in less time. Unfortunately for most young children, the extraordinary time spent in learning letters has simply robbed them of time that could and should have been spent at other kinds of learning and playing activities.

Kids vary considerably in their readiness to read. Schools sort kids by chronological age, but that does not make them all the same. Just as they didn't all walk at twelve months, they don't all learn to read at six.

In fact, research has shown that kids who don't get formal reading instruction until age seven read as well as kids who start at six by the time they all reach the fourth grade. Perhaps even more significant is the fact that by junior high school, the later starters turn out to read with more enthusiasm and spontaneity than the early readers. It may be that starting a bit later makes a real difference between kids who *can* read as opposed to kids who *do* read. It's another case of "haste makes waste."

Quite naturally, both parents and children view these beginning years of school with great expectations. First and foremost, these expectations center on learning to read. Although formal reading instruction used to begin in first grade, many kindergarten programs today are rushing children into reading. Of course, there have always been some children who come to school already knowing how to read. And there have also been many six-year-olds who were not ready to begin reading. One of the problems kids face today is measuring up to those great expectations—their own and others'.

## Supporting School Skills

> I work with him every day. He comes home and we sit down for an hour or as long as it takes. We go over his work. I make him read it and reread it until he gets it right. Sometimes, I have to admit, it doesn't seem to help.
>
> —Mother of a second grader

Small wonder this mother's approach is not succeeding. Indeed, it may be doing more harm than good. All parents are eager to find ways to help their child with schoolwork. Unfortunately, some parents are overeager. As a teacher of sixes and sevens, I often found that some of my students went home to another day of school. In parent-teacher conferences I was asked:

"Do you have a harder reading book?"

"I'd like a third grade math book; she wants to learn the times tables like her sister."

"Don't they need more homework?"

Although well intentioned, many parents think "harder is better." In their eagerness to teach, they end up overloading both the intellectual and emotional circuits.

An absence of homework does not mean parents can't or shouldn't be involved with school-related skills. But workbooks and schoolbooks are not the only way to help.

There are games and activities you can share with your child that reinforce skills and positive feelings between both parent and child, and the child and his schoolwork. The trick is in knowing what your child is ready for—not what you want or wish he was ready for.

Take your clues from the papers she brings home. Are they working on sounds, writing, counting? If you're not getting papers, there may be several reasons:

- Your child's teacher may not send them home.

- Your child's teacher may not use many duplicated task sheets.

- Your child may be leaving them on the bus.

- Your child may not want you to see anything but perfect papers.

Whatever the case, you can certainly find out from his teacher. You can also ask the teacher what kinds of skills your child is working on and how he is doing. Teachers often have suggestions for things parents can work on at home.

Whatever the suggestion, remember that many normal and bright children are simply not ready to read—just because they're six! What you have to keep alive is the child's belief in himself as a doer. Keep in mind that children of this age are particularly sensitive to criticism. They need lots of praise and success. Pushing them to the next level may lead to a dead end rather than a step forward. Kids need plenty of practice to make math and reading skills part of themselves. Not everything needs to be hard and new. While the games in this section are directly related to school skills, they are no more important than other activities in this chapter. Indeed, it's important for parents to understand that these are a very small and narrow part of what children need to learn from their play.

## Early Reading Games

Learning the names of letters and the sounds they say are two different skills. Just knowing the names of the letters won't help you to r-e-a-d one word on this p-a-g-e, will it? It's learning the sounds they say that helps kids break the code. If your child needs help with this kind of skill, try some of the following games:

### Cat in the Box

Here's a lively game that doesn't require sitting still or writing letters. You'll need to do some homework before you can play.

- Save three small boxes.

- With permanent marker, write a different letter in upper and lower case on each box. Draw a picture that begins with the sound of each letter.

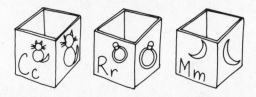

- Gather a collection of small household objects and miniature toys that begin with the same sound (i.e., candle, cookie, car, comb; roller, rabbit, ruler, rubberband; monkey, mouse, marble, marker).

- Store all the objects in a basket or in a big box. The child reaches into the basket and must decide what box the object belongs in.

- Gradually add more boxes and objects as the child learns the sounds and letter names.

- This is a game your child may enjoy playing alone. You can also involve the child in finding objects to match the sounds.

## Letter Lotto

This sound game requires a little cut-and-paste work your child will enjoy helping with. Finding pictures of relatively uniform size may be better done by parent. But trimming and pasting can be fun for your playing partner. You'll need index cards, magazine pictures, paste, scissors, paper, and buttons.

- Cut out a variety of small pictures from magazines that begin with three different sounds (you'll be adding more gradually).

- Paste each picture to an index card or use old playing cards.

- Make playing boards from paper or pieces of cardboard. Label the playing boards with the same three letters in different positions.

- To play, put your cards in a stack.

- Taking turns, the first player draws a card and puts a button on one box that matches the sound he drew.

- Second player picks next card and covers the letter on his board that matches picture.

- The winner is the first to have three in a row—across, down, or diagonally.

As your card collection grows, you'll be able to play other games such as *Gotcha!*

## Gotcha!

- Deal out all the cards evenly.

- First player puts his first card in middle of table.

- Second player puts his first card out. If his card matches card on table, he takes both cards, saying, "gotcha!"

- Winner is the player who gets the most "Gotchas!"

## Sound Detector

This is a riddle game that parents can play without any equipment.

- You say, "I'm turning on my sound detector . . . I see it in my scanner . . . it's made of wood . . . it has one, two, three, four legs . . . it is round . . . it starts with the same sound as 'tiger' and 'tuna' . . . what is it?"

- *Variation I* You can make it tougher by telling less about the object and more about the sounds . . . "I see something in this room that starts like 'lion' and 'lamb' . . ."

- Here the answer is more open-ended since there may be a lollipop, a lamp, and a leopard in the room—who knows?

- *Variation II* Let the child switch on his sound detector and give the clues . . . but remember that giving the clues is a different and sometimes more difficult skill.

- *Variation III* This one is good when you're on the road. Play "Invisible Sound Detector": give clues about something that is not in sight—something you're thinking of. Good clear clues are important here.

- Remember, not being able to see the object makes it tougher and the clues more essential.

- For a further variation, see if your child can give you the clues.

### Oh, No You Don't

This is a variation on the old favorite game "Grandmother's Trunk." Tell your child you're going on a make-believe journey. You have to take lots of things—only everything that you're taking must begin with the same sound. Tell your child you need a little help—if you say something that doesn't begin with the sound of, for instance, "s," they have to holler, "Oh, no you don't!"

- Now you begin. Say, "We're going to Seattle and I'm going to take a seal, a sock, a safety pin, soap, a bottle. . . ."

- *Variation I* Pack a bag with rhyming words. Your child must shout if the word doesn't rhyme (i.e. "I'm going to take a pear, a chair, a hair, a hose. . . .").

Note: Kids really love the power of saying, "Oh, no you don't." Here they're in the position of correcting you instead of the other way around.

## More Than Sounds

Learning to "sound it out" is just a small part of reading. If you doubt this, try reading an engineer's manual or a monthly journal for biochemists. You may be able to read every word. But putting the ideas together is something else. Building quick recognition helps the child past the one-letter-at-a-time habit and over the hurdle of understanding what they read.

You may remember flashcards bringing on sweaty palms and butterflies in the stomach. Here are some self-correcting games you can use in their place. These are word games that should strengthen comprehension and rapid recognition of whole words. You can expand some to phrases as well.

### Pumpkin Patch Match

You'll need white construction paper, scissors, and crayons. Cut out a dozen pumpkins (or shoes, socks, hearts, flowers). Now you (or your child) color six pairs. Each pair should match.

On the blank side of each pair, print words that mean the opposite of each other.

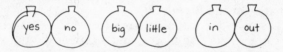

You and your child can brainstorm more opposites than you'll need. Knowing them is the first step to reading them, so build the list together.

To play:

- Mix up the cards, picture side down.

- Child must make word pairs with opposites.

- Once they're paired, the child flips the cards over. They're self-correcting, remember.

- *Variation I* Brainstorm a list of things that go together like shoes and socks, bread and butter, bat and ball.

- *Variation II* Brainstorm words that mean the same: easy/simple, fast/quick, little/tiny, cold/freezing.

### Captain Action Words

Acting out action words is a lot more fun than just saying them. You'll need a stack of word cards (index cards are great). Print action words on these: RUN, DANCE, JUMP, FALL, etc.

- Child draws card from stack. He reads card to himself, then he must act out the word.

- Other player must try to guess what the card says. If other player guesses, he gets the card.

- Players take turns drawing a card and acting it out. If a player can't guess, the card goes back under the stack.

- *Variation* You could write phrases on the cards. For example, "Clap your hands two times," "Put the card on your head," "Turn the light off," "Jump three times and sit down."

### Off the Board

Most games you buy are played on game boards. They're played by the rules (sort of) that others make up. Here's a game that's Off the Board.

You'll need index cards, scissors, crayons or markers, buttons or coins as playing pieces, and a coin or die to toss.

- Cut the index cards in half.

- Print easy-to-read directions on the cards. Some cards may have pictures of objects or numbers or colors.

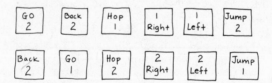

- To play: Child lays the cards out in any order.

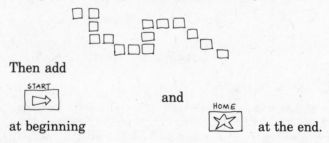

Then add

and

at beginning                    at the end.

- Players toss coin: Heads = one move; tails = two moves. Or toss die: Odd = one move; even = two moves.

- Each player takes turns and must do what the cards say. This is a good game for building recognition of "little" words, which are often most confusing.

In the storebought department, there are several reading games that may be fun to add for sixes and sevens:

Scrabble for Juniors
Spill 'n Spell
Anagrams
Silly Sentences (word cubes)

Basically, kids like to experiment with these on their own since they are obviously no match for competing with a parent or older sibling. They may play such games with a visiting friend, but not for long.

Activity books with beginners' crossword puzzles and word games may be entertaining for a child who sees adults doing crossword puzzles in the newspapers and magazines.

## *Books*

He reads the same books over and over. Why does he do that?
—Mother of a six-year-old

She reads to me every night. You know, I bought those easy-to-read books. She loves them.
—Mother of a first grader

### *Easy- and Not-So-Easy-to-Read—*

One of the best ways to support school skills is to continue sharing books with your child. Beginning readers today have a wider range of easy-to-read choices. These are books your child will enjoy reading to you or to a younger brother or sister. Their limited vocabulary gives the child a sense of success. In fact, you may need to hear the same book again and again. The need for repetition is something you've seen from the earliest days, when they were eagerly playing fill-and-dump games.

Gaining a sense of success as a "doer" comes with reading easy books with real ease.

Being a good listener doesn't mean parents should give up reading to their child, though. A good many rich and delightful children's books are beyond the reading ability of most sixes and sevens. Sharing these books enlarges your child's motivation to read and the richness of their own language development.

In picture books children find humor, adventure, suspense, and drama. For a small stretch of time they escape into another world of make-believe. Inside the pages of a book, they find small creatures and people like themselves or as they wish they were. So, picture books offer emotional release and another way of walking in someone else's shoes. They also fuel your child's own imaginative play and their own original stories.

Here's a sampling of picture books and slightly longer story books fives to sevens will enjoy listening to:

*Amos and Boris; Sylvester and the Magic Pebble,* by William Steig

*Where the Wild Things Are,* by Maurice Sendak

*Five Hundred Hats of Bartholomew Cubbins,* by Dr. Seuss

*Everyone Knows What a Dragon Looks Like,* by Jay Williams

*The Stories Julian Tells,* by Ann Cameron

*The Garden of Abdul Gasazi,* by Chris Van Allsburg

*Pinkerton* series, by Steven Kellogg

*Grimm's Snow White,* by Nancy Ekholm Burkort (illustrator)

*Crow Boy,* by Taro Yashima

*Ramona* series, by Beverly Cleary

*The House at Pooh Corner,* by A. A. Milne

*Paddington Bear* series, by Michael Bond

*Mary Poppins,* by P. L. Travers

*Charlotte's Web; Stuart Little,* by E. B. White

*Just So Stories,* by Rudyard Kipling

For more ideas, check with your local librarian.

On the other side of the coin, kids are hungry for information about the real world. While books alone are a poor substitute for the real thing, they can supplement the child's growing interest in how things work.

Trips into the community can be supplemented with a follow-up trip to the library for finding out more or helping to recall what has been seen. Books may have more information than children want or need, so parents may need to paraphrase the information or discuss illustrations, taking their clues from the child's questions and interest. You need not be limited to children's books. Indeed, the prospect of sharing "grownup" books builds a kind of appetite, readiness, and motivation for reading. Even if the child is a beginning reader, the opportunity to share books and read to the child should not be abandoned. It will be several years before the beginning reader can read material that matches his interest and hunger for information.

### Making Their Own Books

Long before the child is ready to write down his own stories, the business of composing stories has been part of his play. Make-believe and playing roles are early forms of composing stories.

Your child's pictures and construction with blocks also provide a stimulus for storytelling. This is a good time, if you haven't started already, to encourage the child to dictate stories about their drawings or buildings. Young children have much bigger stories in their heads than they can write or even copy on their own.

Seeing you write down what they say helps the child make the connection between what they say with the printed squiggles on a page. This is a real leap in learning. As they watch you write they also see the mechanics of writing from left to right, how a pencil is held and letters are shaped. You don't need to make a big deal of the mechanics—just let them happen.

Sometimes a collection of a child's drawings has a common theme. Suggest putting them together in a book by stapling them together. Your child may want to label or have you label the pictures to tell a story.

> Amy and her friends drew a delightful collection of flowers. They were growing into a blooming garden. So we put them together and the idea of a bookful triggered even more fanciful flowers. It's a treasure.
> —Mother of a second grader

If you help with the spelling of words they need, some sixes and most sevens like to write and illustrate books about themselves, their family, toys, trips, special events, animals, food, machines, numbers, and colors.

Keep a supply of note pads and blank paper of varying sizes available. You can even staple some blank books together and have them ready for bookmaking. Construction paper or pages from old wallpaper-sample books make nifty covers.

Remember, all books need titles and the author and illustrator's name on the cover. These first books, written or dictated by children, often become part of their early reading library. Since they are written in the child's own words, they have the structure and rhythm of the child's own language.

In addition to their own pictures, children also enjoy collecting print and pictures from magazines to illustrate their books. Collections of planes, trucks, and cars may fill a scrapbook of a transportation lover. Animals and furry creatures may fill another. Such collections are a way of classifying and ordering the world with pictorial symbols.

Beginning book writers are as different as the grownup kind. Some tend to favor facts while others prefer to spin fantasy. Some are verbose, others concise. Accept the child's early stories as they are told to you. If you want to help the writing juices flow, don't make a big issue over spelling and penmanship now. Mechanics come later.

## Writing vs. Penmanship

Sometimes these two words get mixed up—writing and penmanship. Although they are closely related, they are definitely not the same thing. Penmanship refers to the mechanical act of forming letters, while writing refers to the act of putting ideas down on paper. Both skills begin developing through play long before schooldays. Pretend playing, storybook, and real-life experiences all feed the growing ability to dictate and then write one's own stories.

Penmanship, or shaping letters, on the other hand, is essentially a fine motor skill involving eye-hand coordination and seeing things in spatial relationships. Basically, penmanship is dependent on physiological development and cannot be rushed. Indeed, too much practice with pencil and paper can be painful to small fingers and not necessarily productive. Practicing poor habits can actually be destructive to penmanship and create bad feelings that overflow into writing. A good many grownups, who today claim they can't write, really mean they hate penmanship and all the cramped feelings that surrounded their early experiences.

Kids do need plenty of practice in learning to control the line their eyes and hands are trying to make. However, practicing on lined paper with pencil is not the only way to gain control. Paint, marker, crayons, and chalk continue to be useful at this age in developing eye-hand coordination. Indeed, learning to control the fluid, sweeping movements of paint and markers offers less restricting and tiring practice.

- Magic slates that can be written on with fingernails or styluses give children a nonpermanent surface to practice on. Mistakes get abracadabrad when the plastic sheet is lifted from the carbonlike board.

- Plastic baggies with taped tops or zip-type closings can be filled with a few spoonfuls of ketchup or pudding. Close top securely! Flatten bag and then trace letters or drawings with fingertips. Like the magic slate, mistakes vanish by smoothing the bag and starting again.

- Watercolor markers are fun to use on acetate folders. These are found in school supply sections and are usually used by high school students for report covers. If you load lined paper and practice letters in the folder, your child can trace over the letters with wash-off markers. The thick lines and fat shape of watercolor markers give the child an extra helping hand.

- Chalkboard and chalk for playing school is both non-permanent and appealing.

- A tray full of sand or flour is great for tracing letters in and helps give the child a real feel for forming letters.

- Cut-out letters of sandpaper can be mounted on cardboard and are also handy for getting the feel of letters.

- Plastic magnetic letters, both upper- and lowercase, are appealing to handle and shape into words on the refrigerator.

- Keep a supply of wide-lined writing paper and fat primary pencils.

- Keeping a variety of sizes, shapes, and colors of papers available makes writing-type activities appealing.

- Shaping letters with cookie dough is yet another way of playing with letters. Shaped by hand or cookie cutters, these letters can be baked to spell the names of family members.

- Big block printing alphabets and stamp pads are fun.

### How to Shape Up

Knowing how to shape letters and what directions the lines should go means learning the right way, rather than practicing mistakes. This chart is for reference, not drill. Avoid practicing too many letters at one time.

Practicing on paper can cramp small fingers. Here are some other nonpencil tasks that are fun and may be of real benefit.

- Write letters in the air. Have the child use her whole arm writing giant letters in the air.
- Suggest that the child "write" a letter with footprints—you write one and let the child guess what letter you've made . . . then have the child write one. This is another way of getting the feel of letters.

### *Finding Reasons to Write*

Just practicing the same letters again and again can be deadly. But finding reasons to write legibly is central to being understood. Writing a note to a friend exercises the same skill and is meaningful to the child, as are:

| | | |
|---|---|---|
| labeling collections | signs | birthday cards |
| letters to grandma | games | shopping lists |

These are the things that help children to make the connection between penmanship and communicating.

### *Related to Writing*

Quite apart from practicing letters directly there are a variety of play activities and toys that develop fine motor tuning needed for school skills.

- Sewing with a blunt needle and thread requires refining the grasp of small fingers—sewing puppets, pincushions, dolls' clothes, or decorative wall hangings is ideal. Remember, sewing is not for girls only.

- Doing needlepoint, using big-mesh canvas and fat yarn, children develop both eye-hand skills and stick-to-it power. Start with small but usable pieces that can become bookmarks or rugs for dollhouses—quick results are a must.

- Small play tiles or mosaic-type toys that fit into peg-type boards require small fingers to grasp and arrange tiles in patterns. Encourage your child to create his own designs and pictures, as well as reproduce the picture patterns that come with the games.

- Parquetry blocks come in many sizes and with patterns that can be reproduced. Keep in mind that learning to write requires the ability to copy letters and to notice the direction of the patterns they form. Parquetry blocks and tiles offer this kind of practice without the letters.

- Small wooden beads that can be designed into wearable jewelry—or any bead and jewelry kit—give your child another playful way to sharpen the fine-tuning muscles.

- Don't overlook the old-time toys—jacks and pick-up sticks—that really put eye and hand to the test. Wooden pick-up sticks are hard to find, but much better than plastic sticks.

## Math Games

*One potato, two potato,*
*Three potato, four—*
*Five potato, six potato,*
*Seven potato, more.*

Perhaps no school skill is more intertwined with the child's everyday play life than math skills. Jumping rope and bouncing balls, kids count by ones, fives, and tens, practicing both physical and intellectual feats over and over again until both become quite automatic. Mention math and most parents, and too many teachers, think of computing. But counting, adding, and subtracting are just the mechanical pieces of mathematical thinking—just as phonics are a narrow part of reading.

Blocks (see pages 98–103) continue to give children concrete experiences with a variety of concepts that are the underpinnings of understanding size and space relationships of higher, taller, wider, longer, and straighter.

Although some concepts of time remain confusing, abstract ideas, kids are trying to pin them down in personal and meaningful ways. Counting the days until a birthday, a holiday, or a planned event can be happily anticipated on a good-sized calendar. Keeping track of the weather by drawing on symbols for rain, sun, clouds, or snow makes the calendar a daily kind of journal. Sequences of events like the days of the week, dates of the month, months of the year, are built into the events that dot a child's calendar. Parents can extend the child's growing awareness by referring to the first Sunday, the last Saturday, and day before or after an event.

Outdoor thermometers, scales, tape measures, rulers, and clocks are tools kids want to know about on their own childlike terms. Clocks tell when it's time for bed, dinner, school, the movies, and other urgent hours. Toy clocks, clock puzzles, wristwatches, and old alarm clocks will be especially welcomed by sixes and sevens. Learning to tell time is more important when it has personal relevance.

Bathroom scales, kitchen scales, and toy balance scales all lend themselves to interesting experiments with measuring volume by pounds, ounces, and grams. Nuts, pine cones, styrofoam pellets, small blocks, or shells satisfy the child's need to count, weigh, and compare real things. Accuracy is not the object. Children need to make generalizations before they pin down particulars in exacting terms. Playing with real tools moves them toward such learning.

Just as the kitchen was a learning center for your toddler, it continues to offer rich ingredients for learning and play. Cooking together opens the door to:

- reading recipes—in sequence

- measuring liquids and solids, cups, spoons, pounds, ounces, grams

- timing on clocks

- measuring with thermometers

- first-hand observations of how things change from solid to liquid, from thin to thick, from soft to hard, from small to big.

Any excuse to cook together is a golden opportunity to mix skills and play into nourishment for mind and body.

### On the Go—Numbers Everywhere

Counting telephone poles or green cars remains an age-old favorites of the under-eight crowd. If the counting gets to you on long hauls, you might set up a highway hunt for an assortment of sights. Be sure to sprinkle the list with highly probable finds as well as hard sightings.

For prereaders, a sheet with drawings rather than a word list may make more sense and spark their awareness.

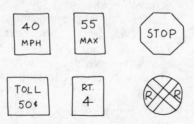

### I'm Thinking of a Number

Here's a good riddle game you can play on long hauls with children who are learning their addition facts. Say, "I'm thinking of a number that's less than ten." The child may not ask, "Is it two?" He must ask you if it is less than something or more than something. As he zooms in on the number he must ask, "Is it the same as three plus four?" or "Is it one more than six?" The final question must have an addition or subtraction fact.

### What's My Pattern?

This is another listening game for kids who are learning to count by twos, fives, and tens. Say, "See if you can guess my pattern. Listen: Four . . . six . . . eight . . ." or "Twenty-one . . . thirty-one . . . forty-one . . ."

Many of the games in the reading section can be adapted to beginning math skills. The Pumpkin Patch Match could have pairs of cards with matching numerals and objects

or numerals and equations

or make broken hearts:

- Cut the hearts on the dotted line.
- Mix them up.
- This is a self-correcting toy.

### Math in Motion—Action Dice

A good many store bought games come with dice that are rolled and counted for moves on the board. But dice can be used for putting kids in motion, too. Buy two big cubes—three or four square inches—of foam rubber and mark them with dots like dice (use permanent marker).

There are many games they can be used for. In fact, your child may invent some games of her own. To begin with, give her some time just to throw them. Maybe it's the novelty of throwing a "square ball," but they are very appealing. Then play:

### *High Tosser*

- Keep a simple score card.

- Players take turns tossing and adding their throw. High tosser scores a point. Game is won by first person to get ten high rolls. If you lose, demand a rematch.

### *Dots of Jumping*

On the sidewalks use chalk; inside use tape. Either way, make a grid.

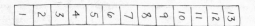

*Plan One:* Use two dice. Players jump to number they throw. This game moves you back and forth. Winner is first to roll a twelve.

*Plan Two:* Use one die. Players take turns. You add dots to number you're standing on. Magic moment comes when you have a combo that adds up to twelve.

*Plan X:* Keep the fun alive . . . let your child invent the rules. She might want to start at ten and use one die to substract . . . or only move forward on even numbers . . . the fun is in keeping the options open.

## Clap-a-Number

This is a terrific listening game. Once your child gets the drift, let her be the leader. For openers, say, "I'm going to clap a fact. . . ." Then clap once . . . pause . . . clap two times. Child must tell you what you clapped . . . not just three, but, one and two are three. You can use a drum or sticks, but hands are always handy.

The big thing about all of these games is taking the drill off of paper and pencil and letting the child experience numbers in real and active ways. Until kids are seven they still need concrete and meaningful experiences to understand abstract symbols like numbers.

Learning to simply count to 100 is very often meaningless gibberish. Although kids are eager to count to a zillion, be on the lookout for opportunities to make their number play count. It may be as simple as counting out the pretzels in a bag to share, the shells gathered at the beach, or pine cones found on a hike.

Losing their place in counting may lead them to find a more systematic way of counting. Pennies in stacks of ten, scoring in packs of

all lead to a way of using numbers in their everyday life.

## Hide-and-Seek Numbers

Once sixes and sevens have the drift of numbers, they'll enjoy practicing with this number game. They'll have just as much fun helping you construct it.

You'll need a big piece of cardboard, a ruler, a permanent marker, a hundred poker chips. Draw a grid on the cardboard. Print numerals from one to a hundred.

- To play: Cover the board with chips.
- First player calls a number.

| 1 | 2 | 3 | 4 | 5 | 6 | 7 | 8 | 9 | 10 |
|---|---|---|---|---|---|---|---|---|---|
| 11 | 12 | 13 | 14 | 15 | 16 | 17 | 18 | 19 | 20 |
| 21 | 22 | 23 | 24 | 25 | 26 | 27 | 28 | 29 | 30 |
| 31 | 32 | 33 | 34 | 35 | 36 | 37 | 38 | 39 | 40 |
| 41 | 42 | 43 | 44 | 45 | 46 | 47 | 48 | 49 | 50 |
| 51 | 52 | 53 | 54 | 55 | 56 | 57 | 58 | 59 | 60 |
| 61 | 62 | 63 | 64 | 65 | 66 | 67 | 68 | 69 | 70 |
| 71 | 72 | 73 | 74 | 75 | 76 | 77 | 78 | 79 | 80 |
| 81 | 82 | 83 | 84 | 85 | 86 | 87 | 88 | 89 | 90 |
| 91 | 92 | 93 | 94 | 95 | 96 | 97 | 98 | 99 | 100 |

- Other player must lift chip to reveal the number. If he's right, he keeps the chip.

- Second player calls a number.

- Winner is person with greatest number of chips.

## Science—Taking a Closer Look

Most of the science activities suggested in the preschool chapter (pages 115–18) will continue to be of interest. Given a magnifying glass, kids are eager to take a closer look at the natural world. A pail full of pond water, scoop of soil, a leaf, or a piece of bark comes alive in new ways under magnification.

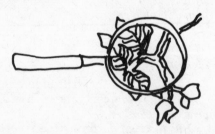

Magnets, too, are fascinating tools for discovery. Give them a roll of stick-on dots (from stationery store) and let them stick a dot wherever the magnet sticks. These dots come off easily, but help the child see how many things in the world are made of iron. A pair of rod magnets with north and south pole clearly marked is harder to find than the usual horseshoe magnets, but worth searching for. Help your child discover what happens when north meets north or south meets south.

From magnet to compass is a natural leap for sevens—especially if you talk about the earth's North Pole being like a giant magnet that pulls the compass arrow north. Learning how to turn the compass and line up the arrow is a concrete step toward understanding abstract ideas about direction.

Gardening on the windowsill or in the backyard demands crops with quick results. Outdoors try beans, radishes, and lettuce. If you haven't any yard space, don't overlook the possibilities of potted plants. Everything from tomatoes to sunflowers can be contained in a deep planting tub.

Kids will be fascinated with windowsill gardens. Bulbs that flower, such as paper-white narcissus or amaryllis, are available in most supermarkets. They give quick and flashy shows.

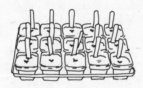

Taking cuttings from ivy or philodendron and rooting them in water is a kind of life-cycle show kids can see with their own eyes. Keeping a log of dates and changes with illustrations may be interesting to the young scientist. Plants from cuttings also make lovely "homemade" gifts for giving.

Fall is a perfect time to gather small plants from the field for terrariums that require little care but grow greener as the outdoors grows gray. Look for gardening books in the library for details. *Bottles and Cans,* a Puffin Book (Penguin Books), is a clear, easy-to-follow book for setting up terrariums and other projects using found materials. Get your child involved in gathering the stones, soil, containers, and plants.

Bird watching is of interest to both city and country children. A pair of inexpensive field glasses will be welcome, along with a simple bird watchers' guide book (try *Child's Book of Birds,* by Kathleen Daly). This is a good time for starting a life list—collecting the names of kinds of birds spotted. In winter, hang suet and bird seed in nearby trees and enjoy helping our feathered friends through the lean time. In the spring, put some lengths of colored yarn on low branches for the nest builders. Then keep your eyes open for the telltale thread.

## Electronic Toys

There are now numerous "educational" electronic toys on the market, some as small as hand-held calculators, others to be used with personal computers. They promise to teach your child how to become a math buff, a spelling demon, and an all-around whiz kid. Most of these claims are questionable. At best, these toys offer a way of drilling skills that the child is trying to master. In a sense, they are probably better able to do that drilling without creating an atmosphere charged with parental judgments or the child's shame or fear of failing. A button that lights up, showing "try again" may be less difficult to take than a parent or sibling who says, "No, that's wrong; you're not trying," or "What's the matter with you?"

On the other hand, the skills drills cannot enlarge upon or make meaningful connections beyond what they are programmed to do. The electronic toy can neither understand nor clarify the reasons that underlie a child's repeated mistakes. It only knows the right answer. A limited tool for expanding the child's need to become a problem solver or question asker, it may fail to show the child a variety of ways to arrive at answers. Unfortunately, a good many parents and teachers consider knowing the one right answer the beginning and end of learning. Yet too often rote learning leads, at best, to quick recall and, at worst, to easily forgettable facts. Kids who grow up with the expectation that learning is as easy as spitting back answers or pushing the right button may be unwilling or unable to grapple with digging in on nitty-gritty problems that demand time and multiple steps to arrive at solutions.

Recognizing electronic toys for what they can and cannot do, parents had better not rest assured that machines can do the whole job. On the list of priorities, kids may use pushbuttons— but they are a poor substitute for real people who say, "Try it another way" and can suggest ways to try, instead of just "try again."

Given their limitations we must also acknowledge that kids love the magic of electronic toys and that such enthusiasm has real value. For those who need extra practice and drill, the learning machines put spelling and number facts in a new and appealing format. Indeed, the novelty and sense of control offer positive motivation for independent practice.

A generation ago parents with even limited funds scrimped and saved to buy their kids an encyclopedia. Today's parents are likely to feel the same way about electronic teaching machines—especially home computers. There is no doubt that children are becoming computer literate at an ever-earlier age. (See Playthings, chapter 9, pages 275–80.) As more personal computers are bought for home use, manufacturers are producing a wider variety of educational software. Some have done little more than put boring workbooks on discs. Others have combined games with skills in playful formats.

Like all electronic media, these new playthings have a hypnotic appeal. It is hard to turn away from the light and sound, even if the show is less than great. So parents are going to have to evaluate the value of the lessons and the time it takes from other forms of play.

Throughout this book we have pointed out the need for a variety of play experiences. Parents who understand the learning value of multiple kinds of play will see the need to set limits and help kids find a balance between passive pushbutton answers and the active business of learning through play. The allure of the new should not replace (or displace) the lasting value of the old.

## Music

Music continues to be a physically, emotionally, and intellectually stimulating part of the young child's daily life.

Dancing and marching to music opens the door to a pleasing release of body tension after prolonged sitting sessions. It is also a way to use the body expressively, casting one's whole self into pretend roles of animals, monsters, machines, you name it. Indeed, kids may welcome some suggestions, both from your words and the music you choose to play. Circus music, jazz, rock, dramatic symphonic music, bagpipes, brass bands, lyrical flutes, and rhapsodic harps all lend themselves to very different interpretations. The key here is offering a wide variety of music and space to skip, gallop, slither, slide, and twirl. Barefooted is best, but a soft, flexible shoe will do. Lengths of cloth, scarves, net, or headgear will add to the pretense. Although an occasional activity record with directions to follow may be of limited appeal, allowing children to explore what their bodies can do should play a large part in their play.

Adult suggestions need to be open-ended rather than demonstrations of particular steps to be done the one right and only way. That doesn't mean you can't join in and dance, too. Just don't forget to follow as well as lead. After a trip to the circus, the best souvenir turned out to be a record of circus music. My sons and their friends loved to act out their own version of walking an imaginary tightrope, a clown's act, lions and tamer, and elephants on parade. But don't limit the choices to obvious storyline music. Give them some exposure to a wide range of sounds that lend themselves to interpretive movement. These experiences give more rein to the child's own creative and physical potential. In the act of dancing, the child is both choreographer and performer.

Although many parents consider dance instruction or gymnastics at this time, it may be more desirable to postpone the discipline of formal training for another year or two. Some sevens may be coordinated enough for tap dance classes or dancing classes that encourage creative dramatics and movement. But exercises at the barre and formal routines are more appropriate a bit later.

### Instruments

This is a time when children often begin piano and guitar lessons. There are different views on how desirable this may be. Although your child may be able to pick out tunes on the piano, learning to read notation and time signs may be an

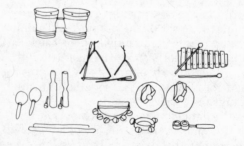

overload. Kids who are struggling with breaking the reading and number codes may not need the extra challenge of another set of abstract symbols. Often, the child who starts piano at eight or nine makes more progress in six months than his friend who started a year or two earlier. In the meantime, there are all sorts of simple instruments to experiment with. Xylophones, harmonicas, wooden flutes, ocarinas, and ukeleles are good for picking out a tune or creating your own songs.

Homemade instruments (see chapter 5, page 131) continue to serve well for keeping rhythm to the beat. Sixes and sevens are intrigued with tuning a set of water glasses to a full octave and tapping out familiar tunes on their glasses.

Setting up the glasses calls for some spoon tapping, spilling, and filling until the notes ring true.

A good toy drum with a skin head that can take a beating, and small finger or hand cymbals have a less abrasive sound than pot lids at this age. Sandpaper over a pair of wooden blocks makes an altogether acceptable sound for apartment dwellers, as do rhythm sticks and maracas. If you're the expansive type, tambourines and bells will definitely be pleasing

ways for kids to punctuate the beat. Of course, no child needs all of these, but they are offered as choices for young music makers.

You can expand the child's listening skills by calling attention to other musical values of volume and pitch. Playing a drum from "as loud as thunder" to "soft as raindrops falling" calls for interpretive skills and physical control. Clapping over your head when the music goes up or clapping way down to the floor when the music gets low—this combines action with understanding.

> After reading about several kinds of sea creatures that live inside of shells, my daughter and her two friends asked if they could act out the totally factual material I'd read to them. Frankly, I was puzzled. But I played them some "watery music" as they requested. Lo and behold, they were suddenly clams opening and closing their shells as they propelled themselves across the room. One child, hunched over with both feet stuck firmly together, moved ever so slowly to the music. "I'm a bivalve!" a clam called. "So, I'm a univalve!" old snail boasted. Again, it was a clear demonstration of how kids transform information and practice what they're learning through play and action.
> —Mother of a seven-year-old

### Song Fests

Children continue to delight in songs with repetitive choruses and predictable patterns. If it has a good beat, or simple lyrics and a loud chorus, it's bound to be a hit. This is the time for open-ended songs, where kids can construct some part of the verse. If it has animal sounds, machines, or nonsense verse, so much the better.

"Old MacDonald" now becomes a feat of repeating every animal sound that is added to the collection as the song builds. The same is true of "Comin' 'Round the Mountain" which grows from Toot Toot, Whoa There, Hi Babe, Chop Chop, Yum Yum, to snoring sounds.

It takes a good many miles to exhaust that one. But when you do, try taking words away instead of adding sounds, as with this old favorite:

> John Brown's baby
> Had a cold upon its chest (three times)
> And they rubbed it with camphor oil

After singing it through once, you sing it again, leaving out first one word and, the next time, still another. In the end you have just a frame of the song left:

> *John Brown's* ——
> *Had a* —— *upon its* —— *(three times)*
> *And they* —— *it with* —— *oil.*

It takes a long time and a lot of control to remember what not to sing. The old song about Bingo works on the same principle.

Of course, there are many folk tunes, holiday, and nonsense songs that are part of your child's musical heritage. Learning to sing these songs with the family is good fun and equally good preparation for group singing in school. Check the library for collections of folk songs on records and in books. Look for: *American Folk Songs for Children*, by Ruth Seeger; Woodie Guthrie's *Children's Songs*; *You'll Sing a Song and I'll Sing a Song*, by Ella Jenkins; *The Corner Grocery Store* and other records by Raffi.

Once kids have a repertoire of songs, they may enjoy playing Clap That Tune—you simply clap out the rhythm of a favorite song. Try "Jingle Bells" or "Row, Row, Row Your Boat." No humming or singing allowed! The other members of the family must guess what you're clapping. The person who guesses claps the next tune. This is a surprisingly quiet game that demands listening. Or try Sound Rounds. One member of the family begins singing a rhythmic chant. It can be as simple as dee-dum-dee-dum. First person must keep going with same sound as second player adds a very different rhythm and sound of his own. Depending on how many folks are in your family, you'll have some pretty interesting and sometimes comic compositions overlapping each other along the way.

Choose records that call attention to the distinctive sounds of various instruments. *Tubby the Tuba* and *Peter and the Wolf* do this in story form and have long been favorites. But don't overlook records in your own collection or at the library that feature percussion ensembles, harps, piccolos, or brass. Symphonies that conjure up images of trains and animals, clocks and cowboys, enlarge the child's understanding of music as another form of expression. These are not merely for sitting still and listening to. Sixes and sevens love to dance with, accompany, and even conduct the great music of the world—if it's shared with them on childlike terms.

## Woodworking

Given the proper tools, scrap lumber, and nails, both boys and girls love to make their own toys—boats, planes, dolls' beds, trains and cars. They are ready and eager to work with wood and real tools. Woodworking has a lot of learning built in with the fun. It gives kids concrete experience with relating parts to wholes, seeing spatial relationships, solving problems, dealing with frustration and success, cause and effect, and developing stick-to-it-iveness. Quite apart from the products they create, kids seem to love the rhythm and repetition of sawing and hammering. They need something sturdier than toy tools, but lighter than those found in the family tool chest.

Most mills or lumberyards will give or sell cheaply a supply of scrap lumber. Soft woods of quarter- and half-inch widths are ideal. Craft shops also have inexpensive bags of assorted wheels and ends of turned dowels. Balsa wood and plywood scraps are also useful for the young builder.

A low work table with a vise to hold wood in place is a must for sawing or drilling by hand. Naturally, no power tools will be used for years to come. Fives are ready for a real but lightweight hammer and short but real crosscut saw. Sandpaper, nails, glue, and wood soft enough to saw are basic materials for getting started. As with all new materials, kids need time to experiment with how things work. But a demonstration of how to use the tools correctly should precede the child's independent use of any new tool. It may even take more than one demonstration, so hang in there and be patient. By six, your child will welcome the addition of a hand plane, pliers, screwdriver, screws, rasp, file, hand drill, and coping saw. Essentially, these are all the tools needed for the next few years.

As they go beyond the experimental phase of exploring tools and wood, young builders like to make simple birdhouses, boats, airplanes, and dolls' furniture. They may also enjoy sharing Harvey Weiss's book *Hammer and Saw*, an introduction to woodworking with simple step-by-step plans for easy (and not-so-easy) projects.

### Parents' Role

Aside from assisting in gathering materials, you'll want to be sure that your child understands how to use and store the tools safely. He or she may also need help in planning the stages of a project. Encourage your child to sketch out the plans.

Building a toy wagon (or doll's bed) requires some measuring and forethought, so that the sides of the wagon are approximately the same. Of course, kids of this age are impatient with painstaking details. So projects that take too long are apt to be abandoned. But somewhere between doing things "any old way" and making them perfect is a meeting ground for getting results that satisfy. Parents should always remember that these activities are closer to play than to mastering the craft of fine carpentry. Building with wood is yet another way of building the child's sense of competence as a doer.

Parents can help build that sense by discussing the order of doing things. These are very real problem-solving tasks that are built into the fun of working with wood.

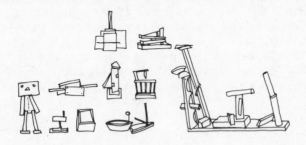

## Art Experiences

By six or seven, children may begin to paint people working or playing together. Swimmers, runners, climbers, jumpers—

their active play life is reflected in their symbolic drawings and paintings.

Unlike the preschooler who names what he's made accidentally, your child is now more likely to name what he is going to make before he begins. If he's had experience with art materials, he will know just what colors, textures, or tools he wants to start with. This doesn't mean that things won't change as he begins to work, but he has more of a plan in mind. His work may be representational or pure design.

> Amy started painting a tree with apples dangling on every branch. It was a lovely composition. Then, when I looked again, the apples and branches had disappeared under a mass of muddy green paint. Of course, she was right, a tree with apples has leaves . . . but it was a shame.
>
> —Mother of a six-year-old

Often, the unfinished work looks more like a finished product than the final outcome. But the process of painting or constructing or modeling has a logic if we tune into what's happening. The story inside the painting has more significance to the child than the final product.

At the upper range of this age group, children often become somewhat critical of their own efforts. Their expectations often fall short of their ability to command the brush. Often, drawing with pencil gives them the controlled line they seek. As always, their ability to draw realistically outstrips their ease with brush. Yet crayon and pencil drawings are more tiring to small hands. So children should be encouraged to use a variety of sweeping, fluid materials for their pictures. This may be a good time to introduce oil pastels which spread with greater ease and can be blended with interesting effects. Markers of various thicknesses and colors continue to offer colorful alternatives to crayons and pencil drawings.

Often, children of this age ask, "How can I make a plane?" or a dog. Or they say, "It doesn't look real." Rather than drawing a picture for the child, talk about the objects and actions he's longing to represent. Help the child describe the form, texture, colors involved. Instead of saying, "Why not paint an elephant?" you might say, "Paint the time we went to the circus and saw the elephant." This gives the child an action image linked to personal experience. Often this is enough to fire the child up and help him bring things into focus. Children of this age are not usually concerned with realistic perspective. Indeed, they are apt to draw the front and side and top of a house, as if one could see all of it at once. Emotional importance rather than reality dictates the size of things and people. Interest in perspective and horizon line generally comes later and should not be rushed.

At five, children become much abler at mixing colors and caring for their materials. They will welcome a variety of paper, in different shapes and colors, from time to time. Tempera paint (see chapter 5, pages 105–107) is still preferable because of its bright and full-bodied color.

At five and six, kids like to paint about their friends, pets, family, and things they like to do. You can help your child think about these things in terms of the color choices or materials he will use. Your comments can help the child extend his painting by commenting on what you see. "Is the car on a road?" or "I see you painted a house. Let's see, it has a door and a chimney, two windows . . ." Your comments are not judgmental, but help the child look at the relationship of parts to the whole in making symbols.

## Collage

Children continue to use a variety of textured materials to make collages that may be pure design or representational. Sometimes the child who is not satisfied with his drawing ability finds greater satisfaction in combining materials in more free-flowing designs. If fabric is used, be sure the scissors are sharp enough to cut with ease. Here are some suggestions for materials to save for a collage-supply box:

- fabric of various textures (velvet, corduroy, burlap, satin)

- paper (patterned, metallic, transparent, corrugated)

- yarn of various thicknesses

- cotton balls, feathers, seeds, grass, weeds, wood shavings, sand, leaves, egg cartons, buttons, toothpicks, wallpaper samples.

For backgrounds, a box top or firm piece of cardboard is fine. White liquid glue can be applied with fingers or brush.

## Constructions

Many of the materials used for collage will also be useful for making constructions called stabiles that stand in one place or mobiles that dangle in the air and move. However, materials for constructions present a new set of problems to be solved (see page 109). Not only must the child decide what looks good, there are real structural considerations of how to hold things together and in balance. A mixture of flexible and rigid materials will be needed:

| | | |
|---|---|---|
| paper tubes | sticks | wire |
| paper cups | staples | foil |
| paper clips | string | corks |
| plastic or Styrofoam scraps | tongue depressors | bolts |

Children may need help in setting up their hanging base for mobile constructions. There's really no way to do this without hanging a line of yarn or wire to work on. A coat hanger that's freely suspended makes a good base . . . or a string with paper clips and string and wire attached.

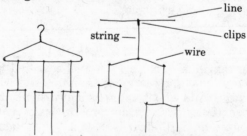

## Clay and Plasticine

Plasticine which does not harden takes on new interest as a prop in dramatic play. Children now have the dexterity to create miniature foods and accessories for their mini-

world constructions with bright
pieces of plasticine.

Working with real clay, children
are fascinated with making objects—animals, bowls, monsters,
cups, plates, and other specific
things. They may be interested in
adding textures to their clay with
toothpicks, combs, and shells. To
keep clay from drying out, children
will need to learn to cover work-in-
progress with a damp cloth or plastic
wrap.

Children will welcome some simple instruction on how to pull or
pinch the shapes they are trying to
form from the ball of formless clay.
Adding on legs or arms or heads, the
child needs to learn how to poke a
hole or trench and then join the
pieces of clay together by wetting
and smoothing the two pieces into
one. Simply sticking one piece to another will end in disaster once the
pieces dry. So take a little time to
demonstrate.

### Printmaking

If your child has not yet tried his hand at printmaking, go
back to chapter 5, page 107, for ways to start. Printmaking is
such a wonderful art form for making special occasion cards
and gift wraps with little expense or mess.

Sixes and sevens will enjoy making prints with styrofoam
meat trays from the grocery store. Simply cut off the curved
edge and you have a drawing surface. Using a sharp pencil, the
child presses a design or picture into the styrofoam. Using
printing ink or thick tempura, the surface of the tray is covered
with color. Then a sheet of blank paper is placed over the inked
surface and *voilà!* You have a print. Your child may enjoy
washing away the paint and printing the same picture in other
colors.

Unlike linoleum printing which requires sharp tools, this is a printing process young children can do safely with great satisfaction.

Children of this age are also fascinated with print rubbings they can make by placing paper over various textured materials and rubbing the paper with crayon or pencil. Coins, fabrics, leaves, feathers, and shapes all appear magically as the printmaker discovers pleasing ways to produce rubbings.

## Weaving

This is the time for a variety of weaving experiences. Spool and yarn looms and loop looms are widely available in toy stores. Don't overlook the possibilities of weaving with paper. Try this simple method:

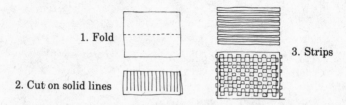

1. Fold

3. Strips

2. Cut on solid lines

Fold and cut paper as indicated. Use another sheet of paper cut in strips to weave—over, under, over, under. These can be made into placemats for parties or handsome wall hangings to be framed.

Or string a tree branch with grass and yarn to make a loom . . . then weave found objects from the field (leaves, weeds, bark, dry pods, feathers, reeds) into the loom and hang in a breezy place.

All of these art experiences are part of a continuing process in giving children opportunities to experiment with materials and to make personal and meaningful symbols. Although your child may have art classes in school, having art supplies at home gives him opportunities to explore materials in greater depth and at his own pace. Some schools offer only rare experiences with paint and clay and rely heavily on drawing. In part, this is a matter of time limitations and available space for setting up materials for twenty-five to thirty children. Sometimes it is a matter of philosophy, and art classes are essentially craft-making sessions with everyone making a copy of what the teacher presents. Such exercises may teach something about following directions, but they are limited in any other real sense. If your child is in such a program, it is all the more urgent that you supply him with space, material, and opportunities to create his own works at home.

## Summing Up

During these early school years children are finding new friends, learning new skills, and shaping new images of themselves. Your once-wary kindergartener grows more world-wise—at least in terms of those journeys out and back into the bigger world of school.

Playing alone or with others, children continue to stretch their physical, intellectual, and emotional growth. They want the facts about where babies come from and how to balance a bike, but still cling to the magic of the tooth fairy and Santa. While you were once the center of the universe, your child's universe is now expanding to include others. Although they still want and need your praise and support, children now long for acceptance outside the family. It is in the classroom and schoolyard, the playground and the backyard, that they stretch and measure themselves. As preschoolers, their self-images were reflections of your view of them. Now they see themselves as they think their agemates see them. They long to see themselves as able doers and welcome players among their peers. It is in play that they practice what they are learning about—the important things and people in their world. So play remains central to understanding. Play is not separate from work; it is still the way children come to understand themselves and others.

=== **Chapter 7** ================

# Middle Years—Eight to Eleven

### You Wanna Be in Our Club?

| | |
|---|---|
| Kelly: | I was the one with the idea of a club. |
| Caroline: | Let her be the president. |
| Jessica: | That's no fair; let Maureen be president. |
| Caroline: | Maureen can be next time. |
| Jessica: | I'm quitting. We'll make our own club and no one will bother us. |
| Kelly: | You're not the boss. |
| Caroline: | I'll tell the rules. |
| Kelly: | I'm not following. |
| Caroline: | If I'm the leader, you could be president. |
| Jessica: | What am I? Just a kid? |
| Kelly: | Hold it, I got a rule. You all got to promise not to fight in this club. |
| Jessica: | No way . . . |

—Three eight-year-olds

Of course Jessica is right. There's "no way" to avoid fights in the typical fly-by-night clubs that kids form at this age. While preschoolers played games of pretend and tried on roles of power, the clubhouse is only part pretend. It parallels the real developmental struggle that is central to the middle years child. What kids want most at this age is to be an accepted member of the group.

Unlike adults clubs that have a real purpose in serving the community, basically these little clubs serve the common need kids have to belong. They are instant groups that band together—not just as mutual admiration societies, but also as mutual exclusion societies.

Debbie's friends formed a club. There were four girls.
Then Debbie's friend Stacy wanted to join but the others refused. Not only was Stacy not welcome, Debbie
had to say she didn't like Stacy. Well, Debbie refused.
She wouldn't do that. I was really pleased. Debbie used
to be chubby and she knows what it's like to be left out.
—Mother of a ten-year-old

Debbie's story is typical of the struggle kids have within the
many groups they encounter. It is a sign of real growth that
Debbie begins to see a situation from her friend Stacy's point of
view. Her sense of justice outweighs her desire to belong—at
least to that group, at that time. So, in a variety of play situations children stretch and test their values and those of their
peers.

Inevitably, these little clubs fall apart almost as quickly as
they are formed. What everyone wants is to be president, to
make the rules, and to accept or reject others. With their secret
handshakes, passwords, and complex codes of rules, they
create a small world where they are in charge. It is a real
contrast from the everyday world where teachers and parents
make the rules. In a way, these clubs express the child's real-
life needs to become a member of his age group and establish
some independence.

### More Talk than Action

Compared with their younger brothers and sisters, eights
and up spend a good deal of their time talking about playing.
Agreeing and disagreeing, making and changing rules, picking leaders, choosing teams, arguing and settling things—
often they spend more of their playtime in talk rather than in
action.

Talk is the way they establish themselves, test their power

to persuade, lead, negotiate, and get along. Not only do they talk together, they whisper. Life is full of secrets, signs that

say "Private! Keep Out!" and vows to "cross your heart and hope to die."

## New Self-Image in the Making

This new desire for privacy and greater independence from adults is another significant step forward in development. During these middle years, your child is forming a new self-image. While your preschooler's feelings about himself were a reflection of your image of him, the middle years child shapes his new self-image from the way he thinks his agemates see him. Although your child still values your approval, there is a real shift at this age to needing approval and acceptance by his peers.

On the playground and in the clubhouse, the middle years child measures himself and others. Playing with and against each other, they test themselves as runners, skaters, builders, swimmers, riders, skiers, and jumpers. In their day-to-day play life, they discover what they're good at and not so good at, what they enjoy and what they dislike, who they can lead and who will follow.

While much of their play is independent of adults, parents

# jordan marsh NEW ENGLAND

**A Unit of Allied Stores**

| EMP. NO. | STORE TERM. | TRANS. NO. | TRANS. TYPE |
|----------|-------------|------------|-------------|
| 238816 | 07155 | 44920 | MC/V |

ACCOUNT NO.
4128699123548

| DESCRIPTION DEPT./CLASS/STOCK | QTY TAX | AMOUNT |
|---|---|---|
| WOMENS DRESSES | | |
| 1370-510 257/4936 | 1N | 59.99 |
| 1 | DIS10N | 6.00- |
| 3300 | | |
| MC/V | | 53.99 |

11/16/88  15:21

NAME

STREET

CITY, STATE, ZIP

IDENTIFICATION

**CUSTOMER'S SIGNATURE**

X

may be assigned

S40N 4/87

# Thank You!

We appreciate the opportunity of serving you, and trust this transaction has been completed to your satisfaction.

May we serve you again soon?

## jordan marsh

| | |
|---|---|
| (1) BOSTON | (15) SOMMERVILLE |
| (2) FRAMINGHAM | (16) NEWINGTON, N.H. |
| (4) PEABODY | (17) HANOVER |
| (5) BEDFORD, N.H. | (18) WATERFORD, CT. |
| (6) BRAINTREE | (19) ALBANY, N.Y. |
| (7) BURLINGTON | (20) NASHUA, N.H. |
| (8) SO. PORTLAND, ME. | (21) TRUMBULL, CT. |
| (9) WARWICK, R.I. | (22) DANBURY, CT. |
| (10) WORCESTER | (23) DERBY, CT. |
| (11) LOWELL | (24) SOUTHBURY, CT. |
| (12) METHUEN | (25) YORKTOWN, N.Y. |
| (13) BROCKTON | (26) BRIDGEPORT, CT. |
| (14) HYANNIS | (27) POUGHKEEPSIE, N.Y. |

can give support to the child's development in a number of significant ways.

## Open-Door Policy

> They've got friends over all the time. I don't mind. I'd rather have them here. I know where they are and what they're doing.
> —Mother of nine- and eleven-year-olds

> He's never alone anymore. I feel like a full-time den mother. I've got the whole neighborhood coming in and out for drinks, the bathroom, the telephone, the time, and, whenever possible, for lunch.
> —Mother of a nine-year-old

Recognizing how important friends are at this age, parents can do a lot by keeping an open-door policy on visitors. It may mean a little more noise, scuffed floors, and extras for dinner or snacks—but the benefits outweigh the bother. Without intruding, parents can support kids' play by providing space and back-up skills for ambitious projects.

> When we were ten, I remember a big show we had in Kay's backyard. Kay had a real playhouse with furniture, windows, a door, and a porch. We managed to organize every kid in a two-block area and put on a show—dancers, singers, magic tricks, and acrobats. I'm not sure if we charged admission, but it was a big-time production.
> —Sixteen-year-old

Thinking back on that show, you'll note that there are no grownups in the picture. But it's unlikely that such an event could have happened without parental approval and support. In the city or suburbs, kids still need adults who are willing to drive them to the skating rink, act as advisor, audience, and aide.

## Distorted Images

Life on the playground, in the classroom, and even on the schoolbus can be pretty bumpy at times. When Stacy is closed out of the club, or Jeff doesn't make the team, the hurt is real. Kids of this age can be very hard on themselves and others. Often their perceptions are not quite on target and they get distorted images of themselves. "I'm no good at swimming. . . ." "Nobody ever picks me for the team. . . ." "The teacher likes her best."

Talking things over with an adult helps kids to clarify what's going wrong. Parents can help kids find ways to handle the ups and downs of group life. What kids need are parents who are willing to listen and take their seemingly small problems seriously. Along with a sympathetic ear, they need optimistic attitudes about themselves and the future. Often, kids at this age have impossible expectations of themselves. They honestly do want to be instantly best in everything. Parents can do a great deal to help kids balance their expectations with reality. Instead of trying to be great in everything, parents can help kids focus on improving one or two skills at a time. In the backyard, a parent must be part-time coach and full-time fan. Helping the child see small gains from his efforts encourages more effort.

Jan was terrified of water. She was always afraid of getting her face wet. In three lessons, the coach had her putting her head under. "But I don't want to go in the deep water," she said. "Who's telling you to?" the coach asked. "Last week you wouldn't get your face wet." "Yeah, well, that's easy." Jan laughed. "So is swimming in deep water—but not today," the coach agreed.

—Father of a nine-year-old

Jan's coach understood the importance of doing things one step at a time. Jan was already worried about the next step instead of finding satisfaction in her real achievement.

### Other Adults

Although kids at this age are eager for greater independence, they recognize and admire the skills caring adults can offer. During these middle years, learning how to ski, skate, play tennis or other sports becomes more urgent if that's what the peer group is doing. Kids don't have to be champs, but they do need to know how to hold their own. Occasionally, an older child or capable agemate can play the role of coach. However, big brothers can be hard to take.

> If Kenny doesn't do well, he doesn't want to play. He really won't play with someone who is much better . . . a kid, that is, like his older brother. If his father goes out and plays catch, that's okay. But not a kid who plays better.
>
> —Mother of a nine-year-old

Sometimes, a tactful parent can offer the time and patience needed. But some kids feel more comfortable about learning skills from adults other than their parents. Clubs, camp, or after-school coaching can provide opportunities for your child to learn new skills. Such learning situations are less charged with the emotional strain of living up to real or imagined parental expectations. Whoever the coach is, the key issues remain—teaching competence without tearing down confidence.

## Joining Up as Dues-Paying Members

With their great desire to belong, middle years kids quite naturally gravitate to ready-made clubs such as Scouts or 4-H or other formal youth groups. Joining up, taking oaths, secret handshakes, wearing uniforms, earning badges—all this gives kids a sense of belonging. Of course, adults play an important part in leading these ready-made groups.

Fortunately, membership is such groups is usually based on age, neighborhood, and common interests. With an adult to smooth out the bumps and structure the meetings, such organizations give kids a framework for working and playing together. Their uniforms, pledges, and songs unite them as a team. Their individual and cooperative efforts earn them rewards and recognition. Often, some project involves them in an effort for the community in which they live—thus broadening their outlook and involvement. Collecting and repairing toys for the children's hospital, visiting and entertaining the elderly, collecting paper for recycling—all these activities help kids develop a sense of social responsibility through action. Best of all, formal clubs offer kids a way of belonging without the total responsibility for keeping things going.

## Taking Lessons—Are You Practicing or Playing?

Dance classes and gymnastics are another kind of instant way into a group situation. Middle years kids are ready now for some of the discipline and direction the teacher provides. While few are destined to become prima ballerinas or Olympic champs, all children can benefit from the physical and intellectual demands put on muscle and mind. Such first-hand experiences enlarge children's esthetic and athletic view of themselves.

Every music student must, at one time or another, have heard the question . . . are you practicing or playing? The answer, of course, is both . . . or at least it ought to be. At this stage of the game, learning to play an instrument demands skill and persistence. Yet at the early end of this age group, lessons tend to be more a matter of exploration than dedication. If the love of music (as opposed to performing) is to flower, parents may need to accept some playing along with the practicing and much more experimenting than expertise. As in all things, there are some rare children who exhibit both exceptional talent and intense interest. Such children may benefit from opportunities to study with master teachers in the late middle years. If, however, like most parents you have no child prodigy on your hands, music studies should be a blend of both playing skillfully and playing for pleasure. Indeed, one of the great lessons kids learn is how practice builds skill and skill builds pleasure—but this discovery takes time and patient instruction. Care needs to be given in selecting a teacher who can keep alive the joy of music which attracts children to lessons in the first place. Treated with care, that joy can enhance not only the child player, but the adult music lover as well.

Unfortunately, many of these benefits are lost when too much emphasis is placed on recital performances and competition for medals. When trophies become the dominant objective, kids who would benefit most from participating are the ones who bow out. Too often, adults are the ones who set kids up in competitive performance situations (see page 208). Dance classes that spend eight months of a ten-month class preparing for a recital are out of step with kids' needs. Recitals and meets are just part of the bigger picture. What kids need at this age is the opportunity to explore their talents without losing their joy in themselves and others.

## Dabbling in the Arts

Somewhere between dedication and bowing out, there are kids who tend to dabble in the arts—changing from piano to flute and back to piano again. Others simply start and stop then beg to start again. Though parents may despair at their dabblers' short-lived enthusiasms, these are the years for tasting and testing a variety of possibilities.

Exploring the arts opens the door to new ways of communicating ideas and feelings in nonverbal ways. Finding a place for that kind of ventilation can be personally satisfying for the child and a resource for the adult-to-be. Museums, concert halls and theaters are not filled by artists and performers alone. Chances are that every audience has its share of former and lifelong dabblers.

### Ventures

Ventures in the arts offer a legitimate way for kids to expand both their own individual talents and to begin to appreciate others' more fully developed talents. Well-chosen visits to the ballet, opera, theater, symphony, art galleries, and museums add new dimensions to weekends and the child's developing esthetic sense. With any luck, these early flirtations with the arts may grow into long-term love affairs that will enrich their lives.

## Teams

Playing on teams, like forming clubs, is a principal way that middle years kids join the group. While the chief purpose of a club is to belong, teams are formed to play against other teams. So it is on the teams that kids get their first experiences in formal competition. The team acts, in a positive sense, as a cushion for these early encounters with winning and losing.

Kids of this age do not generally compete in individual sports—one against the other. Although there are more and less skilled players on a team and skill is valued, it is the whole team that wins or loses, rather than the individual.

Although young players prefer games without complex rules, their sandlot baseball, kickball, and football teams do have a framework of order and agreed-upon rules. "Cheaters" or "sore losers" are dealt with by the team, so playing fair (and, sometimes, not so fair) is part of the built-in learning. Individuals may have status within the group—as a pitcher or a kicker—but a game requires teamwork and cooperation from all the teammates.

### Becoming a Skilled Player

Of course, playing on the team is not without its ups and downs. In contrast to the carefree running, jumping, and climbing young kids enjoy, the eight-and-up crowd begins to take its sports seriously. Games have rules. There's a right way and a wrong way to hold a bat, swing a racket, pitch a ball. There's a real shift right now to measure up as a skilled player.

> Sandy really practices hard. She works at things—like her skiing or gymnastics or whatever she's learning.

The better she gets the better she begins to feel about herself. There are older kids she admires and she realizes that to be like them she has to work at doing well and she's willing to stick to it.

—Mother of a ten-year-old

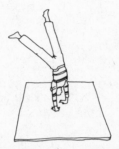

Some kids are less willing to try or less able to succeed than Sandy. Some shy away from active group sports, preferring not to play if they don't play well. Their expectations of themselves may be unrealistically high. Kids at this age can be extremely tough on each other and themselves. This is where parents play a vital role in helping them build skills as well as good feelings about themselves. Your time and attention are the patient gifts of parenting that build stronger bonds than the purchase of expensive equipment. Sure, kids need a mitt, but they also need a helping hand that can pitch a ball *and* pat them on the back.

### Parents' Role

Suggestions for coaching (chapter 6, pages 153–54) may help both skill and confidence. Parents really need to wear several hats—acting as coach, player, fan, and philosopher. As coach, you will no doubt have some helpful pointers on how to swing, bunt, and pitch. But, mixed with that advice, don't forget your job as part-time fan. Praising your child's small gains helps reward big efforts and strengthens the desire to keep trying.

As philosopher you may need to recycle those golden oldies: "If at first you don't succeed, try, try again," or "Rome was not built in a day." Some old sayings are worth passing along. Often kids of this age have heard a lot about your successes. Try sharing some stories of your athletic defeats as well. It's really quite a burden when kids have to live up to a legend, real or imagined. Perhaps the hardest task of all is helping kids accept their own strengths and weaknesses. Learning that "no one is great at everything" is part of the process of discovering what time and experience teach. Giving kids a hand with these lessons lasts longer than the best mitt in the sports shop.

## Competing

> My kid is really good. He practiced and practiced and he made the majors . . . he's the youngest kid on the team. Of course, he hasn't played in one game . . . I guess he'll sit on the bench all summer, but he's on the best team.
>
> —Father of a nine-year-old

Poor kid. He's really in a no-win situation. Too often, kids compete to get on the top teams and then spend the season on the bench. The status of making the better team seems to be more important than getting to play. Somewhere along the line, we make winners into losers by valuing the competition more than the game.

> Kenny's in the Little League and he really enjoys it. It brings the kids close together. They just get out there and try. Kenny didn't get one hit. But that seemed to be all right with the kids . . . though not with the coach. He wanted a winning team, I guess. But the kids stick together. They encourage each other.
>
> —Mother of a nine-year-old

### Developing Attitudes—For Better or Worse

Both coaches and overeager parents often bring their own competitive yearnings to the ballpark and lay them on kids. These adults are actually denying the kids opportunities for learning and enjoyment. Heavy emphasis on learning to play "like a pro" leaves no room for just playing ball. In fact, it can lead to feelings of anxiety and, in some cases, encourages cheating.

Most parents have very strong feelings about the value of competition. Some see it as instructive, others feel it is destructive. Essentially, competition has the potential for being both. Rather than labeling competition as all good or all bad, let's say it's inevitable. Whether we like it or not, kids are highly competitive at this age. For better or worse, it is during the middle years that they develop attitudes as well as skills. These attitudes are no less important than their batting skills. Indeed, their attitudes are carried off the playing field and into life. Adults who are too short-sighted to see the bigger picture ought to be benched, or find their satisfaction elsewhere.

Anyone who coaches youngsters in sports knows only too well that everyone wants to win. The real trick is in helping kids learn how to compete rather than how to win. We can't say, "Be a good sport," and in the next breath holler, "How could you miss that shot? Are you blind?" Despite their frequent bravado, school-age kids feel less than secure about how they're doing. Too much harsh criticism and feelings of shame and guilt can have long-lasting effects. Their internal scorecard will last a lot longer than the score of today's game.

Coaching kids to compete requires thoughtful words and positive action to build both competence and confidence. When kids feel good about themselves and their efforts, they are free to win or lose, without losing their self-esteem. No one wants to lose, but everyone needs to learn that "you can't win them all."

## Competing with Oneself

> According to the brochure, the camp we chose offered "noncompetitive sports." So on parents' weekend, we were dismayed to find our nine-year-old son in tears after failing to swim the lake. Sure, there was no race against others, just the width of the lake, a counselor in a rowboat, and a fear of deep water. Swimming the lake meant he'd win a red feather at the big campfire ceremonies the next night. It's become family legend that his swim the next day set a record for the slowest swim ever, but swim he did. I still have mixed feelings about that red feather.
>
> —Mother of a nine-year-old

Mixed feelings or not, children compete against themselves as well as others. We all do. Taking a jog alone along a country road, one competes against yesterday's time or distance. Such competition can have positive value in spurring us on to test and stretch our abilities. It can be a healthful release of energy and enhance feelings of success.

Even in noncompetitive settings there are goals to strive for. The key is finding satisfaction in reaching for realistic and personal goals. It is in such reaching that kids find out what they're "good at" or "rotten in." Such discoveries need not be permanently defeating or devastating. They are part of the healthy business of discovery. In learning to know themselves, children grow better able to pick and choose where and when they'll compete. Without such understanding, they can get caught in the trap of trying for feathers they don't even want.

## Individual Sports

While team sports offer kids an outlet for using up their high energy, don't overlook the value of individual sports. Kids who don't make or join the team, most especially, need alternative ways to develop skills and spend that energy. Skating, tennis, hiking, biking, swimming, or other individual pursuits should be encouraged. Sometimes gaining competence in one sport builds up enough confidence to carry kids into other physical challenges. In any case, the child who develops ability in individual sports may be better prepared for long-term activity than the kid who only plays on teams. After all, how many people at thirty-five (or even twenty-five) still play on baseball teams? Recognizing the lifelong need we have for physical pursuits, even team members would do well to develop some individual sporting skills that can still be enjoyed when the gang's not there.

## "All in Together, Girls," or "Girls? Yuk!"

Growing up male or female today is quite different than it was twenty or thirty years ago. Just as adult roles and opportunities have been changing, so too has the nature of children's play. Traditional all-boy sports are now open to both girls and boys. Space stations come equipped with toy people of both genders. Unisex sneakers, jeans, and sweatsuits are the uniform of the day.

Yet, in forming friendships and groups, middle years kids tend to separate into girls' groups and boys' groups. Although brothers and sisters may play with each other at home, the school-age child generally chooses friends of the same sex. It is almost as if by clinging together they strengthen their own identity and sense of belonging. The age-old debates over who's smarter, stronger, or better are still continued. But today there are new role models emerging as men and women break out of the old stereotypes society has cast them in for generations.

Parents can actively call attention to the women and men in the news—from the front page to the sports page. Around the house, parent/child cooperative ventures need not remain sexist. Kitchen and workshop offer opportunities for both daughters and sons. Chemistry sets and erector sets are now packaged with girls and boys on the label, for good reason. By offering all children opportunities to explore their talents, we can challenge both boys and girls to fulfill their human potential.

## Change of Pace

In contrast to their physical play, kids need activities that offer a change of pace . . . active doing for the fine muscles rather than big action. These activities can engage them in the company of others or develop into hobbies to pursue on their own. Being realists, kids find great satisfaction in making honest-to-goodness, usable things. Candles to light, belts to wear, even toys that can be played with.

## Crafts

With their new and more refined dexterity, kids in the middle years are interested in exploring a variety of crafts. Often, the interest grows out of their studies of the past. Indeed, one way to bring history alive is to put tools into the hands of children so they can experience what it was like to weave cloth, dip candles, or tool leather. Visits to folk art and history museums, or craft fairs may spark interests in projects the family can enjoy together.

While kits are limited and often come predesigned, sometimes they're as good a way as any to explore the tools and techniques involved in a small way.

> I remember a patchwork pillow that became boring, with a capital B, to every member of the family. Thank goodness we didn't start with a quilt!

Remember, interests at this age are often fleeting, and expensive experiments are no better than inexpensive ones.

Naturally, you'll need to be on hand to go over safety rules in using craft equipment and tools. Hot wax, irons, and ovens should not be used without adult supervision. Unless you're a perfectionist, doing crafts together is another great way of connecting with each other.

Among the crafts most favored at this age are:

| | | | |
|---|---|---|---|
| weaving | leather tooling | lanyard | macrame |
| candle making | bead looms | enameling | batiking |
| woodworking | soap and woodcarving | tin work | tie-dying |

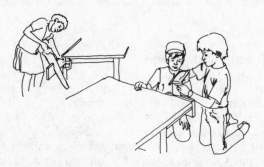

You'll find wonderful books on the craft shelf in the library or bookstore. Two of my favorites are *Making Things,* by Ann Wiseman (Little, Brown) and *Play Book,* by Steven Caney (Workman Publishers).

## Art Experiences

In addition to the art materials suggested earlier (see chapter 6, pages 191–97), kids may now enjoy exploring the feel and look of opaque water-based paints in tins and acrylic or oil paints in tubes. For drawing, they'll like experimenting with pressed charcoal, colored pencils, or pen and ink.

While young school-age children have found ways to depict people, animals, houses, and cars, older children are no longer satisfied with these ways. They yearn for more skill and greater detail. Their attention is more focused on fine details such as clothing, hair styles, facial features, and machines with dials, buttons, and antennae. But their desire to draw the real world runs far ahead of their ability.

As in all skills, the middle years child becomes quite self-conscious and critical. This is the time for several kinds of support:

- Parents can help the child become a close observer by calling attention to how light and distance change the size and color of things we see.

- On trips to museums or sharing reproductions in art books, call attention to the many ways artists picture reality without photographic realism.

- Encourage the child to continue exploring clay and collage, which invite freer expression and inventiveness.

Sometimes we forget that drawing, painting, and modeling with clay continue to be a great joy for kids. In their fact-filled world of numbers and words, art provides a nonverbal form of expression. Through art they can find release from tension as well as another way of dealing with ideas—real or fantastic.

In school they may have art classes once a week or less. There the teacher is structuring the lesson, directing their attention to specific skills and techniques. Unfortunately, schools facing budget cuts tend to cut art classes out entirely. Kids who are caught in such systems most especially need opportunities at home to fill the void. At home, there's more time to explore materials in depth, with more individual style, and to carry things further than the allotted forty-minute class in school.

## Construction Toys

In the ready-made department, Erector sets, models, and jigsaw puzzles demand eye, hand, and mind to work in concert. Following directions puts reading skills to work and a finished product is a reward. Constructions are frequently put on display as part of a collection and as proof of successful workmanship.

## Who Took My Scissors?

Since model building and crafts take more than a day, kids need a workspace where younger brothers, pets, and neat mothers do not tread. Desks where homework must be done or the kitchen table are too temporary for any long-term projects. A shelf near a window, or surface in a well-ventilated garage or cellar, or the corner of a room is now a real plus in supporting play and order.

Hooks, pegboards, and shallow containers hung on a wall prevent the "where's my ———?" syndrome and make clean-up quicker.

## Collections—But I Need That!

Ever wonder what happened to those collections of yours? Chances are your comic books, postcards, bottle tops, shells, rocks, and/or baseball cards started piling up when you were in the fourth or fifth grade. For some, the passion for collecting starts earlier and, for many, the collector's bug continues into adulthood. The bottle tops that began as play accessories for the young child may well become the first items in the collections of the avid hobbyists of the middle years.

## How Many Pitchers Have You Got?

Early collections tend to be prized on the basis of sheer quantity. Interest in any particular collection may be rather short-lived. Last month it was baseball pitcher cards, this month it may be stamps, and next month rocks. Collectibles tend to be faddish, dictated by whether they're desirable to others in the group. Swapping marbles or cards is all part of being a member of the group. Although parents may need to veto excessive buying, some participation in the bartering business may be beneficial. Learning how to negotiate, to make decisions, and to live with the consequences may be well worth the low price of some marbles or baseball cards.

While some collections reflect group interests, many collectibles are more personally connected to the child's individual interests. But even these collections may be short-lived, since school-age kids tend to change their enthusiasms frequently. This changeability is not a sign of flightiness, but rather a reflection of their great thirst to know about, experience, and embrace many things in the world.

As they become more experienced, young collectors may become more interested in quality as well as quantity.

> At nine, my daughter began collecting political buttons. By ten, she had narrowed the collection to presidential buttons. Her interest led her to books about buttons, presidents, and, I think, a small but real feeling of holding a piece of history in her hands.
> —Father of a ten-year-old

While some collectibles are rare and costly, many are quite affordable and fun to hunt for in antique stores, rummage sales, and flea markets. They are tangible pieces of the past that can spark an interest in history, politics, and people.

This is the age when the passion for Barbie dolls with all their clothes and accessories reaches its height. It's also the age when miniature cars, trucks, planes, animals, and people are prized in great quantity.

Amy's friend Linda spent the weekend with us. It was a Barbie doll marathon. I really hate it. They want to look like, dress like, and be like Barbie.

—Mother of a ten-year-old

Of course, one of Amy's and Linda's great interests is in becoming grownup, in looking ahead to the next stage. While a few years ago they stomped around in mom's high heels, now they dream their dreams by putting high heels and earrings on Barbie.

While some collectibles are used as accessories to play, others fall more into the hobby category and are purely for looking at. Foreign doll collections, glass bottles and figurines, postcards, and ticket stubs are souvenirs of places and people.

Not all collections need to cost a great deal. Saving stamps from the mail for your child's collection feeds the child's interest in variety and quantity. It's a way of saying "I'm interested in what your interests are and I thought of you when I saw this."

Parents can also help by providing young collectors with orderly places to display or store their collections. Scrapbooks, cigar boxes, or shelves help establish order out of chaos and build pride instead of frustration.

Here are just a few of the treasures kids like to collect:

| | | | |
|---|---|---|---|
| stamps | postcards | caps | bottles |
| coins | stones | shells | trading cards |
| models | books | dolls | comic books |
| banners | posters | placemats | t-shirts |
| programs | postmarks | spoons | menus |
| penpals | miniatures | hats | ticket stubs |

Don't be surprised if your child comes up with some seemingly valueless collections. My husband's passion as a kid was collecting train time schedules—not just for trains he traveled on; any train schedule would do. A trip to Grand Central Station was paradise. In adulthood, he remains a great armchair traveler and a devoted train buff.

## Visiting Collections

Being avid collectors themselves, kids of this age group seem to have a natural affinity for museums. Just as their own collections reflect their expanding interests, museums can enhance and even spark new interests and enthusiasms.

It's one thing to read about and collect miniature dinosaurs and knights—but quite another thing to stand in the presence of giant fossils and gleaming armor.

While most museums are only for looking, let's not underrate the value of seeing real pieces of the past with our own eyes. Getting a sense of the tools, clothing, and artifacts of the past can make history books come alive. Seeing the variety of living plants and creatures that have inhabited the earth puts the natural world in new perspective. Planetariums, historical restorations, natural history museums, costume collections, and fine art museums are treasure houses waiting to be explored.

Although big city museums may be too far away, small local museums, colleges, and libraries often house regional collections well worth a visit. A local train buff, rock hound, or amateur astronomer may be delighted to share his enthusiasm and welcome a visit. Parent organizations in schools can sometimes seek out such adults and encourage them to invite hobbyists/specialists into the classroom. Parent groups may also find museums with collections that travel, or sponsor field trips to nearby cities.

Increasingly, museums today have instituted programs and exhibits that encourage "hands-on" experiences for kids. Some offer art classes, puppetry, bird watching, star gazing, and rock hunting. These are mind-expanding alternatives to Saturday cartoons and the Sunday what-should-we-do blues. Such experiences may stir interests that are meaningful now and in the years to come.

## More Fun in the Kitchen

Both boys and girls of this age group need very little encouragement to get involved with cooking. Although you may view cooking as work, kids tend to see mixing, measuring, stirring, and tasting as play. In many ways, cooking is a lot like game playing. It is a series of critical moves with an unpredictable (and hopefully edible) ending.

Since most kids of this age are apt to get the urge to experiment in the kitchen, this is a good time to establish firm rules about safety. You may not want them to cook alone, but better to teach them how to do things properly than to leave learning to chance.

It was my father-in-law who taught my husband how to cook. He really believed everyone should know how to prepare a simple meal for himself. My husband has taught the same thing to our sons. They really love to cook.

—Mother of a nine- and twelve-year-old

Knowing how to make scrambled eggs or a salad, even a spaghetti dinner, gives kids a sense of being able to care for themselves. It's also a skill that can make them feel like a useful and productive member of the family. Using recipes, kids learn to read, measure, and mix their ingredients in a sequential order. Cooking from mixes or completely from scratch requires following a set of orderly procedures. Measuring and mixing their ingredients, kids discover that numbers and fractions serve a useful purpose in the real world. Not that everything needs to be a serious learning experience. One of the most memorable cooking sessions in our kitchen ended in an inedible glob of terrible taffy that still brings memories of a silly, enjoyable time. While eating is something we all do daily, cooking together takes some of the matter-of-factness out of mealtimes. Unlike playing a board game, cooking together is a cooperative venture with rewards you can eat.

## Games: That's Not in the Rules!

Now games with rules come into full play—not that rules can't be modified, negotiated, or challenged. In fact, learning to play with the rules is a large part of the action. Kids really watch each other and the rules to be sure no one gets away with anything. What with rules being so hard to live with, young players demand that rules must be rigidly adhered to.

As they become more experienced, making up new rules may

be as much fun as playing. Unlike young kids who believe that rules have a life of their own and can never be changed, parents can help kids understand that people make rules. Naturally, rules can't be changed in midstream—unless everyone agrees—but they can be negotiated for future games. My husband's grandfather used to play a card game called 501. Everyone started with 501 points and the object was to subtract points and end up with none. But if a grandchild was playing and his score was going up instead of down, Grandpa would say, "If you get a thousand points you also win." Obviously, Grandpa understood that along with the pleasure of playing, the hope of winning needed to be kept alive. He used the rules to keep both possibilities of playing alive.

After dinner with the family or after school with friends, middle years kids can settle in with a game that challenges their minds and competitive natures. With experience at the gameboard, they continue to learn: You win some and you lose some. Within limits, they begin to expand their skills in planning ahead, using strategy to block moves and capture pieces in checkers, chess, and battleship.

Monopoly and other board games with multiple pieces of equipment and built-in rules are a test of skill, taking chances, making deals, and, often, endurance.

Games of Scrabble, Spill and Spell, and Anagrams can support spelling skills, just as Dominoes, Triominoes, and Parcheesi support math skills. Or, forget the gameboards and try some of these:

### Twenty Questions

- Leader thinks of name of famous person, but doesn't tell.

- Members of group take turns asking questions that can only be answered with "yes" or "no." All together, the group may ask twenty questions.

- The person who guesses becomes the new leader.

- Here are some leading questions:
    1) Is the person living?
    2) Is this person a woman?
    3) Is she an athlete? In government? A performer?
    4) Does her last name begin from A–G?

### Coffeepot

This is good for a party or a rainy day.

- *It* goes out of the room while group decides on an action word which *It* will have to guess. E.g., the group chooses "swim."

- Now *It* comes back and can ask questions: Do I coffeepot? Do animals coffeepot? Do I coffeepot in the house? In school? (You may want to put a time limit or number limit on questions asked.)

- After *It* gets the answer, let *It* choose new person to go out.

### Geography

This old favorite can really make the miles fly by in a car or bus.

- First you have to agree on categories. Using countries, cities, states, *and* bodies of water gives the greatest flexibility. But some like the challenge of using *only* cities, or only states.

- First person says name of place. Second person must name a place that starts with the last letter of first person's place—e.g., Texa*s*—South Dakot*a*—Alabama.

- Variation: Use food names.

### Salt and Pepper

Here's another good one for the car.

- Leader calls out a word that often goes with another word—e.g., "salt and pepper," "bread and butter."

- First person who gets the match for leader's word becomes new leader and gives new word. (Other examples: "bacon and ———," "bat and ———.")

### Ghost

This is a word-building game, but the object is *not* to be the one who finishes a word of more than three letters. Two to four players is best.

- First player gives any letter.

- Second player adds a letter to first.

- Third player adds another letter, but be careful: It must be part of a possible word or someone can challenge you.

- Fourth player adds another letter, but again, be careful. If the letter you add turns the letters into a word, you're on your way to becoming a G-H-O-S-T!

There are other games you can make up as you go. A friend recently recalled a point game he played on Sunday drives with the family. You got five points for spotting a horse, ten points for a mule, one point for a barn, one point for a bridge or train tracks. But if you passed a cemetery on your side of the road, all your points were wiped out! Today's roadside point sites might have to be updated to include airport or hospital signs, road repair trucks, soft ice cream stands—maybe a billboard for cigarettes could be your wipe-out sight.

## Books—New Pathways for Pretending

As kids shift into the late middle years, they tend to abandon their games of pretend. Now they play at real games that demand real skills. Twenty Questions proves how smart they are. Home runs prove how fast they are. Building a model of a real plane, playing the flute, dancing on point: Their play life is geared to mastering real skills.

Yet as skills become central, kids still need some corners in their lives where imagination can find expression. Sure, they need to learn spelling and grammar, but their old gifts of spinning stories need not be squelched. Knowing the dynamics of flying a kite should not diminish the possibility of casting daydreams aloft. Belonging to groups is great, but enjoying one's own company demands being resourceful. Yes, schedules are important, but so is the ability to use free time. Acquiring facts and skills should not drive out the capacity for imagination.

Kids still need pathways where feelings as well as facts can be expressed and explored, where dreams and fantasies can be played out. Keeping these pathways open strengthens their capacity to be playful with feelings and ideas. It's that creative capacity that artists, scientists, and even statesmen call upon in going beyond the paint, numbers, or facts of a situation. It is the difference between playing music with technique and with expression. Even in everyday life, we see the differences in the ways people approach cooking a meal or solving a problem. Seeing possibilities beyond a recipe or quick answer is the difference between "getting it over and done with" and finding pleasure in the process. These are gifts children have in the early years, but often lose as they tool up with skills. Though spontaneous games of pretend all but vanish, the need to keep imagination and fantasy alive must find new direction.

For many children, books open a pathway into other worlds where they can step into other people's shoes. Realistic fiction about kids who have friends (who are not always friendly), relatives (who are not always perfect), and problems (that are often confusing) offer young readers a peek into the lives of people not unlike themselves. Such books offer another view of how others cope with the familiar ups and downs of friends and family, hopes and fears. But realistic fiction is just one departure point.

Fairy tales and myths take children farther afield into imaginary lands where danger is faced with courage and good triumphs over evil. These are soul-satisfying tales for the middle years child whose daily journeys into the world demand another kind of courage and independence. Unlike their preschool brothers and sisters, the middle years child now has a firm grasp of what's real and make-believe. So the witches' spell and the ugly giant provide the pleasure of a safe scare. Framed in a world of the "once upon a time," the young reader can become, for a time, the cruel giant or the brave hero. He can thrill to the danger and be assured that all will end happily ever after. This offers the middle years child confidence as he takes those big steps toward independence.

For those who prefer their adventure in modern clothes, mysteries and capers are another path to pretend. Many kids start with *Nancy Drew/Tom Swift,* and gobble them down till they've read them all. These books in series serve several functions. For the inexperienced reader, they are reasonably easy to read and follow a comfortable format. Breaking out of picture books into "big" books with chapters marks a new step forward as an independent reader. Seeing the books lined up on the shelf satisfies the collector's bug and represents visible proof of being a real reader.

Unfortunately, some kids never get beyond those first books, although the library and bookstores today have collections of mysteries, animal stories, science fiction, and historical novels that take kids into the past. Adventure lovers will enjoy Bantam's *Choose Your Own Adventure* series in which kids get to choose what happens next in the story from multiple options. They'll also find mystery and entertainment in Knopf's *Caper* Series.

Sometimes, by reading the opening chapter aloud, parents can help launch the reluctant reader on a new path. Time to browse in the bookstore or library can lead to new discoveries. The children's librarian or salesperson in the bookstore can help kids match their interests with books. Perhaps no one can make that match better than parents who have, ideally, been sharing books with their kids for years.

### Information, Please

Naturally, with their interest in facts, middle years kids are ripe for informational books. Young athletes are hungry for books about famous players as well as how to hit, punt, and pass. Budding naturalists need handbooks on bugs, snakes, plants, and animals. Future astronauts want information about stars, planets, galaxies, and black holes.

Encyclopedias, field handbooks, and even record books that match their expanding interests are welcome tools that feed their curiosity. So books and play serve each other in a back and forth way. This is especially true if adults help children find the connections and lead the way. It's not just homework time that produces questions. Day-to-day experiences often stimulate the need to know more. Even if you know the answers, take the opportunity to lead your children to other sources. A captured bug, a strange plant, a story on the news— all can lead to digging in together in the atlas, encyclopedia, or nature handbook.

TV and movies may also act as stimuli to reading. Today's

kids are likely to want a copy of a story they've seen played out on the screen. In a sense, the viewing has showed the story to them and then reading gives them a chance to see a rerun. Don't despair. If a program encourages them to read, chalk up a plus for TV and reading.

### Comic Books

During these years, most kids also go through a craze for comic books that parents find disturbing. Yet comics are part of the group thing—a shared and relatively harmless fascination that tends to wear thin in time. Part of the pleasure of comics is the sheer joy of ownership—the collector's bug again. But comics are also a quick and easy form of entertainment that at least requires more initiative than watching the TV screen. While their literary quality may be limited, they are rarely the only things school-age kids read. So, rather than banishing them (and thereby making them desirable), just try to balance them with a rich supply of tempting alternatives.

## Puppets

Puppet shows for each other and for the family or parties continue to be of interest as a vehicle for dramatic expression and storytelling. The impromptu show of the past may now become a scripted adaptation of a TV show, familiar story, or an original play.

Unlike their improvised puppet shows of the past, some kids now prefer to write out scripted plays with lines that are read by the players. Ambitious productions of this kind may be helped along if adults are willing to type scripts for budding playwrights.

Hand puppets continue to be useful and more elaborate, as does scenery, curtains, lights, and even music. At this stage, your child will enjoy making hand puppets that take a bit longer, but last longer, too. Puppets with papier-mâché heads and fabric bodies take several days to construct. But this may be an interesting, cooperative family project.

You'll need: half a piece of a toilet paper roller, a small balloon, masking tape, shredded newspaper, white liquid paste, paint and markers, scraps of yarn, scissors, fabric scraps, needle, and thread.

## Pattern for a Puppet

Trace a pattern with white chalk on a piece of fabric, folded in half, like the one below. An adult may need to cut the fabric if it's heavyweight.

Folded fabric

Cut pattern on dotted line

With a little help, kids can sew the puppet's body together with relative ease . . . just remind them to leave the neck open! Blunt tapestry needles are easy to thread and save small fingers from being pricked.

Step-by-step construction of puppet head:

1) Blow balloon up to size of a large apple and tie.
2) Tape toilet paper roller and balloon together.
3) Dip shredded pieces of newspaper in white glue and smooth pieces onto balloon . . . continue till balloon and roller are covered . . . allow to dry a day or more.
4) When balloon is dry, paint with one color and add facial features with marker . . . paste on yarn for hair or whiskers.

Now the fabric body of the puppet may be glued to the puppet head and it is ready for action.

If the head-making seems too hard, try a stuffed sock with glued or sewn-on features, or less permanent but quick paper bags with faces painted on.

bag ———

string ———

For odd-shaped creatures try heads made of big matchboxes or small cereal boxes.

## Theater Games

Family or party games need not be limited to board games with rules and tokens.

Next time you're rained in, or the family clan gathers, or the doldrums set in, try a new form of charades that everyone can play.

### That's No Chair, That's a . . .

- Place a chair in the middle of the room.
- One person goes over to the chair and acts out something to convey what the chair now represents and what she's doing. She doesn't tell with words . . . just actions. For example, it might become a space ship, an ironing board, a carriage.
- Others in group must guess what she is doing.
- Variation: When players get skilled, one person starts the action and another person, who recognizes what's going on, goes in and joins the action until the others guess what they are doing.

### Pass It On

- Pretend you have an ice cube, a lit match, a cup of tea, a snowball in your hand.
- Tell what it is and pass it around the circle.

### Once There Was . . .

This is fun to play in the car or on a rainy day.

- One person starts the story with an opening sentence.

- Next person must add another.

- Story keeps going round and round, until someone brings it to a close with his sentence.

- Variation: Build story one word at a time. Each person adds a word until one player stops the game with the word "end."

## What a Surprise!

This is another kind of acting game.

- You can make up a list of presents on cards (or let the players dream them up as they go).

- No talking allowed.

- The actor picks a card. He must pretend to unwrap an imaginary present, and then act out what it is by the way he uses it.

- Other players must guess what the surprise is.

## Fortunately/Unfortunately

This game is based on a funny picture book by Remy Charlip and it makes a wonderful game.

- First person opens story with "Once there was a ——— who wanted to ———. Fortunately, he had a ——— so he started to . . ."

- Now the second person picks up the story by saying, "But, unfortunately, the ——— did not have ———, so he had to . . ."

- Third person comes in with the next "fortunately" event.

## Statue Maker

This game requires handling others delicately and cooperating without talk—good skills and good fun.

- Two people work together; one is the sculptor, the other is clay or marble.

- The sculptor arranges the clay into a statue (no talking).
- Others in the group must guess what the sculptor has done.
- Variation: Exchange roles.

If your family warms to these games, you will enjoy looking at Viola Spolin's book *Improvisation for the Theater*. It's full of theater games grownups and kids can enjoy.

## Writing

Writing and drawing offer other avenues for story-spinning skills which used to find expression in dramatic play. While school may be putting the accent on book reports and grammar, kids of this age are ripe for writing everything from comic strips to diaries to action-packed adventures. These flights of fiction may begin with characters and plots closely related to television or the stories and books they're reading; or they may be thinly disguised reflections of their own struggles. Such stories can serve as a safety valve for ventilating powerful emotions that may otherwise be bottled up.

Diaries and journals give the child a time for reflection and a legitimate place to express not only what's happening, but how it made them feel. Naturally, such writing should be respected as private and personal, and not subject to scrutiny for spelling, grammar, and punctuation. Aside from providing a special notebook or diary and guarantee of privacy, parents can promote expansive journal entries in a number of ways.

In her book *When You're Alone It Makes You Capone,* Myra Livingston Cohen shares a journal idea that goes beyond "Today I had orange juice for breakfast." What she suggests is a two-column story:

*Objective—What I Saw*    *Subjective—How It Made Me Feel*

Under the Objective column, one might describe what one saw, smelled, heard, tasted, or touched. Under the subjective heading, one would describe how it made them feel and what it reminded them of.

Here's another exercise, a family favorite my daughter claims still works in college. Faced with a decision or personal problem, talk can only go so far . . . after a while you start talking in circles. That's usually the time when sorting-out lists can help. Making a *Pro* and *Con* list helps to clarify and weigh one's thoughts about a situation. Writing it down can help kids see that there are things that can't be changed and things that are temporary. When outcomes are in doubt, you can sort out the worst that can happen from the best that can happen. Somehow, putting it all down on paper defuses the emotions that surround some issues and puts them in sharper focus.

While journals, diaries, penpals, and story writing may seem a long way from play, they do in fact retain many of the qualities formerly found in dramatic play—not merely personal expression, but playful modes for problem-solving.

## Summing Up

In sneakers and toeshoes, on skis and skates, swinging bats and strumming strings, joining teams and forming clubs— middle years kids play at complex games that test and stretch their growing skills. Socially, intellectually, and physically, the school-age child is hungry for greater independence and new challenges. Now, perhaps more than ever, work and play complement each other in a back and forth way. Even fun has a serious side, with rules to be followed and points to be scored.

As kids measure themselves against their peers, adults continue to play a vital role in supporting competence and confidence. With their expanding interests outside the home, parents need to act as soundboard, coach, fan, philosopher, facilitator, friend, and chauffeur. Keeping the door open to both friends and communication, parents can provide leverage as kids shape their attitudes, values, and skills through play.

# Chapter 8

# *Playmates*

You're my friend, right?

—Preschooler

You're not my friend anymore!
So—you're not my friend either!

—Two six-year-olds

You wanna come over and play?

—Eight-year-old

Our team is going to win!

—Eleven-year-old

With each stage of development, we have seen how children's play expands and becomes more complex. Not only does their play change, so does their need for a variety of playmates.

Of course, as a parent, you are the first playmate. But your early role as plaything, playmaker, and playmate shifts gradually from center stage to somewhere in the wings . . . or backstage. Let's look at how the cast of players changes over the years.

## *U R #1*

To begin at the beginning, U R #1, but for a relatively short time. Playing with your infant, you help your child discover the pleasures of playing with objects, with others, and, miracle of miracles, even how to play alone. These are significant discoveries. While the players and playthings may change, these early forms of play are the foundations for future play. Children who have a good relationship with their mothers and fathers have the easiest time forming play relationships with others.

It is in these early years that children learn whether curiosity is rewarded or punished, if independence is supported or thwarted, and if trying is safe or unsafe. With their parents, they soon discover that people are warm or distant, predictable or unpredictable, friendly or unfriendly. These are just some of the pieces that your baby picks up as you play together. Indeed, most psychologists believe that during the first two years in the small circle of family (and significant caretakers), the foundation is laid for the child's future relationship with others.

## Significant Others

### Brothers and Sisters

If there's more than one child in the family, each child has the extra advantage of a built-in playmate. Although parents tend to worry a lot about sibling rivalry, too often we overlook the positive value of sibling relationships.

As senior playmate, the older child gets pleasure and learns from playing the role of teacher, model, and entertainer. Though their judgment may be faulty and your supervision needed, the benefits to both players are real. "Do it this way; watch, I'll show you," the how-to teacher says. In demonstrating, the older child proves his own competence as a doer, building his own sense of accomplishment. At the same time the younger child, with "me too" motivation, is stretching to learn what the other is teaching. Since children quite naturally enjoy repetition, the "big" brother or sister may be a more patient and delightful playmate than a hurried adult. Surprisingly enough, studies show that when children of mixed ages play together, they are less competitive than playmates who are the same age. They are also more inventive in playing with toys than kids who play alone.

But of course that doesn't mean that brothers and sisters are always patient, thoughtful, and kind to each other. Nor does it mean they don't compete and fight with each other. The fact is, however, that some of the turbulence that rumbles out of sibling fights has positive value in learning how to get along with others.

Learning how to share, the demands of give and take, the ability to stand up for one's rights, to respect others' needs for privacy and rights to property, to know how to negotiate, and even how to make up, to fight fair—these are some of the positive social skills brothers and sisters can learn from each other over the long haul.

One of the chief problems that heats up sibling relations and play is the issue of *mine* vs. *yours*. In other words, *things* often set the stage for bitter contests. Preschoolers are especially sensitive to toddlers treading on their turf. Remember, preschoolers still feel that their toys are extensions of themselves. That sense of entitlement is not a sign of selfishness or weakness of character. Expecting older kids to give up or share their things with the younger child— "because you're a big boy"— may lead to more angry feelings than brotherly love.

At any age, it should be possible for siblings to have some space of their own for their possessions. It may be no more than a shelf, a drawer, or a corner of the room, but it should be respected. When we give kids that kind of respect, then we can teach them to give the same kind of respect in return—to our things and to siblings' things.

Naturally, there are some things in a home and yard that are common property. The swing set, the slide, the sandbox— equipment kids must learn to take turns with and share. Learning to negotiate—who goes first and for how long—may cause storms to erupt, but the less you get drawn into it the better.

With very young children, parents can often divert attention with a simple alternative. By stepping in with suggestions you may redirect a situation that is going downhill. The trick here is to anticipate and intervene before things fall apart.

Older siblings can usually settle their arguments without interference—even if it means that the game ends. Of course, if fighting escalates to fists and feet, then parents may need to step in and stop the action—but not the fight. It's absolutely normal and even healthy for sibs to get into heated arguments, but once kids have the power of speech, parents can expect them to use words—not fists.

About the best words to stop the fights are: "I won't let you hurt Saul and I won't let Saul hurt you." By saying this firmly and consistently, you are telling them that you will protect them from others and themselves, that it's all right to be angry and to say so, but that it's not alright to hit anyone.

Some years ago I filed away a legal document concocted by my then-school-age sons. Since their dad is a lawyer, the idea of a contract had elements of dramatic role-playing as well as negotiating. It was, as I recall, one step beyond "no taking it back"—a hedge against "but you traded, fair and square." (James, incidentally, is now a lawyer who can write real contracts.)

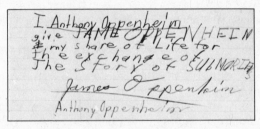

*Life* refers to a game. *Submarine* refers to a book.

By the time kids reach school age, most—given the choice—much prefer to play with children their own age. Some of the skills learned in the circle of the family will help them in their play with others. While siblings may continue to be playmates for life, developmentally we know that children also need to play with others outside the family.

### Not All in the Family

Did you ever notice how animated small children become when they see another child? Just watch two toddlers in strollers as they approach one another. It's as if the sight of another child sets off a spark of recognition; they seem to say, "Ah-ha, there's someone like me." At the park, toddlers may spend more time watching than actually playing with other children. Yet such watching has value—a kind of sneak preview that helps them figure out the rules of the social game.

### More than Side by Side

Historically, American children had little continuous contact with playmates outside their extended family until they entered school at five or six. Today, increasing numbers of infants and toddlers leave home with their working parents every morning. They spend much of their waking day in the company of other children. For years, developmentalists thought that very young children were not capable of interacting with each other. Yet recent studies show that toddlers who are together on a consistent basis do more than simply play side by side. Indeed, children who spend their days together appear to learn social skills of interaction earlier.

Whether your child goes to a day-care center or goes visiting with you, the opportunity for early socialization can be rewarding and pleasurable.

Of course, an inexperienced toddler is likely to poke, jab, and explore another toddler as he would a stuffed doll. Or two toddlers may play next to each other with little or no contact. Toddlers have to go through the process of learning how to get a response from another child. They may do this with sounds, actions, or objects.

Few twos are ready for extensive lessons in sharing. Better to have an adequate supply of duplicates to distract them with than to make a big issue over taking turns. The objective here is to make being with others pleasurable. While twos may give up a toy without much protest, by two-and-a-half, kids are likely to become both vocal and physical. Few kids of this age can settle their own battles. They really do need the help of an adult who mediates.

Amy wants the carriage Suzy is pushing. "When Suzy is finished you can push it," mother says. Mom is telling Amy that she knows what she wants. "It will be Amy's turn soon." Now mother is telling Suzy what to expect.

Sometimes, if the waiting child is offered a temporary alternative until Suzy is ready, she becomes so busy with the distraction that the original toy is forgotten. Since kids of this age don't generally stick with one thing for long, Amy and Suzy will probably both get their fill of carriage time.

If your child is in a day-care situation, you'll probably become aware of a special friend. Even in small playgroups, children as young as two and three seem to gravitate toward a particular playmate. Often, young children prefer others who are much like themselves. So an active toddler is apt to play most happily with another active tot, while two quiet kids are drawn to each other. Kids also seem to pick up clues from the way their mothers and caretakers interact. Seeing adults enjoying each other's company serves as a positive model for inexperienced players.

In group situations, toddlers advance from side-by-side play to one-to-one play. They're really not ready yet for much group action. It takes time before three, four, and five kids can hold each other's attention and play cooperatively.

### *Being a Guest*

> She's with kids all morning. I just don't see why she needs company every afternoon.
>
> —Mother of a four-year-old

Well, maybe not every afternoon, but attendance at a day-care center and nursery school, or even elementary school doesn't mean that kids don't need other kids after school hours. Actually, opportunities to play with one friend, undistracted by the group action, is much to be desired. Having a guest and being a guest are two very different sides of the coin. Your child needs opportunities to play in both situations.

Playing the role of guest gives kids a chance to step out on their own a bit. Naturally, you'll want to be sure there's a caretaking adult on hand. You'll need to agree on how long the visit should last and where you can be reached—just in case. Shy kids may need their mom or dad to stay for a while until they feel at home.

For kids who are new at playing guest, it's important to be prompt about picking them up on time. Some young children are apprehensive about being left in any new environment, even one they want.

Playing at a friend's house gives kids an inside view of how other people live. They get to play with what the host says they can play with. Away from home, they must make themselves understood. Mom isn't there to guess what they want. At least for a little part of the day, they must know and say what they want.

They may visit homes stricter than their own or others more

relaxed than their own. Both kinds of situations give kids a wider perspective and, eventually, a base for comparing.

### Playing Host

As host, your child must do some of the planning and preparation for guests. With young kids, this should include putting unsharable toys away to avoid fights.

You might do well to set up some activity to warm things up with inexperienced players. Some playdough or potato printing (see pages 74 and 107) might start things rolling.

> After nursery school, Jeannie's mom always let us help in the kitchen. We used to make lace cookies. Then we'd play and later we'd have warm cookies and cold milk. I wish I had the recipe for lace cookies.
> —Six-year-old girl

While baking cookies may be a hassle, doing something together sets the tone for a visit and helps kids get the idea of cooperative action. Nursery-school-age kids are learning this in school as well. Of course, there's no need to hover over them all the time. Kids need time to play independently, but they also need to know there's somebody available to turn to.

## *You Wanna Be My Friend?*

### *How Friendships Develop*

Children as young as three or four may begin to choose a preferred or "best" friend. Yet their definition of "best friend" is quite different from the ten-year-old's. Ask four-year-old Lorrie why Beth is her friend and she'll say, "I like her." An hour later she may tell Beth, "You're not my friend anymore."

Studies show that kids from three to five are like the fickle leprechaun in *Finian's Rainbow* who sang, "When I'm not near the one I love, I love the one I'm near." It's not that kids don't have long-standing relationships with other kids. But they don't see beyond the moment-by-moment aspects of it. In a sense, that's what makes it possible for young children to connect so easily in a park or on a beach.

> On a train between New York and Washington, my five-year-old daughter was immediately attracted to a child a few rows down. For the first few miles, they went through the business of staring at each other—taking stock. Before long, the other youngster came up the aisle with crayons and paper in hand. "Wanna color?" she asked. In moments, the two were launched on a four-hour playathon. In recalling the trip, the "friend" from the train became as important as saying she saw the White House.
>
> —Mother of a five-year-old

This five-year-old's concept of a "friend" sounds a lot more like a playmate than a friend. Mere physical presence is the basic requirement for an early playmate. In fact, according to the dictionary, a playmate is "a companion in play or recreation." This is quite different from the definition of a "friend"— "a person whom one knows, likes, and trusts." Little children make "friends" with a variety of playmates whom they barely know and can hardly trust. Indeed, "You're not my best friend" usually means one is not doing what the other child wants. It's not until they have greater experience and a less self-centered view of the world that kids can conceive of the mutual satisfaction of friendship.

Studies show that most kids don't reach this stage until they are somewhere between the ages of nine and twelve. Their ability to look at things from another's point of view comes about slowly, along with their new intellectual power to think about things they can't see or touch. It is in contact with others, both young and old, that kids come face to face with issues beyond good and bad, right and wrong, fair and unfair. It's at this point that they begin to understand friendship as a two-way thing. It's not really until adolescence that kids see friendships as continuing and intimate relationships in the dictionary sense of "a person whom one knows, likes, and trusts."

During the course of childhood, kids have many playmates—some of whom become friends. Although some lifelong friendships are forged in the early years, most children find and need different kinds of friendships as they grow up.

### You're Not My Friend Anymore!

As children grow older, their view of friendship changes. A best friend is no longer a sometime thing. But friends are supposed to be loyal and true. They're supposed to share your likes and dislikes, your troubles and triumphs, your secrets and dreams. In short, a best friend is supposed to be perfect. Unfortunately, it takes time and some pain to discover that not even the best, best friend can be perfect.

So, in their friendships, kids discover that no one always agrees with them, praises them, goes along with all of their best ideas. Indeed, one of the great discoveries best friends learn from each other is how to make up.

Yet sometimes friendships fall apart and, like Humpty-Dumpty, they can't be put back together again. During the course of childhood, most children go through the crisis of losing a best friend more than once. Such breakups are not usually over an isolated incident, although the final blow may seem to center on a single event.

Most often, the root of a broken friendship lies in the fact that kids' interests and needs change as they grow. Indeed, changing friends may be a healthy sign that your child is developing new interests and/or skills. Your child may be ready for the swimming team, while his pal is hooked on computer games. Your child may see herself as a dedicated dancer in training, while her friend sees herself as dancing with dates.

Physically, emotionally, and intellectually kids don't all mature at the same rate. So it is altogether normal and natural that their close friendships will inevitably change as they develop new interests.

Natural and unavoidable as it may be, the loss of a best

friend is, nevertheless, a painful experience to most kids. Few close friendships break by mutual consent. The child who wants out may feel guilty over telling the other one to "get lost." And, on the receiving end, the child who is cut loose may be left with feelings of "nobody likes me."

Although parents cannot shelter their kids from the aches and pains of such events, they can help their child through the rough spots. It's not enough to say, "You'll find another friend." It may be true, but kids need to deal first with their feelings about this particular friend. They may need help in seeing that the reasons behind the breakup have more to do with the way people's needs and interests change rather than in some failing of their own. Parents can give support by listening and talking through the hurt and angry feelings of being rejected and lonely.

Rather than playing up the other child's faults, try to help your child find his own strength and value as a likable person. What parents need to keep alive is the fact that while friendships may have positive and negative points, the value of both is real and worthwhile. By showing the child you understand the immediate pain, you can also lend assurance that as people change and develop, they find others who are changing and looking for new friends, too. It's not that the old friend will be replaced but, in time, people do find other friends.

### But I Don't Want to Move!

Unlike friendships that end because people outgrow each other, many childhood friendships end when families move. While the ache of parting is not tinged with one child rejecting the other, the pain of involuntarily losing a close friend is no less real. Preschoolers and teenagers seem to feel such break-ups most intensely.

For both the child left behind and the child who leaves, there is a void that may be filled with bouts of irritability and depression. Although the child left behind has the benefit of remaining in a familiar environment, parents need to recognize the feelings of loss the child is dealing with. Sometimes, keeping in touch by mail, phone, or occasional visits may ease the empty feelings. However, for some kids the contact is only a sad reminder of what was, but is no more. Kids are generally pretty resilient and bounce back, but they may continue to talk about their old friend. Young kids may even play pretend games, keeping the memory of their lost friend alive.

Rather than pushing the idea of finding a replacement, parents can lend assurance that eventually their child will find other friends to enjoy. To kids, the idea of finding a replacement is a breach of loyalty to the old friend. Better to acknowledge that special person as something valuable. Without rushing the idea, parents can still convey that it's altogether possible to find other rewarding relationships in time.

For the child who moves, the problems are multiple. Not only is there a sense of loss, there is the stress of finding a way into new groups and starting all over again. While young school-age kids may be open and curious about a new child, older kids tend to travel in cliques and closed clubs.

Parents may need to make special efforts in helping their kids weather their displaced-person feelings. Take the time to appraise the new setting. If you've moved from a tie and shirt school to a jeans and t-shirt setting, put the ties away. New kids need all the help they can get to fit in, not stand out.

Don't wait to get everything company-perfect before visitors can come over. Encourage your child to join open-admission groups (such as Scouts, 4-H, dance class, craft clubs) where they may find agemates with common interests. Encourage them to invite new acquaintances for lunch, dinner, or a family outing.

Accept the fact that there will be some looking back and loneliness that comes with giving up old friends. Here's an area where you, too, are having to deal with separation. Let them know you understand how they're feeling.

Unfortunately, some kids who are forced to move repeatedly give up on the business of establishing close friendships. Their repeated experiences with having to separate become so painful that they prefer to avoid the problem by not making friends. Corporate and military families face this problem every few years. These are the kids who may need even more help and support from their families.

In making the transition from one place to another, parents may have to take a bigger role as confidant and friend, lending security and support as their children test the new show in town. Having known the pleasure of friendship, it's altogether likely kids will eventually find new friends to grow with.

## Saving Face and Furniture

In a big old country home, it's a lot easier to set limits on where kids can and can't play. With rooms to chose from and out-of-doors, too, there's less of a problem than in a city apartment. Yet, in either place, the space needs to be defined in positive as well as negative terms.

As a kid, I had a friend whose upholstered chair and quilted bedspread were off-limits. Also forbidden were the living room, dining room, and other bedrooms. Yet playing was no problem since there was a small but unfussy guest room where we played everything from movie stars to Monopoly, cut out paper dolls, told jokes and "cross-your-heart-and-hope-to-die" secrets. There was also a porch, a backyard, and the hallway and stairs for more active pursuits. After-school snacks had to be eaten in the kitchen and snow boots came off at the front door. There was plenty of fun—but no funny business with the house rules. In large part, those were enforced by the host child with little need for personal interference. Clearly, the rules were defined and understood before any playmate arrived.

In today's more typically tight quarters, the child's room or living room may need to be furnished for dual roles. It may mean keeping breakable treasures out of harm's way. Sometimes an attic, garage, porch, or corner of the kitchen can be set up for play. Establishing the boundary lines goes a long way in preventing problems before they arise.

Naturally, you may have to step in if things get silly or wild. Usually, a reminder of the limits is sufficient. What you want to avoid most is embarrassing your child in front of friends with long, loud lectures and harsh criticism. Better to save the big message for later and simply but firmly call a halt to unacceptable action.

"Running in the house disturbs our neighbors," tells kids why they must stop. "You can go outside or find a quieter game," gives kids an alternative. There's no need to holler,

"You know better than to run and scream in the house and if you don't behave you won't have company again!" Putting your child down in front of his friend is humiliating to your child and embarrassing to his friend.

## Friends You Wish They Didn't Have

Somewhere along the line most kids find a friend you wish they didn't have. While young kids generally pick friends like themselves, school-age kids sometimes befriend others who are quite the opposite. It may be exactly that difference that attracts your quiet child to her bossy, loud friend, or visa versa. As a kid, I had a friend who walked pigeon-toed. I thought it looked so sensational, I started imitating her. It wasn't until the man in the shoe store suggested wedging my shoes to correct my new walking style that I understood who had the problem.

Like it or not, opposites often attract simply because both kids offer each other something they need, want, or admire. Talkative kids need listeners, followers need leaders, timid ones need braver ones—at least for a while. Since many childhood friendships tend to be short-lived and kids themselves keep changing, few of these opposite arrangements last for long.

> Robbie's friend Dan was two years older and knew how to fly kites, spin gyroscopes, build a clubhouse, pop wheelies, and tell unbelievably off-the-wall stories to prove his prowess. Robbie was in awe of Dan. He was fascinated and pleased to be called a friend of this big kid who lived in the neighborhood. But I was always just a little bit worried about Dan's derring-do and slightly wild ways. He wasn't mean—just fearless and a lot abler physically. And there were jokes and language I'd overhear. I'd try to tell myself that boys will be boys. I kept suggesting that Robbie invite some other friends over sometime. But it was Dan's BB gun that ended it. Robbie kept telling me that a BB gun was harmless and wouldn't hurt anyone. I didn't want Robbie playing around with a kid with a gun and I said so. So Dan was allowed to come visiting without his gun, but a few weeks later, Dan was using rabbits for targets and that was it for Robbie. I guess Robbie

realized that Dan and a gun might not be a good combination. Their friendship just sort of faded out—no fight, we just gradually saw less and less of Dan.

—Mother of a ten-year-old

Banishing certain kids from your home may actually do more harm than good. On the other hand, if you have reservations about the supervision (or lack of it) or questionable atmosphere in a friend's home, you can encourage their after-school visits in your home.

Much as you wonder why your child is attracted to a particular friend, try to avoid picking and choosing your school-age child's friends. What really counts is how well it is working for the kids. If the friendship is not destructive or dangerous, there's no reason to interfere.

## Bullies

On the other hand, some kids get themselves embroiled in relationships that are potentially harmful and, at best, unhappy. If the neighborhood bully has bamboozled your child into giving in or taking the consequences, you may have to step in. Young kids are often the victims of such behavior.

Tommy came off the schoolbus complaining constantly about some kid named Duane. At first I thought, stay out of this. He has to learn to take care of himself. Then one day he came in with teethmarks on his arm. I called the school and discovered that this kid had been terrorizing all the kindergartners. Well, they took Duane off the bus for a week and that took care of it. I guess Duane's parents read him the riot act. They had to pick him up and deliver him for a week and that did it. I wish I had called sooner.

—Mother of a five-year-old

While it's true that we can't fight their fights for them, parents do sometimes have to act on their child's behalf.

Not long ago, I had a seven-year-old student who was taking karate lessons. His parents believed that it would give him confidence to "take care of himself." In effect, they were arming him for violence and saying indirectly that "the world is full of violence, so you'll have to be violent, too." Unfortunately, when seven-year-olds get such messages, they are apt to find what they expect. They may even invite opportunities to prove how strong they are. True, kids should not allow others to push them around, but few seven-year-olds need karate lessons to know how to defend themselves.

Kids who are constantly putting on a tough act and engaging in physical fights are sending out trouble signals. Young kids often lack social skills to interact with others. They may not yet have the social knowhow to engage others without stirring things up. Instead of asking, "Do you want to play?" they intrude upon a game in progress and smart if the players reject them. While some kids will wander off and find another game, others respond by teasing or making physical assaults on those who reject them. The kid who is "out" compounds his problem and is seen by others as a troublemaker.

Parents and teachers can sometimes help kids negotiate their way "in" by suggesting a role the third child can play (banker, scorekeeper), or suggesting that the player who is "out" join the next round or play the winner. Adults can also help by verbalizing the facts: "Johnny doesn't want to fight, he really wants to play with you . . . do you think he could be the banker (or whatever) in the next game?" Here, the adult is clarifying things out loud for both sides rather than laying a guilt trip on either side.

## Taking the Bully by the Horns

While the lack of social skills is often a matter of inexperience, the child who is slugging his way into one confrontation after another may have problems that outweigh but color his problems with his peers. Often, these kids are embroiled in a family crisis over which they are powerless—but hurt and angry. One of my second graders got into fist fights every Friday. It took a while to discover that his weekend visits with daddy were preceded by mommy's long list of daddy's shortcomings. Kids who are forced to become confidant, confessor, and referee in adult concerns may be so overwhelmed that their angry feelings overflow into their relationships outside the home. Both parents and kids may need professional help in this kind of situation.

One second grader's parent told me that she couldn't understand why her child was getting into fights on the bus, in the classroom, and on the playground. She said she'd tried everything to make him behave. By everything, she meant using a belt and the back of her hand in repeated episodes of physical punishment. Small wonder that this child, who was constantly assaulted by a big and powerful adult, was using the same approach to get his way with others. While this may appear an extreme kind of case, the rising incidents of child abuse demonstrates that it is far from unique. When parents rely on physical force to punish children, they give their children a loaded lesson in how to deal with children. Kids who are physically abused frequently find someone to strike out at.

Unfortunately, parents with misplaced loyalty may indirectly support and defend their child's misbehavior by blaming the other kid who started it. One of the hardest things a parent has to face, somewhere along the line, is the fact that even their child may not tell the whole truth and nothing but the truth. We don't have to love them less for not being perfect— but loving them will not replace their need for getting along with others. It's not enough to say, "Oh, he's just like his father," or "He's always been difficult." If your school-age child is constantly pushing his weight around with fists and feet, you may need professional help to get at the underlying causes of the problem. Learning karate is a poor substitute for helping kids to develop social skills.

## Friendship Skills

Some kids have more trouble than others making their way into any group. In new situations, they may not know how to get the attention of another child. Some kids hang back and watch; some clown for attention. Others know how to oil the wheels—asking questions, offering information, and extending invitations to play.

### Friendly vs. Unfriendly

Nursery-school-age kids who have the easiest time making friends are those who accept others more than reject them. They pay more attention when others seek them out. They give help and praise to their peers and are therefore well liked. Often these social skills reflect the way children have been treated by adults.

When disagreements arise, kids need to know how to handle conflicts. Aggressive kids need to learn how to listen, instead of socking someone or grabbing. Submissive kids need to learn how to stand up for themselves with a firm but controlled stance. Learning how to negotiate with tact and a sense of other people's feelings takes time, but it is an essential skill.

In large part, these skills are learned gradually as kids interact with each other. Playing one on one, in small groups, in school and at home, the skills of friendship are learned largely by trial and error. Adults may act as models in their own relationships with others, but they cannot teach these skills directly by telling kids how. Parents can help best by making it possible for their kids to play with others on a regular basis.

Sometimes an older child (neighbor or sibling) can provide the kind of modeling the younger and less experienced player needs. Although neither child should be locked into this arrangement exclusively, it can help both players develop social skills.

### Forget the Popularity Contest

While some kids are "social butterflies," others are content with limited contact. Trying to make your child into something she is not can only produce more harm than good. The object is not to make your child into the most outgoing, friendliest kid on the block. Rather, parents need to accept their child's social style and give it room to grow. Some of that growth will include conflicts as well as cooperation, and tempers as well as tact. For learning social skills, there simply isn't any shortcut or substitute for learning from experiences with others.

### Can Danny Have Dinner Over?

Allowing kids to have an occasional guest for dinner is one way parents support farm subsidies and kids' friendships. Actually, dinner need not be super-special or fancy. Just having Danny over is special by itself.

School-age kids (and even preschoolers) often taste and enjoy new or more varied food away from home. If the young guest isn't eating with gusto, don't make an issue of it. Eating dinner away from home has less to do with nutrition than socialization. Avoid, too, the business of comparing kids' appetites and table manners. Praising one child at the expense of the other does nothing to promote friendship—only competition.

### Can Sara Come Along?

A trip to the beach or the museum may be twice as enjoyable when a friend comes along. School-age kids especially appreciate having a friend's company on a day-long outing or a work-a-day trip to the supermarket. A drive in the car or a walk to the store is just less boring when there's a playmate who likes to play Ghost or Twenty Questions along the way. Giving friends new and broader experiences to share enlarges, and may extend, their common interests.

It's not that you don't want to save some times for parent/child outings. But adding an extra child occasionally can enhance rather than distract from the fun.

Don't overlook the possibility of involving your child and a friend in projects close to home. Raking leaves, painting the porch, planting a garden, polishing the furniture, washing the car—these may be more play than work for older kids and their friends. Taking the time to teach the "how-to" skills gives kids a chance to play at real things. One of my daughter's closest friends had to help her mother with house cleaning every Saturday. Whenever she could, my daughter spent Saturday at her friend's house, learning how to make countertops and sinks shine. At first, I was appalled. But then I came to realize that she was proud of these newly learned and practical skills.

## Parties

Birthdays and holidays parties are eventful times when playmates get together. Celebrations for the preschool gang are generally happier if they're scaled down to size. Better to have a small, short, happy event than an oversized disaster. If you must have the whole neighborhood, be sure to have back-up adults on hand to lend support. Whatever size party you're having, set a time limit so parents know when they should return.

### For the Younger Set

Most twos and threes may want their moms to stay, at least till they're feeling at home. Although you may remember games and prizes when you think of birthday parties, save these for the school-age gang. Preschoolers are not ready for much competition. Better to pick games that are fun to play for their own sake, rather than for winning and losing. Rather than prizes, each guest will enjoy going home with some small party favor pulled from a big, fussy favor box. Small cars, bubble pipes, toy jewelry, bean bags, or crayons make good favors. Choose one and make them *all* the same.

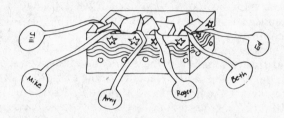

Party favors can sweeten the new and sometimes painful experience of bringing a gift and leaving it. Supplying a name-tagged loot bag for each child will also simplify homebound hats, candy, and noisemakers.

As guests arrive, have an area with toys available for playing together. Playdough, hat making, or crayons and paper give kids a chance to warm up to each other. Once all the guests have arrived, bring on the cake and candles. If you're serving lunch, keep it simple. Serve finger food that kids can manage on their own. Rather than filling glasses to the brim, serve a half-filled glass and offer refills.

After eating, kids will enjoy some time for cooperative games if you're ready to lead them. The Farmer in the Dell, Looby Loo, Follow the Leader, and Simon Says are preschool favorites. Don't overlook the possibility of their pleasure in playing in the sandbox, on the swing set, or blowing bubbles. If you're caught indoors, kids enjoy playing informally with the host child's toys and each other. In the line of prevention, have your child select in advance the toys he will share and put the others out of sight and reach. Doing this in advance gives your child a chance to make choices he can accept about the hard business of sharing.

As parents arrive to pick up their kids, the remaining guests may enjoy a storybook. Some youngsters may get anxious about their mother or father's arrival. You might also help the time fly for such kids by inviting them to help you with the pick-up jobs.

Although the job of planning and preparing will be chiefly yours, try to involve your youngster in some of the choices. Paper goods and favors, making decorations, setting the table —all are part of the happy anticipation.

### For Older Kids

Older kids should definitely play a larger part in planning their parties—from invitations to clean-up. School-age kids can help in making and hanging their own decorations, writing invitations, and planning the games and menu. Often, parties at this age center on a theme that dictates the decor, menu, and even the games. For instance, a spaceship party may feature Pin-the-Tail-on-a-Rocket (instead of a donkey) and a cake in the shape of a rocket or spaceship. Find a theme and play around with the ideas that flow from it. This is an opportunity to put kids' imaginations in flight.

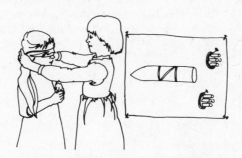

In planning the party, set up the limits of where kids will play and how long they will stay. If weather permits, some outdoor team games give them a chance to play boisterously. Indoor games for this age group should be well planned or the party can fall apart. You'll find suggestions in chapters 6 and 7. Chances are you won't play all the games you plan, but that's okay. Better to plan too many than end up with kids wrestling from restlessness. Mix the games—some active with some quiet times. Don't overlook the possibility of involving the guests in some make-it-yourself activity. Make-your-own party hat, paint-your-own pumpkin, scoop-your-own sundae all add to the pleasure.

If your space is limited, you may want to consider a party away from home. Taking a few friends to the bowling alley or skating rink may cost no more than having a big crowd at home. Consider, too, the possibility of some sit-down entertainment. A family-produced puppet show, a teenage magician in your neighborhood, a film and projector borrowed from the local library, may add that extra touch. On one occasion, we had a Japanese feast (on the floor, of course) followed by an impressive origami (paper-folding) demonstration by Papa-San. Our daughter and her friends soon forgot about all other games and everyone went home knowing how to turn a square of bright paper into a small bird with flapping wings.

Good planning can go a long way toward making a party work, but don't get locked into schedules that must be rigidly adhered to. If a game is going over well, let it be rather than hurrying kids on to the next event. Kids just generally get charged up with the excitement of big events, so try to develop a blind eye and a deaf ear to the inevitable messiness and noise. Naturally, you can't let kids run wild, but don't expect party-perfect manners at all times. Like the old *Mission Impossible* prologue—this is an assignment you may choose to ignore. If you decide to go with it, remember that the word that goes with "birthday" is "happy." Don't let that message self-destruct. Good luck.

## Pets as Playmates

Unlike human playmates, pets don't argue, talk back, or criticize. They're generous with their affection, companionship, and loyalty. No wonder kids have such an affinity for pets.

Of course, young children can't be expected to take full responsibility for the care of another living creature. They can and should help, though. If you're considering a pet, better prepare yourself for most of the heavy-duty grooming, tank- or cage-cleaning chores involved. If that's not your speed, better postpone the pets for the late middle years. Even then, kids will need to be reminded that feathered, finned, and furred pets cannot care for themselves.

## What Pet?

Where you live will naturally affect your pet choice. Apartment dwellers may want to consider gerbils, birds, or fish. They don't wag their tails or lick your face or cuddle with you. But they can fill the bill as companionable listeners.

If you have the space, you'll probably want to consider a cat or a dog. Of course, cats are less likely to be just where you want them at any given moment. Though they're playful, their independence may not quite satisfy the child who is eager to lavish attention and affection on a pet.

Dogs, on the other hand, demand more attention and, if treated gently, give their owners great affection. Just a word of caution: Little dogs tend to be snippy and therefore iffy pets for kids. About the best rule to keep in mind is—the smaller the child, the larger the dog should be.

## Value of Pets

In their day-to-day activities, kids rarely have a better chance to try on the role of caretaker. Pets offer that opportunity. Even if the child can only help, he'll be learning small lessons in being responsible for a dependent creature.

Coupled with such lessons is the parents' responsibility to see that kids treat pets gently, not as toys. Recent reports indicate there has been a rise in the incidence of children under four being bitten by the family dog. Teaching tots to respect pets is no easy task. If you don't have a pet, specialists suggest that it may be best to postpone owning a pet until your child is older.

Teaching pets tricks, grooming them, feeding them, playing with them—all give kids a pleasing mixture of skills, fun, and commitment.

Pets also provide many kids with the earliest experiences of the mysteries of life and death. The arrival of guppies or puppies gives kids some first-hand knowledge of sexual reproduction and the birth process. Watching a mother cat feed, clean, and protect her kittens speaks to the hearts of children who are not that far removed from dependence.

It is also with the death of a pet that many children experience their first permanent loss and the grief it brings. Painful as this may be, psychologists believe such losses are better faced than hidden or replaced. Dealing with the sad feelings and the happy memories helps kids come to grips in some small way with the bigger issues of life and death. Rather than rushing out to find a replacement, give your child time to mourn the loss. In time, a new pet will be welcomed with a fuller understanding and appreciation of beginnings and endings.

In their own way, pets open the tap on a whole range of emotions and questions that kids need to deal with. More than

many playmates, a pet adds new dimensions to a child's understanding of himself and other living creatures.

## Some-er-Time Friends

I went to school in a small town. In school I was always the next-to-last kid to get picked for the team. Then I went off to camp with city kids who had never played volleyball or kickball. All of a sudden, I was a captain, a jock! Nobody knew I was a klutz in jock's clothing!

### Sleep-Away Camp

One of the beauties of summertime and vacation friendships is this opportunity to try on new roles. School-age kids, particularly, get hooked into playing certain roles in their peer group. Given a new set of peers, kids can break out of the mold and discover new strengths and skills. Often, the benefits of enlarging the child's view of himself are carried home at summer's end.

Unlike school friends who go home every night, the camp group is thrown together for the camping season. Together they learn the give and take of shared responsibilities and cooperative living. For the middle years child, hungry for independence and group life, camp may be an ideal opportunity.

In selecting a camp that's right for your child, you may need to do some shopping around. While the cost, distance, and length of stay are practical considerations, they are not the sole factors in choosing an appropriate camp. Basically, parents need to look at their child's interests, talents, and temperament in assessing the program and philosophy of a camp.

> As a kid I was sent to a sports camp. For six years I was the next-to-worst kid on the playing field. The worst kid never came back. I don't know why they sent me there, or why I didn't refuse to go. I want something better for my son.
>
> —Father of a nine-year-old

Today there are camps for jocks and nonjocks. There are camps for musicians, dancers, gymnasts, and computer buffs. One of the dangers of a highly specialized camp may be its narrowness. As seriously directed as your child may seem, middle years kids should be continuing to explore their possibilities and new interests. Finding a camp that does nothing outside its specialty may lead to premature limitations and unrealistic expectations. It may also feed all that's most damaging in setting kids up in endless competition.

Selecting a camp to match your child's needs and your philosophy may require some research. Camp registry services are a first step in the right direction. Talking to friends and their children who have attended camp can give you useful leads. If possible, the best bet includes a visit the season before you intend to send your child. Brochures are fine, but they are hardly a substitute for seeing the camp in operation.

## Day Camps

For many kids, day camp is a viable alternative to the sleep-away camp. Not only is it less financially taxing, day camp does not demand the total separation from home and family. Some kids at eight, nine, or even ten are simply not ready to live full-time in a group situation. They still need to touch base with the security of home on a nightly basis. If there are choices in your area, try to find the time to visit the camp while it is in operation. Check to see what kind of indoor facilities they have for rainy days, for rest time, and for eating. Chances are your on-site visit will give you a feel for the camp and its staff that a brochure can't describe.

## Vacation and Weekend Friendships

Whether kids go away or not, summer, weekend, and vacation times offer opportunities for kids to expand their circle of friends. While their day-in, day-out relationships tend to be with kids of the same age, same class, same sex—vacation friendships tend to be more varied. Indeed, some of the fascination comes in discovering the likenesses and differences of their common experiences. "We don't play it like that!" they say, or "You're lucky; in our school we have to . . ." Exchanging and comparing notes and rules, kids find out that there are other ways of doing things and enjoying them.

My own kids, who grew up in the country, looked forward to the arrival of our summer neighbors down the road. Unlike their local friends, these summer friends took no bug, berry, or blossom for granted. They brought with them their own brand and variation of games, chants, and jokes.

Separated from their usual school friends and routines, this mixture of country and city-wise kids formed a seasonal bond that renewed itself from the Fourth of July to Labor Day each year. While most vacation friendships tend to be short-lived, their value in enlarging the child's perspective is no less real. Opportunities to break out of the home-base group can add new dimensions to the child's view of himself and others.

Parents with weekend visitation rights often overlook the value of inviting some kid-size company along. Eager as they may be to spend time with their youngsters, it may be better to make that shared time. Kids who have only weekends to play with their friends may have mixed feelings about giving up one or the other of their pleasures. Rather than forcing the choice, try to combine the pleasures. Allowing your child to invite a friend along, or welcoming a next-door neighbor's child in, may enhance your weekend time together.

## On Their Own—Sort Of

Sleeping away from home is a big adventure for kids. Overnight or weekend stays at gram's, daddy's, or a friend's house give kids a chance to spread their wings and taste a bit of independence. Eager as they may be to take off, most kids (and parents) have mixed feelings about leaving home and liking it.

> At four o'clock, sleet started falling and the roads became instantly treacherous. There simply wasn't any way to get her home safely. Poor Steph was in no way prepared for sleeping over. We spoke on the phone several times in the early evening. Her friend's family did everything possible to make her feel at home. But I know it remains one of the longest nights in her record book.
>
> —Mother of a five-year-old

## Parents' Role

While most young visitors are not unexpected, even the most longed-for visit may have its moments of stress. Young children, particularly, are creatures of habit and their nighttime routines are close to ritual observances, with doll tucked, pillow fluffed, and kisses given in an exacting sequence. Naturally, there's something to be said for a little changing of the routine now and then, but the smaller the child the smaller the changes should be. Sending along a familiar "comfie"—doll, pillow, or blanket—can go a long way toward easing the discomfort of sleeping in a strange bed.

School-age sleepover guests are apt to feel at home if they're treated like one of the family. They don't need a special dinner or the best dishes. In fact, they'll feel more comfortable if they're treated casually. If kids set the table in your family, let the visitor take a hand in helping. Avoid making comparisons of the guest's superior eating habits, posture, good manners. This will just embarrass your child's guest and irritate your own child. Most kids (including yours) travel with company manners. You can show your approval without turning it into a production or a put-down.

Sleepover guests generally prefer sharing a room with their friend, even if a guest room is available. Naturally, this may lead to late-night giggles, long after the lights should be out. Face it, it's part of the fun. Within limits, a late night once in a while is not such a terrible thing.

## *Everybody—Off the Brooklyn Bridge!*

Marcy:　But, Mom ...
Mom:　I said no.
Marcy:　It's not fair . . . why can't I? Everybody else is . . .
Mom:　You mean if everybody else were jumping off the Brooklyn Bridge, you'd jump too?

Is there a school-age child anywhere who has not quoted that eminent authority—Everybody? Along with their homework, lunchbox, and dirty gymsuit, it's safe to predict your middle years child will be telling you more about the Everybodys than you ever wanted to know. You may not see them, but they'll be at your dinner table, in the car, and especially at the shopping mall!

According to Marcy, these privileged Everybodys get more allowance, stay up later, and all have ten-speed bikes. Everybody who's anybody is allowed to go to the movies, the ball game, the party, and the arcade.

Quite apart from your child's best friend, the Everybodys represent a different and powerful force in your school-age child's social development. To the middle years child (eight to eleven), there's probably nothing more urgent than gaining membership in the peer group. It is with their agemates that they gain a sense of belonging (or rejection) and of participating (or being left out). In the group they test their strengths in leading and following, making rules and changing them, agreeing and disagreeing.

### For Better and for Worse, the United Way, or Together They Stand, Sort Of

On the bright side, the Everybodys are giving each other support in the tough business of gaining a measure of independence. You don't get the gift of thinking for yourself on your eighteenth or twenty-first birthday. Learning to stand on your own two feet is a long-term process. It begins by standing together with others.

In forming and joining groups kids give each other a kind of Social Security system to support independence. However, there are some real flaws in the system. Becoming a member demands conforming to the group's styles and values, bowing down to a new kind of authority. Being "in" means becoming more similar than dissimilar. So your daughter suddenly needs a metal racket—not wood. Or your son needs a particular kind of bat or mitt. Conforming on the outside represents the child's admission ticket to the group.

Matching up to the group's uniform and fad of the day should not be major issues, unless they are dangerous to health, safety, and the family's financial reality. Where such matters are at risk, parents will need to be firm and consistent. Too much volume and static may blow out the speakers, so try to keep the sound level down. Too often, during the middle years, minor issues escalate into major confrontations. Yet it's during these years that parent and child set the stage for the teen-age turbulence ahead. It's important to set patterns now for dialogue rather than dramatics between parents and kids.

> I've told Wendy that rock music is out. I won't have it in my house. I don't want her listening to it!
> —Father of a ten-year-old

Wendy's dad may bar the Top Ten from his house, but unless he locks earplugs in Wendy's ears it's unlikely his ten-year-old will stick to Papa Bach alone. In fact, she may overreact to dad's dogma and abandon Bach completely.

Trying to legislate against the Everybodys on small issues

may lead to power plays on bigger and more crucial issues. It's not that parents should give up their values and hand the child over to the group. But it should be possible for Wendy to hear both Bach and the Top Ten. In the long run, kids are more likely to turn your values into their own if they are given some freedom to form opinions, especially on small issues.

### Parents' Role

With all their bravado and their newfound Everybodys, entry into the group is by no means painless or automatic. At one time or other, everybody who's anybody knows the pang of being "out" and the feelings of rejection and self-doubt. Kids of this age see themselves as others see them. So the power of acceptance and rejection are of deep-felt importance to the child's self-image. In their search for social security in the bigger world, home and family continue to be the safe haven kids return to for warmth and support.

While accepting the Everybodys, parents can continue to promote individual skills and interests and values. During the middle years, parents often look ahead with great anxiety to the teen-age years. In their eagerness to establish "who's in charge here?" they sometimes hasten to lock the door and keep the Everybodys out. Too frequently, in taking a rigid stance they discover they've locked their own child out as well. Better to keep a revolving door in motion if you want to get your messages through. At this stage, kids need dialogue—not uninterrupted parental monologues. Kids who know they can turn to caring adults are less likely to be enslaved by group dictates. Such adults offer communication, not just dictation. And they provide strong role models that give kids a clear view of what they value and care about.

According to Gary, everybody had a moped and there was no reason why he shouldn't have one, too. In the first place, I explained, it was illegal for kids under sixteen to ride a moped, and it was also unsafe and expensive. When he pointed out that his combined birthday checks and saved allowance would cover the bill, I told him, "You can buy it, but we can't let you ride it. You're not going to break the law."

—Mother of an eleven-year-old

Difficult and argumentative as they may be, kids of this age do not want or expect to take total control. They may not like the why-nots, but they do respect and need parents who say "no" as well as "yes." Gary may still want a moped, but he also knows his parents care about him, as well as values and laws that are part of living in the bigger world. Interestingly enough, kids with overly permissive parents often feel their parents are uninterested in them. Anyone who's ever been engaged in a long-winded sales pitch by a ten-year-old knows it's often a lot easier to say "yes" than "no."

Yet somewhere between deadly defiance and complete compliance is a two-way path for a new kind of parent-child alliance. It's on that path that kids have always had to test what their parents believe and what the group believes in order to begin to discover what they believe. Parenting in the middle years doesn't require surrendering, but rather a little acceptance of the Everybodys and the child's search for independence.

## Summing Up

At every stage in their development children need playmates. From their crib when U R #1 . . . to the sandbox and

swings where tots play side by side . . . to the preschoolers who gradually grasp the give and take of cooperative play . . . to the school years where agemates turn into teammates . . . and some playmates into devoted best friends. Growing and changing, playmates enlarge and enrich their understanding of themselves and others, the pleasure and pain of becoming a social being. Such experiences are the foundation of forging meaningful relationships with others throughout life.

# Chapter 9
# Playthings

## Toys, Toys, Everywhere

But Mom, I NEED it!
—Child to mother

Now, let's make a choice . . . we can't spend the day here.
—Mother to child

Is this a good toy for a four-year-old? He's very bright.
—Grandfather to salesperson

Oh, look at this . . . I had this . . . it was my favorite when I was a kid.
—Husband to wife

Honestly, these trucks . . . they're falling apart already. How come they don't make things that will last?
—Wife to husband

But I saw it on TV and they said it could . . .
—Child to parent

## What's New?

Anyone who has walked the aisles of suburbia's vast new toy supermarkets or visited a small-town shopping center or local stationery store knows that children's toys are a big business. Indeed, each year the toy industry adds around 3,000 new choices to nearly 150,000 play-related products already on the toy stores' crowded shelves! So how come kids are always saying, "But, Mom, I've got nothing to play with!"?

All kids need toys. Most kids have toys. The sad truth is, some kids actually have too many toys.

## Toy Overload

He's got a roomful of toys, but I never see him playing.
—Mother

Of course, few kids would ever admit that they have too many toys. Yet one sure symptom of a toy overload is the lack of play. Faced with too many options, kids often develop a habit of flitting about rather than settling into any sustained kind of play.

Chaos in the toy chest is a lot like chaos in the kitchen. Have you ever found your kitchen cabinet or drawers in a jumble? Did you ever have trouble finding the right lid to match the pasta pot or the cake pan you use only occasionally for a special dessert? Too many gadgets in the kitchen (or the playroom) may create more problems than pleasure. Is there really any reason for me to have a special tool to hull strawberries or a super-duper cake-testing pick when a knife will do the same job? Besides, who can find the one right gadget when it's needed? Kids have similar problems with toy overload.

Parents might do well to take a clue from classroom teachers who change available play materials from time to time. A shower of birthday or holiday toys can be opened and partially shelved for future consumption. The old adage—"Saving up for a rainy day"—has real value, even on a sunny day with "nothing to do" complaints. Old toys often become found treasures when they reappear from cold storage.

The other side of saving is clearing out toys kids have outgrown. You wouldn't throw away a perfectly good down jacket that doesn't fit, but you wouldn't save it, either. Toys, like clothes, can be recycled, passed on to younger cousins, yard sales, or thrift shops. Toys could have a second life if more parents' groups ran toy swaps.

### Toys 'R' Tools

Toys are to a child what cooking utensils are to a chef. Toys are the tools kids use for their playmaking. Like our kitchen tools, they need to be kept in an orderly fashion so that they are accessible. Some need to be discarded, others replaced.

Kids, like chefs, need an assortment of tools to match their various play needs. Just as children change physically, intellectually, and emotionally, so, too, does their need for toys to match their growing developmental skills and changing interests.

How can parents and kids choose from the glut of toys touted on television, in toystores, drugstores, and supermarkets? When we shop for toys, how do we control the child inside ourselves who says, "I had one of those; it was my favorite!" or "I always wanted one of those but nobody bought it for me!" If the box says "educational," does that make it good and important? How do we tell a staple from an unnecessary frill? Let's look at some basic criteria for selecting toys that enhance play.

## First Things First: Is It Safe?

Shocking as it may seem, every year 134,000 children are rushed to hospital emergency rooms because of toy-related injuries. That figure does not include mishaps on bikes or playgrounds which account for a million more accidents. In spite of the efforts of the U.S. Consumer Safety Product Commission and the Public Action Coalition on Toys, unsafe toys, bikes, and playground equipment do reach consumers. Recalls and subsequent bans on unsafe toys come too late for all too many injured kids.

While many accidents may be the fault of poor design and testing, some preventable accidents have more to do with poor toy-buying choices. Small wooden beads may be delightful for a six-year-old but deadly for a toddler. When it comes to safety, make no assumptions. Examine toys carefully in terms of the age and play style of the child they're intended for.

Check all toys for rough spots that have splinters, sharp edges that can cut, pointed parts that can puncture, and moving parts that can pinch. Consider, too, the hidden hazards of a toy: The paint, stuffing, springs, wires, and strings may be dangerous. Kids don't necessarily use toys as they were designed to be used. Ask yourself:

If it drops will it shatter?

If it's dirty can it be cleaned?

Steer clear of plug-in toys that get too hot and gas/water-powered toys that may soar in the wrong direction.

Before buying major outdoor equipment or bikes, take the time to check out consumer testing reports in your local library. Be sure equipment is installed properly (see pages 114–15) in your backyard and on the playground where your children play. Establish clear but simple limits on where, how, and when equipment can be used. Supervise the use of equipment until you are sure it can be used with safety and independence.

Naturally, parents and kids have the right to expect that the toys they buy will not endanger health or safety. However, the Latin phrase "Caveat emptor" says it all: "Let the buyer beware."

## *Safety Check List*

Some toys are hazardous to begin with. Some get that way through use. Check for potential danger before and after you make purchases.

### *For Young Children*

*Dolls and stuffed toys*

- Check seams for sturdy construction.

- Avoid metal armatures inside that may pop through.

- Remove bows, bells, and doodads that may be swallowed.

- For infants, stick to dolls and animals with stitched-on features rather than buttons or decorations that can be swallowed.

- Avoid dolls' hair until they're past the mouthing stage.

- Stay away from battery-operated dolls that can't get wet.

- Avoid wind-up keys that may hurt if fallen on or slept on.

- Avoid small squeeze toys that can fit totally in child's mouth.

*Wheel toys*

- Be sure ride-on toys are not easily tippable.

- Child should be able to touch ground when sitting on toy.
- Check edges of fenders for smooth seams.
- Look for easily grippable handlebars.

## Blocks and accessories

- Check wooden toys for splinters.
- Check cars and trucks for sharp edges and small openings that catch/cut small fingers.
- Watch for sharp points when car wheels fall off.

## Other reminders

- Check plastic toys that crack and have sharp edges.
- Look for nontoxic labels on art supplies.
- Avoid toys with tiny pieces that might be swallowed.
- Avoid toys with flying projectiles.
- Check toys from craft fairs and homemade items for sanitary and nontoxic features.
- Supervise preschoolers with balloons in their mouths —balloons can cause suffocation.
- Check toy chests for lids that may trap or injure children.

## For Older Children

- Supervise use of chemistry sets at all times.
- Supervise the use of any electrical plug-in toys.
- Steer clear of cheaply made imitations that may be less expensive and less well made.
- Avoid toys that do not list manufacturer.
- Avoid darts and other flying toys that may accidentally cause serious injury.

- Stay away from gas-powered and super-powered toys.

- Read consumer guides before buying expensive toys and sports equipment.

- Be sure your child understands when, how, and where to use equipment.

- Avoid toys that heat up to high temperatures and can cause burns or shocks.

For more information about toy safety, ask your librarian for *Guidelines on Choosing Toys for Children,* a booklet published by an organization called Public Action Coalition on Toys.

## Does the Toy Fit?

We spent three weeks shopping for a dollhouse. They're so expensive. Then we spent a fortune on furnishing it, and now it just sits there. I don't understand it. When I was her age, my dollhouse was my favorite plaything.

—Mother of eight-year-old

Spending a fortune or buying an update of your favorite childhood toy doesn't guarantee success. Finding toys that fit really depends more on knowing your child's playing style and interests. As a child I had a passion for dolls. By six, my daughter put all her dolls on a shelf and considered them a great ho-hum bore. She was far more excited about skating, drawing pictures, playing Chinese checkers, and collecting bugs. Anything but the "dumb dolls," as she called them. Knowing the child's interests can go a long way toward selective rather than sentimental toy buying.

Toys often come with age labels—"Recommended for two to six," "Eight and up," or "Perfect for preschoolers." But age labels can't assure the right fit. Those labels are only guidelines, not guarantees. It's like buying clothes by size label alone. Some four-year-olds wear size 4 while others need 6-X. Toys, like clothes, need to be evaluated on a more individual basis.

Whatever age you're shopping for, here are a few questions you might ask before you buy:

## Does the Toy Offer a Challenge without Frustrating?

Toys that require intricate dexterity of small fingers do not build feelings of competence. Toys that demand constant attention or supervision don't build a sense of independence. Buying toys that are too complex is a lot like buying shoes to grow into: They're apt to end up in the closet or leave blisters.

On the other hand, there are some toys worth purchasing because they do involve parent and child in a mutually satisfying activity. Models, chemistry sets, and craft projects may be too difficult or dangerous for the child to use alone. But when you buy them remember that *you* are part of the package.

## Does the Toy Have More Than One Use?

I remember two monkeys that arrived at our house. One was a wind-up monkey with cymbals in his paws. The other was a soft, cuddly monkey with long legs and tail. After the first weeks, the wind-up monkey sat on a shelf gathering dust. The soft monkey led an active life as companion, confidant, and comforter for many years.

The fact is, too many toys have too little play value. Perhaps that's what makes playthings so quickly disposable. Tempting as they may seem, novelty items that turn on and off run down in the high-interest department. Flashy toys with lights that go dead, flimsy toys with parts that break off—all join the clutter that clogs up the shelves, closets, and even the play lives of children.

## Is the Toy Durable?

The key here is in choosing toys that can take it and still keep going. It's not just a matter of breakability. There's probably nothing that's absolutely unbreakable. But some items are predictably destructible. With some games and toys, one missing part and the whole thing's useless. A cheap wooden plane that cracks up on its first flight is not cheap—just a disappointing waste. A china tea set may be a treasure to an eight-year-old and treacherous to a four-year-old. Outdoor toys that can't take rain without rusting or indoor toys that must be handled with constant care end up as refuse rather than in use.

Ask yourself: Does the toy really do what it claims to do? How long will it probably do its thing? Will it still have any play value when it's not fresh from the box? Does it have the potential of being a favorite old thing? Remember, toys are not for shelves—they're for playing.

## Will the Toy Hold Long-Term Interest?

A Jack-in-the-box, a pinwheel, a wind-up car are among the many temporary toys that go from amusement to disuse in short order. Some are inexpensive enough to warrant short-term pleasure. Some have value as a souvenir of an outing to the circus, the park, or a vacation. But most gimmicky toys soon lose their magic.

Most notable of the faddish toys are spin-off merchandise from TV or movies that find their way into toy stores. Buying an occasional "in" toy will probably do no permanent harm. But in spreading out the toy budget, better to put your money on basic staples (see pages 283–87).

## Is the Toy Pleasurable to the Senses?

Ask yourself: How does the toy feel? look? sound? Is the sound it makes grating and intrusive? Is it likely to lead to the necessity for a set of instructions? For instance, there's no point in buying a bongo and then telling the bongo player to be quiet. Is the toy designed to catch the eye or please the eye? On a recent visit to a doll department, I found an abundance of caricature faces frozen in surprise. Such dolls may be appealing to adults rather than kids who range through a variety of emotions in their doll play.

Since toys are the first objects children handle regularly, they should be esthetically pleasing and attractive to the senses. They can be colorful without being crass and child-appealing without being cutesie.

## Is the Toy Well Designed?

Take a good look at the basic item underneath the expendable doodads and disposable packaging. How does it measure up in terms of proportion, craftsmanship, and function? Developing an esthetic sense of taste and form does not begin in art class or by going to museums. It starts with the everyday experience and objects in our lives.

## Does the Toy Have a Hidden Agenda?

As a classroom teacher, it came as a shock to discover that the sample question on a national standardized test tells first graders that a mother bought toys for Ted and Jack and something for their sister. The children are to mark the picture of the toy for sister. Pictured are a toy car, a football, and a doll. Now according to the manual, the only right answer is the doll. But in nine years of giving that test, at least one child in every class looked up at me with puzzled eyes. Not only do we teach sexism at an early age, we even give a test on it.

The fact is, both girls and boys enjoy balls, dolls, and cars. To limit the play choices by sex is to cast children prematurely in narrow roles that can be damaging to their development and the reality of lifelong demands. Both single parents and working couples know only too well that few of us live our lives in such tight compartments. The roles of nurturing, nourishing, and neatening things up are not limited to one gender in most homes today. If there are limitations, they are more apt to be the result of short-sighted expectations we traditionally set for children of both sexes.

While friends and relations may still be bringing dolls for girls and trucks for boys, we need to understand that the playthings we choose for children can convey sexist messages that echo our expectations and shape theirs. On a recent visit to a toystore, I was delighted to find a boy pictured on a box of toy pots and pans. And why not? Many of the best chefs I know are men.

Not only do toys convey hidden sexist agendas, they speak directly to children's emerging sense of themselves in the world. Until recently, toymakers simply overlooked minority children and their needs. Dolls came with blond hair and blue eyes and so did the kids pictured on the packages.

Indeed, the only black doll many generations of children played with was a Mammy-type doll who could be abracadabrad into a southern belle by flipping the skirt and apron over Mammy's head. That particular doll certainly conveyed powerful social messages to both black and white children. So, too, do many dolls today which are essentially white dolls in black face paint, although there are some that are more realistic and pleasing. By being selective and demanding, parents can encourage manufacturers to develop toys and packaging that mirror the emerging self-image of all our children, not just some.

Perhaps the most obvious messages of all are packaged in toys that enhance violence and glamorize war. Machine guns and pistols, cap guns and tanks, are just part of the mighty arsenal of war toys available in your nearest toy store stockpile.

It's not that pretend games of war are signs of a violent

personality in the making. Playing Army, Cops and Robbers, Good Guys vs. Bad Guys—all are a normal part of the classic childhood repertoire of chase-and-catch games. Yet, without arming them with realistic props, such games are likely to run their course and be replaced sooner. Fitting them out in fatigues and battlegear, bazookas and grenades, may only serve to prolong and give a nod of approval to playing with themes of aggression and violence. Neither toy guns nor real ones are necessary props for finding acceptable and healthful release for aggression, excitement, or sport.

## The Shrinking World of Play

While many adults today are increasingly involved in jogging, tennis, exercise classes, and personal fitness, the child's world of play has been shrinking for several decades. Years ago the ritual games and chants were passed along by kids from one generation to the next.

Chances are you put in plenty of inadvertent practice with the alphabet, bouncing a ball to "A, my name is Alice." Your first lesson in odds and evens (and cheaters) was probably learned on your fingers with "Once, twice, three, shoot!" It's not that games were a conscious attempt to learn school skills. A good many chants were delicious nonsense, as in "Mini, Mini, Ha-Ha, went to see her Pa-Pa. . . ." But jumping double-dutch or single file, the rope snapped to "2-4-6-8" or "5-10-15-20." Without any coaxing, kids played with the things they were learning and learned from each other through active play.

Kids today are more likely to recite TV jingles. Their freedom to "go out and play" has been restricted by urban crime and suburban sprawl. Too often, it's easier to take them to the mall or turn on the TV. Indeed, television has become the chief thief of children's playtime.

## TV or Not TV?

When I was growing up, there were so few TV sets that the stations used to send a postcard to every TV owner announcing any special events—the rodeo with Roy Rogers, the circus, the Joe Louis fights. Most of the time there was nothing but a test pattern on the screen. Can you imagine what kids today would do if their TV viewing was that limited? After the shock passed, would our children know how to use the twenty-five hours they currently spend every week glued to the tube?

Some parents believe the only solution is to pull the plug and deny its existence. Others have turned the tube into a full-time baby-sitter and permanent pacifier. Essentially, both extremes are unrealistic. TV or not TV is not the question—nor the answer.

TV is here to stay. It has not replaced newspapers or movie theaters as people once feared it would. It has allowed us to see more distant places than any adventurous explorer in our history books ever visited in a lifetime. Via TV we have seats at the World Series and the opera, the Olympics and the ballet, the good news and the bad. With TV, we've been to the moon and the rings of Saturn. So why all the fuss about TV's negative influence?

## Quantity and Quality

Until recently, the greatest concern has centered on the quality of children's programming. Yet recent studies indicate that the quantity of viewing time is even more significant. Kids who get a big daily dose of any kind of programs tend to display more aggressive behavior than kids who take their TV in moderation. It's as if excessive viewing time eventually leads to an explosion of pent-up energy—like a bottle of warm soda that's been shaken and fizzes all over when it's opened.

Apparently, the quantity of TV viewing also affects children's reading scores in school. Interestingly enough, kids who watch a great deal or very little TV tend to score lower than kids who watch a moderate amount of programming. But just what do the experts mean by "a moderate amount"? In part, that answer must be adjusted to the individual child. Three-year-old Jackie's mother says:

> My daughter hasn't any real interest in toys. She piles them up in a chair and turns on the TV. Jackie knows the alphabet and can count. She loves *Sesame Street* so much she watches it two or three times a day!

This is truly a privileged child—with cable TV she may be ready for *Sunrise Semester* by the time she's five! When I suggested two or three visits a day to *Sesame Street* might be too much of a good thing, Mama's answer was, "But Jackie loves it. And besides, she's learning!"

Kids love a lot of things that may not be good for them. The same mother wouldn't just feed her daughter bananas—even though she loves 'em. Not even the makers of *Sesame Street* would recommend two or three hours a day on their block.

The sad truth is, when it comes to entertainment, parents often consider TV, toys, and play as interchangeable possibilities. Both parents and kids have come to rely on the ready-made convenience of instant entertainment. We play the TV instead of playing. And if it says "educational," so much the better. Indeed, this is where Jackie's mother gets her false sense of security. If it's teaching something, it must be good. Right? Not exactly.

TV, whether it's called educational or otherwise, is essentially a passive activity. Turn the knob and there it is—ready-made nonstop images and sound. No need to dream up little dramas of dangers and triumphs. They're all there, ready-spun, accompanied by music and laugh track. No need to participate on the sports field when you can sit back and watch the pros. No need to understand or make yourself understood to others—when you want company just flick the switch. Rather than relating to others in real situations, the TV offers vicarious relationships. Your child can peep into others' lives, but even realistic programs are unrealistic. Shows with kids feature super kids who are a fiction at best (dressed up as the real thing). Basically, TV kids tend to be super smart and overwhelmingly successful by the end of sixty minutes. A daily overdose of TV may make a regular kid feel cheated or incompetent when real-life problems are less easily solved.

Even if all shows were excellent (which they are not), sitting and staring at the screen for four to six hours of the day can teach lessons you'll wish they never learned!

### Learning to Be Passive—Lesson 1

Kids are, by nature, active explorers. At six months they only gaze at the TV from time to time. If, however, they are consistently within sight and sound of the turned-on tube, their exploration of other things becomes more and more limited. So they play less. By twelve months they'll be staring only 12 percent of the time, but by two-and-a-half it will be up to 45 percent of the time! Even if they've got toys and other distractions in the room, by age four, kids are watching TV 55 percent of the time—*if the set is on*. And by then, they'll even turn it on themselves.

## *Tuning In and Tuning Out—Lesson 2*

From Lesson 1 they're learning to tune in and at the same time they're mastering the art of tuning out as well. We all do this. Haven't you ever turned on the news, waited for the weather, and then realized you missed it completely? Kids who develop that sort of half-attention may be in trouble when the teacher doesn't do instant replays for them.

## *Learning Not to Learn—Lesson 3*

Unlike drawing pictures on a paper or hearing a story and visualizing pictures in your head, the visual images on TV come ready-made, rapidly and predigested. Not only is the child's own imagination left out, so are the visual scanning skills needed for reading. Rather than moving the eyes from left to right, the rapidly changing images keep the eyes in a fixed position. Informational programs are fixed, too. They all start with assumptions about what the child already knows. It is the program, rather than the child, that raises all the questions and gives all the answers. Such one-way teaching is rarely the way children learn. *What a viewer gets is monologue, but what a learner needs is dialogue.* Indeed, TV may even undermine the child's expectations of how you learn to learn. Extensive TV viewing may have a long-term effect on the child's imagination, expectations of what learning is about, and even the physical act of reading.

## *Dialing to Distraction—Lesson 4*

Not only do the images on the screen change rapidly, kids have the power to change the channel entirely. Anything that's going too slowly or is not instantly engaging can be abracadabrad out of sight. Unlike a block building that requires patient planning and balancing, or a puzzle piece that must be turned this way and that, the dial makes it possible for kids to self-distract and, in the process, diminishes their capacity for stickability. This is a hard habit to get rid of or undo. Teachers, particularly, complain that big TV watchers are most easily distracted. Indirectly, kids are also learning to give up on the hard parts and stay with things that are easily and instantly engaging. That can seriously hamper problem-solving, creative prose, and anything that requires digging in.

### Sapping Sensitivity—Lesson 5

Not only do kids get a sensory overload through the eyes and ears, all evidence shows that TV viewing affects their emotional well-being, too. In study after study, researchers have found that kids who watch violent programs display more aggressive behavior in their play. It reveals itself in their relationships with parents and playmates, in their language and actions. Long before kids have a firm hold on reality and the norms for prosocial behavior, they have seen a world at knifepoint with armed robberies, kidnapping, junkies, prostitutes, pimps, and car chases around every corner. No wonder so many kids feel the world is an unsafe place unless you're tough.

While the networks have put controls on new programming made specifically for children, those restrictions do not eliminate reruns of old cartoons, movies, and sitcoms that are often full of violence—and shown during daytime hours. Nor can the networks monitor the hours or shows kids are watching. On a *weekly* basis, the average two- to five-year-old is watching about five and a half hours between eight P.M. and eleven P.M.! Kids from six to eleven average eight hours during the same prime-time hours. So all the controls in the industry will do nothing if parents don't take control!

### How to Be a Selective Viewer—Lesson 6

Clearly, the responsibility for the quantity and quality of TV viewing must begin with parents.

- Putting a limit on the time spent is just a first but significant step in becoming a selective viewer.

- Sitting down and watching with them will help you discover what they're watching. You can't do it all the time, but do it sometimes.

- Check TV pages of the newspaper for programs you think might be interesting. Sit down and watch them together. If it turns out to be a dud, turn it off.

- Discussing the values, both positive and negative, after the show is over can go a long way in helping kids clarify their own feelings, ideas, and fears.

- Have a variety of alternative plans for Saturday morning and after-school hours. The offer of a game of catch or a round of Monopoly is almost always more tempting than any TV show.

• Limit your own viewing. As a model, you can't teach your kids by telling them to "do as I say, not as I do."

## *Electronic Games*

At least they sit down and rest for a while. They need that and at least it's less deadly than just staring at the TV.

—Mother of a nine-year-old

My nine-year-old plays with his cassette games. It's just him. The object is to get the highest possible score. It's not bad. The eleven-year-old prefers TV games. You know, two people playing against each other. He likes the competition, but not the nine-year-old.

—Mother of nine- and eleven-year-old

We don't have one of those Atari games. I guess we should. But when we go visiting to a home where they've got it, it's wonderful. They're great! They play for a long time.

—Mother of ten-year-old

### *You'll Be Back!*

"Help me!" a small voice called as I opened the door of a roadside diner. "Help me!" it repeated in the otherwise empty entryway. What next? I wondered when I realized the plea was coming from a machine—a game machine that begged for players. "You'll be back!" It mocked me as I walked away from it. There was something sinister in that electronic voice calling, "You'll be back!"

Indeed, many kids and adults do keep going back. Some are hooked on the joy of zapping electronic enemies, wiping out bleeps and blasting blobs. They need their fix at the controls and the sense of power a couple of quarters can buy them.

For better or worse, electronic games have become a popular form of entertainment. Kids have been known to skip school, use their lunch money, and even steal in order to support their video game habit. Just recently, a town in Colorado reported a link between game machines and a rise in petty thievery

among school-age kids. In efforts to control their use and mis-
use, city and village governments have been drafting laws to
regulate who can play and when.

Today's hoopla over video games may seem to some a mod-
ern-day version of the Music Man's warnings about corruption
in the pool hall. Indeed, every generation of parents has worried about the places where kids congregate. At the turn of the
century, it was the pool hall; a few decades later it was the
candy store pinball machines. Today's parents are justifiably
concerned about the atmosphere in some of the game rooms
where their kids are playing.

A recent survey of some 700 arcades in New York City indicated that there were drug-related activities going on in more
than 50 percent of them. While arcades used to be a haven for
teenagers, the eight-to-twelve set has steadily moved in on the
turf and is, perhaps, easier prey than their older sisters and
brothers.

Nor is the video game habit confined to public places. Home
video players are supposedly a five-billion-a-year industry that
is now marketing dolls, clothing, coloring books, and enough

spinoffs to turn your head and empty your pocketbook. Indeed, electronic games are now being pushed into the preschool and infant market. So even young children are receiving toys that do most of the action instead of inviting active play.

With games selling at one hundred to three hundred dollars a throw, the pressures to own the "in" toy is tremendous. Like them or not, video games are very much a fact of life. The questions they raise break down into three main parts: (1) What's so great about them that makes them so popular? (2) What's so bad about them that people want to write laws against them? (3) What should you do about them?

Let's take a look at what people are saying. It appears that for every positive statement there's a negative one as well.

### Pros and Cons of Electronic Games

| Positive | Negative |
|---|---|
| The games are entertaining. At least they've got more to offer than just staring at the TV. They're not just passive—they really get kids involved. | A lot of things are more entertaining than TV. Since when is that a measure? Between TV and video games and school, they're spending most of their waking hours sitting. |
| They really develop terrific eye/hand coordination. You've got to be fast. My kids are much better at it than I am. | They're really expert at pushing a button—but that's because they spend so much time at it. It's the rest of their bodies I'm worried about. |
| They can play the games solo or try to outscore each other. Basically, the games are self-competitive and that's good. | Machines are a poor substitute for interacting with others. Even when they're together, kids are playing next to each other, not with each other . . . that's a pretty low level of play for kids past two. |
| Some people think the games may actually help kids develop a greater atten- | Kids who need flashing lights and beeps to focus on are going to have a problem |

| Positive | Negative |
|---|---|
| tion span and train them not to be so easily distractable. | in focusing on a printed page that just sits there. The games build a false expectation. Problem-solving is not so simple as pushing a button. |
| The games offer a good release—they are a modern form of fantasy with all the excitement of rescues and close calls. | The games are essentially aggressive. They play on violent themes of attack and chase. Kids are thrown into a ready-made fantasy rather than spinning their own. |

## Parent's Role

What can parents do about video games? Video games are not going to disappear and the problems they present are multiple. For some people, the games are less of a problem than the unsavory environment in which they are played. For others, the issue is the amount of money kids are dropping into the slot. These are issues on which parents must set limits and stand by them. An occasional round of games in the pizza parlor is not going to do permanent damage. What we're talking about here is the game freak who spends most of his free time and spending money on the machines. We're talking about the kind of habit that was reported in *Dial* magazine:

> An eight-year-old girl confessed to spending around fifteen dollars per week on electronic games. When asked how she could afford such an expensive habit, she replied that she used all her lunch money, her allowance, and birthday and Christmas money.

Giving kids too much money at one time may not be such a great idea if video fever has hit your neighborhood. Earmarking some money for entertainment may help kids by acknowledging some freedom to make choices without handing over a bundle to do their thing. Much as they may balk, school-age children need and expect parents to set limits. It's likely that game fever may bring the "Everybodys" out in force (see pages 256–58). On heavy-duty issues such as this you may have to pull the Brooklyn Bridge out of the mothballs. You know how it goes: "If everybody were jumping off the Brooklyn Bridge, would you?"

In taking a firm stand and sticking by it, parents are telling their kids that they care about them enough to interfere. Discuss your feelings openly and listen to theirs. Listening doesn't mean that you have to change your mind. When kids understand your concern, they may not like your decision but they will at least know the underlying reasons and be more likely to abide by and respect them.

On the surface, at least, the answer may seem to be the purchase of a home video player. Yet such purchases don't always keep the kids down on the farm. They may merely provide another push-button panacea with the parental seal of approval.

Many families find that once the novelty wears off, the games gather dust. If you're considering such a purchase, only you can determine if the price tag is worth it. If your entertainment budget is limited, it might be better to send them visiting where there is a machine and use your money for more enduring toys that engage the child in a variety of ways.

On the other hand, the home video market is gradually changing from joystick games to computer keyboards. What started as a home game industry with computer features is shifting to a home computer industry with some game features. As the market for home computers expands, so, too, is the variety of software. We are beginning to see games that go beyond gobbling, blasting, and zapping moving targets. More games are being designed to encourage cooperative play and logical problem-solving. There are also discs that invite kids to create their own graphics and games by designing their own programs. The learning potential of such software has real value in making kids computer literate with the technology that has become part of our lives.

Of course, the price tag for a personal computer is still more than most people can afford. But even as prices come down, parents will need to evaluate the content and limit the time children spend in front of the new magic screen. There are still unanswered questions and concerns about the long-term effect of radiation and visual bombardment. Like TV, the hypnotic power of the electronic screen is hard to turn away from.

Even if money is no object, you may find the games costly in terms of the time they rob from other pursuits. There are just so many hours in a day, and spending too many of them pushing buttons can become a limiting habit that is more than a waste—used to excess it may even be destructive of the intellectual, emotional, and physical pleasures and values kids derive from active play. Being computer literate should not outweigh the importance of social competence, physical fitness, intellectual curiosity, or creative expression in the lives of children or adults.

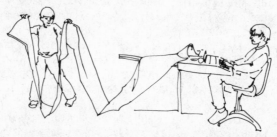

As in all things, the key in this is helping kids find a balance in using a variety of playthings that enlarge the child's world, rather than limiting them to a chair and a button.

## Consumer Ed for Kids

> She saw it on TV. That's all we heard about. I must have driven a hundred miles this week, going from one shopping mall to another. It's sold out everywhere. She's going to be very disappointed on Christmas morning.
>
> —Father of a nine-year-old

If your child is over three, chances are you've been in the same bind as this father. Media purchasing is almost inescapable. The question most parents have is: "What can we do about it?"

First of all, you can pull the plug on the old TV, but don't count on getting rid of the sales pitch. Kids have a network of their own. They get the message and pass it on. Media merchandising is as transmittable as a case of chickenpox. I met a country child who has no TV and asked her what her favorite toy was. She gave me the trade name of the latest craze on TV *and* in her second grade classroom. So pulling the plug can't solve everything.

Secondly, you can fasten your seat belt, open your money

belt, and spend your days tracking down every toy they tout. Of course, be prepared to knuckle under on all issues—from kiddie cars to sports cars. Everybody loves a pushover, right? Just keep that instant gratification button on BUY and don't worry about the payoff—it'll be their problem someday, not yours.

Thirdly, you can stand on your principles. Teach your child the art of broad, sweeping generalizations. Say this: "Don't trust anything you see on TV." At the same time, teach your child to mistrust everything he reads, hears, and sees. This will really teach him how to make choices—he can simply call you. Right?

If, for some reason, none of the above sounds just right, take a little from each and stir. From the first suggestion, accept the fact that some media advertising will get to them. From the second, realize that you don't have to buy everything. And from the third, remember that you don't have to turn them into cynics. Better to teach them the skill of becoming an educated consumer.

A friend recently recalled how her son and his school-age friends would get together with their Hot Wheels and "all that equipment; such a waste," she called it. But was it a waste? To these school-age boys, their toys were tools in the business of becoming social beings. It was their shared interest that brought them together. Their toys were props for fantasy play and real social interaction. Laying out their tracks for races and collision courses produced little dramas that involved both fine muscle tuning and communication antennas. No boy had all the equipment, but several boys together learned the value of joining together and sharing the wealth. These are experiences kids need to learn with other kids—and hardly what should be classified as "a waste."

Some acceptance of what's current and part of the play life of most kids need not turn your child into a conspicuous consumer, a patsy for all pitches. You can teach more about becoming a wise consumer by letting your child make some decisions (including some that turn out to be duds).

> Our sons saw a toy robot on TV. It looked huge and magical on the screen. It was "the" toy of the holiday season. A trip to the store would cure it, I thought. Wrong. The box was tremendous—almost as flashy as the ads. And, even though it needed six batteries and cost ten dollars more than their combined checks from

grandma, they wanted it desperately. We suggested a number of options; still no deal. Finally, they sold dad on a cash advance. An hour later, they were shocked to discover that the robot was one-half the size of the box. Two hours later they knew the robot was rubbish. It fell over more readily than it followed commands. They wanted their money back. Of course, the dealer would not refund money for a used toy. He sent it back to the factory and a few months later another robot arrived, who survived for less than a month. It was an expensive lesson they never forgot.

—Mother of nine- and six-year-old

As kids, most of us have gone through the prize-inside stage. We bought candy, cereal, and gum we didn't even like in order to get the prize inside. Given enough experience, we soon learn that with the same money we can buy either a candy or a toy we will enjoy. Let's call it Consumer Ed #1. It's a first step in finding out that you get nothing for nothing.

Now, Consumer Ed #2 can help kids advance to a new level in decision making. Rather than buying nothing or everything, we can help kids best by giving them some opportunities to make less than earth-shattering choices. Sometimes they'll opt for the pop item and it will not live up to its advance notices. We don't have to say, "I told you so." Rather, we can say, "You were told a, b, and c, but not x, y, and z." Next time they're faced with a choice we can remind them to check closely.

We can also take the time to look at other choices. We can point out the differences in workmanship or potential play value. School-age kids can begin to understand that flashy packages and ads on TV cost money and they may be paying for that cost when a less-touted toy may be of equal or better value.

Consumer Ed #3 should include some "hard knock" lessons. Not only do they need the freedom to make some mistakes, we need to let them live with the consequences. When the toy turns out to be a dud, we can sympathize without subsidizing a quick replacement. Let the message sink in or they'll miss the boat.

Now we come to Consumer Ed #4—an advanced course for the gifted child—which might also be called Money Is Power or, as my son James liked to say, "But it's my money so I can spend it any way I please." Growl if you like, but think about it. Unless it's part of a layaway plan for college, gift money from grandma is intended for a purchase of the child's choice. Learning to spend their own money can provide kids with long-term lessons in becoming a smart shopper.

Naturally, kids will not be making all their own purchases. Nor do all of their playthings need to be purchases. As a parent, you will be providing the basic playthings to tool their play. Without making an itemized shopping list of musts, let's look at the staples most likely to fit their growing needs. As we've said in previous chapters, no one needs nor should have everything on this list. Individual interests and playing styles will influence choices. Some kids prefer more physical equipment than sitting-still board games. Yet all kids benefit from a sampling of various kinds of stimulating equipment. You might want to check the main headings and select as you do from the family menu in a Chinese restaurant—some from Column A, some from Column B.

## Recommended Playthings

### Infants to Twelve Months

| | |
|---|---|
| BIG MUSCLES | crib mobile, crib gym, dangling toys for crib and carriage, bright balls |
| LITTLE MUSCLES | small rattles, teething rings, suction-base rattles, music boxes, teething beads, squeeze toys, busy-box board, plastic bottles and toys for filling and dumping, bath toys, rubber blocks |
| MAKE-BELIEVE | unbreakable mirror, washable dolls and animals, roly-poly doll that bounces back |
| ART MATERIALS | variety of bright pictures |
| FURNITURE/BIG EQUIPMENT | infant swing, jump chair, walker |
| BOOKS | cloth books |

## Toddlers

| | |
|---|---|
| BIG MUSCLES  | small wagon to fill and dump, low slide, infant swing with arms and back, ride 'em toys to straddle (no pedals), small rocking horse, push-and-pull toys with noise |
| LITTLE MUSCLES | nesting toys, large pegboard toys, core with color rings, shape-sorting boxes and boards, hammer boards, large pop beads, drum, bath toys |
| MAKE-BELIEVE | housekeeping toys such as mop, broom, vacuum, dishes and pots; tubbable doll, doll's bed, small carriage, soft dolls; toy phone, teddy bear, dashboard and steering wheel toy, pocketbook, big ticking toy watch, toy cars |
| CONSTRUCTION | colored blocks, large hollow blocks (cardboard), oversized plastic snap blocks, sand toys: pail and shovel |
| ART MATERIALS | paper, pencil, fat washable crayons |
| FURNITURE/BIG EQUIPMENT | small table and chair, rocking chair |

## Preschoolers

| | |
|---|---|
| BIG MUSCLES | animals on wheels, small trikes, straddle and pedal-type fire engine, car, tractor; full-size rocking horse, wagon, wheelbarrow, small sled, roller skates; jungle gym, medium-size slide, board for balancing, see-saw, punching bag, adjustable swing; sandbox toys such as tractor, snowplow, steam shovel, dump truck |
| LITTLE MUSCLES | large beads for stringing, wooden shoe for lacing, wind-up toys that make something happen, Jack-in-the-box, |

plastic tiles, parquetry blocks, lacing cards, pegboard, small garden tools, bubble pipe, rhythm instruments such as drum, cymbals, maracas

| MAKE-BELIEVE | housekeeping toys such as mop, broom, pots and pans, play dishes, vacuum cleaner, toy ironing board and iron; rubber (tubbable) doll with easy-on and -off clothes, doll carriage, doll dishes, doll bed and blankets; hand puppets, dress-up clothes and accessories such as pocketbooks, hats, shoes, jewelry, scarves, badges (fireman, ballerina, cowgirl); doctor and nurse kit; mini-world toys such as farms, airports, villages, trucks, cars, and people |

CONSTRUCTION — unpainted wooden unit blocks, non-electric trains and tracks, odd-shaped wooden blocks such as arches, ramps, y's, scaled-down people, animals, trucks and cars for block play, interlocking blocks (Lego-type)

ART MATERIALS — watercolor markers, pregummed stickers, clay, large crayons, paper, pencils, playdough, poster paint, large brushes, fingerpaint, blackboard and chalk, paste, collage materials

GAMES & PUZZLES — screw-type toys, Colorform-type sticker toys, picture lotto, simple puzzles (start with whole-object pieces)

FURNITURE/BIG EQUIPMENT — sandbox, play stove, sink, oven, refrigerator, playhouse/fort (large box); workbench with vise, hammer, nails, saw, wood scraps; phonograph and records

### Early Middle Years*

BIG MUSCLES — jump rope, ice/roller skates, ring toss, skis, scooter, kites, horseshoes, small bike, croquet set, lightweight bat and ball, mitt, fishing gear

LITTLE MUSCLES — magnets, magnifying glass, pick-up sticks (wood are best), flashlight, harmonica, simple binoculars, tops, jacks, marbles, yo-yo

MAKE-BELIEVE — doll furniture, dollhouse, doll clothes and accessories; puppets and stage, toy sewing machine, toy register, miniature gas station, costumes for dress-up

CONSTRUCTION — Tinkertoys, Lincoln Logs, simple Erector sets, Lego construction

ART MATERIALS — plasticine (nondrying clay), self-hardening clay, regular crayons, markers, simple cartridge-type camera

GAMES & PUZZLES — simple board games, card games, puzzles (20–100 pieces), dominoes, anagram letter games, checkers, Chinese checkers, bingo

FURNITURE/BIG EQUIPMENT — tent, desk, bookshelf, phonograph, tape recorder

CRAFTS — small wooden bead kit, knitting spool, simple sewing equipment (blunt needles), hand-operated drill, paper dolls, simple loom for weaving

### Middle Years

BIG MUSCLES — badminton set, basketball hoop and ball, magnetic darts, swimfins and goggles, medium-size bike, large sled, toboggan, skates, skis, regular bat and ball, mitt

*Many toys from the preschool years will continue to be used by this age group.

| | |
|---|---|
| LITTLE MUSCLES | remote-control cars, magic tricks, gyroscope, jewelry kits |
| MAKE-BELIEVE | electric trains, preteen dolls with clothes and equipment, marionettes |
| CONSTRUCTION | simple plastic models, erector sets with motors, models with engines |
| ART MATERIALS | pastel crayons, colored pencils, watercolor paints, papier mâché materials, clay, acrylic paints, oil paints |
| GAMES & PUZZLES | board games that promote number, money, and word-building skills; card games, jigsaw puzzles (100 pieces and up), map puzzles (United States and the world), calculator, electronic games, chess |
| FURNITURE/BIG EQUIPMENT | globe, bulletin board, simple microscope, telescope, typewriter, tape recorder with mike and blank tapes, walkie-talkie |
| CRAFTS | printing set, paper model books of miniworlds, lanyard lace, leathercraft material, wood-burning kit, plaster of paris kit, carving tools, nonpower woodworking materials, bead looms, ceramics |

## *Look What I Found!*

Not all playthings have to be bought. Long before there were toy stores, children found playthings to tool their play. Indeed, the leap of imagination that turns pine needles into pretend soup or transforms a leaf into a boat on a puddle or turns a stick into a magic wand all come much closer to the real gifts of play. That wonderful ability to make one thing "stand for" something else is more fundamental to play than all the costly toys in the world.

Throughout this book we've talked about objects that can be found in most homes or can be made with limited expense into wonderful playthings. Often, these are the playthings that lead children to say with a touch of pride: "Look what I found!"

## *Workaholics Are No Fun!*

Although this book ends with the middle years of childhood, the importance of play continues throughout our lives. You know the old saying: "All work and no play makes Jack a dull boy." Well, that formula is no less true for Jack the boy or man or Jill the girl or woman.

Adults no less than children need exercise to keep muscles toned, circulation flowing, and joints from creaking. Whacking a tennis ball, swimming laps, doing sit-ups or push-ups—all are great for getting rid of tensions that build in the confines of office, shop, home, or factory. Jogging alone or walking together, physical activity can be a separate pleasure or a shared effort.

Nor are sports the only form of play adults enjoy. Playing the piano, a card game, doing a crossword, casting on stitches, sketching a tree, or reading a book are just some of the adult routes to intellectual stimulation, creative expression, and a satisfying change from the work-a-day world.

Indeed, the physical, intellectual, and emotional needs that play satisfies for children are just as important to adults. Unfortunately, too many of us have drawn a sharp line between work and play. We have bought the message: work before pleasure, and the even bigger message that work is no pleasure. Perhaps that's why so many adults seem to find so little pleasure in either their work or their play. In fact, a good many adult players bring the work ethic to their play: jogging into pain, painting for fame, collecting for investment. Somewhere along the way the joy of doing things for their own sake has been lost. Yet, in the lives of children we have seen how work and play are not separate or opposite, but rather overlapping and complementary. The Bank Street philosophy of "developmental interaction" is not limited to childhood. Human development and interaction go on through all of life.

Of course, even in the best of all possible worlds, some aspects of work are tedious or routine. Yet those who hold onto their playful ways bring an extra strength to their work. Faced with a task, such adults risk trying new ways to make things happen, to stretch their skills, to test new ideas, to explore possibilities. These are skills we can take from play to work. Out of such playful approaches ideas emerge—it may be a new way to cook rice or to display merchandise, to negotiate with a tired toddler or a disgruntled customer. Meshing playful ways with work is not to make light of either, but to shed light on both.

Like our children, we need to find a balance between active and passive pursuits, between enjoying our own company and the company of others, between working at play and playing at work.

For those who have put their childish things away or forgotten how to play—it's not too late. Indeed, playing with your children or grandchildren will give you a chance to rediscover some of the pleasures you left behind. With any real luck, you and your family will never outgrow the fun of playing together.

# Bibliography

*Baby Learning Through Baby Play: A Parents' Guide for the First Two Years,* Ira J. Gorden. St. Martin's Press, New York, 1970.

*Child Development and Education,* David Elkind. Oxford University Press, New York, 1976.

*Childhood and Adolescence,* Joseph Church and Joseph L. Stone. Random House, New York 1979.

*Children's Friendships,* Zick Rubin. Harvard Univerity Press, Cambridge, Massachusetts, 1980.

*Complete Book of Children's Play,* Ruth E. Hartley and Robert M. Goldenson. Thomas Y. Crowell Co., New York, 1957.

*Developmental Tasks and Education,* Robert Harighurst. David McKay Co., New York, 1976.

*How to Play with Your Children,* Brian and Shirley Sutton-Smith. Hawthorn Books, New York, 1974.

*Kindergarten and Early Schooling,* Dorothy Cohen and Marguerita Rudolph. Prentice-Hall, Inc., Englewood Cliffs, New Jersey, 1977.

*Love and Discipline,* Barbara Brenner. Ballantine Books, New York, 1983.

*Loving and Learning,* Norma J. McDiarmid, Mari A. Peterson, James Sutherland. Harcourt Brace Jovanovich, New York, 1977.

*Play and Learn,* Volumes I–III, Don Adcock and Marilyn Segal. Oak Tree Publications, La Jolla, California, 1980.

*Supertot,* Jean Marzollo. Harper and Row, New York, 1979.

*The Block Book,* Elisabeth S. Hirsch, Editor. National Asociation for Education of Young Children, Washington, D.C., 1981

*The Child Under Six,* James Hymes. Prentice-Hall, Inc., Englewood Cliffs, New Jersey, 1971.

*The Gift of Play,* Genevieve Millet Landau and Maria W. Piers. Walker and Co., New York, 1980.

*The Hurried Child,* David Elkind. Addison-Wesley Publishing, Reading, Massachusetts, 1982.

*The Learning Child,* Dorothy Cohen. Pantheon Books/Random House, New York, 1972.

*The Magic Years,* Selma Fraiberg. Charles Scribner's Sons, New York, 1959.

*The Middle Years of Childhood,* Patricia Minuchin. Brooks/Cole Publishing Co., Monterey, California, 1977.

*The Parents' Guide to Everyday Problems of Boys and Girls,* Sidney Matsner Gruenberg. Random House, New York, 1958.

*The Pleasure of Their Company* (by The Bank Street College), William H. Hooks, Betty D. Boegehold, Seymour V. Reit, Editors. Chilton Book Co., Radnor, Pennsylvania, 1981.

*Understanding Children's Play,* R. Hartley, L. Frank, R. Goldenson. Columbia University Press, New York, 1952.

*Understanding Your Child from Birth to Three,* Joseph Church. Pocket Books, New York, 1973.

"Video Games—Who's in Charge?", Joan Downs. *The Dial Magazine,* June, 1982, p. 6.

*Your Two-Year-Old,* Louise Bates Ames and Frances L. Ilg. Dell, New York, 1976, 1981.

*Your Three-Year-Old,* Louise Bates Ames and Frances L. Ilg. Dell, New York, 1976, 1981.

*Your Four-Year-Old,* Louise Bates Ames and Frances L. Ilg. Delacorte, New York, 1976, 1981.

*Your Five-Year-Old,* Louise Bates Ames and Frances L. Ilg. Delacorte, New York, 1979, 1981.

*Your Six-Year-Old,* Louise Bates Ames and Frances L. Ilg. Delacorte, New York, 1979, 1981.

# Index

Abracadabra, 129
Accidents, *see* Safety
Acrobatics, 155
Acting games, 226-28
Active play:
    vs. passive play, 4-5, 272
    talking more than, 199-200
    values of, 67-69
After-school programs, 150-51, 155
Aggressive behavior and television
    viewing, 270-71, 274
Alacazam, 129
Alphabet, *see* Letters of the alphabet
Alternatives, providing, 46-47, 78,
    231-35
*American Folk Songs for Children*
    (Seeger), 84, 189
*Amos and Boris* (Steig), 170
Anagrams, 169, 219
Animals:
    feeding, 117-18, 184
    pets, 250-52
    stuffed, 53-54, 60, 94
Art materials:
    for two-year-old, 71-75, 81
    for preschoolers, 70, 104-10,
        135-36
    for middle years, 212-14
    for early school years, 190-97
    recommended, 284, 285, 286, 287
    safety of, 265
    value of working with, 111-12,
        197, 212-14
    *see also* Arts; Crafts
Arts:
    dabbling in the, 205
    formal lessons, 186, 204-5

*see also* Art materials; *specific art
    forms*
*Ask Mr. Bear* (Flack), 113
Attention span, 26, 62-63, 138

*Baby Sister for Frances, A* (Hoban),
    113
Balance beam, 155
Ballet, 204, 205
Balloons, 265
Balls, 28, 40, 81, 135, 153-54
    big bounce-on, 65
    *see also games using balls, e.g.*
        Baseball; Kickball
*Bank Street Two-Gether Books,* 113
Baseball, 153-54, 206
Bathtime, 29-30
    pretend, 61
Batiking, 212
Batting practice, 154
Bead looms, 212
Beads, 263
    making jewelry from, 176
    stringing wooden, 69, 126
*Best Word Book Ever* (Scarry), 113
Bikes, 151-52, 210
    safety, 152, 263
Bingo, 160
Birds, 184, 251
    feeding, 117-18, 184
Birthday parties, 247-50
Blocks, 52, 53, 171
    big hollow cardboard, 65
    math concepts and, 101, 177
    nesting, 70
    parquetry, 176
    for preschoolers, 98-103, 135

298 · KIDS AND PLAY

## About The Bank Street College of Education

Since its founding in 1916, The Bank Street College of Education has been devoted to the study of how children learn and develop, educating children, training teachers and child-care specialists, and helping families. This is still Bank Street's mission in the 1980s, when child-care professionals the world over equate the Bank Street name with a respected, progressive, and humanistic approach to a child's education.

## About the Author

Joanne Oppenheim has been a writer, teacher, consultant, and editor. She has written books, articles, and classroom materials both for and about children. Her recent book *James Will Never Die* was a Junior Literary Guild Selection. A graduate of Sarah Lawrence College and The Bank Street College of Education, Mrs. Oppenheim is presently an associate editor of the Bank Street Publications Department, and also serves as a consultant to ABC's Afterschool Specials. The parents of three grown children, Mrs. Oppenheim and her husband divide their time between New York City and their old farmhouse in Monticello, New York.

## About the Consultant

Edna K. Shapiro, Ph.D., is a developmental psychologist and a Senior Research Associate at Bank Street College. She also teaches child development in the Bank Street Graduate School.